EXPLORING MADNESS

Experience, Theory, and Research

RELATIVITY, lithograph, 1953, 28 × 29 cm by M. C. Escher, Collection Escher Foundation, Haags Gemeentemuseum, The Hague.

Here we have three forces of gravity working perpendicularly to one another. Three earth-planes cut across each other at right-angles, and human beings are living on each of them. It is impossible for the inhabitants of different worlds to walk or sit or stand on the same floor, because they have differing conceptions of what is horizontal and what is vertical. Yet they may well share the use of the same **staircase**. On the top staircase illustrated here, two people are moving side by side and in the same direction, and yet one of them is going downstairs and the other upstairs. Contact between them is out of the question, because they live in different worlds and therefore can have no knowledge of each other's existence.

EXPLORING MADNESS

Experience, Theory, and Research

Edited by
JAMES FADIMAN
and
DONALD KEWMAN

Stanford University

Brooks/Cole Publishing Company
Monterey, California

A Division of Wadsworth
Publishing Company, Inc.

ISBN: 0-8185-0084-0
L.C. Catalog Card No: 72-92044
Printed in the United States of America
4 5 6 7 8 9 10—78 77 76 75 74

Cover painting by Jeanette Stobie.

To those who introduced us
to Altered States of Consciousness
and taught us how to live with
things that go bump in the night

Preface

This book presents many innovative and, in some cases, radical ideas for the investigation, understanding, and treatment of madness. Included are personal and literary accounts of madness, theoretical positions, and research findings. Our intention is to present the contributions of individuals who extend or go beyond current conceptions in abnormal psychology—to survey alternative models that emphasize inner experience in the development of further theories and research. Many of the writers view madness as an altered state of consciousness that causes certain perceptual, emotional, and behavioral changes; however, each viewpoint is based on a different way of exploring and interpreting the experience.

Section I presents firsthand accounts of the world of madness. These raw experiences are offered first so that the reader may form his own opinions before turning to the theories of others. Each selection has been chosen for its clarity, immediacy, and dramatic impact.

Section II contains theories that attempt to explain the various aspects of madness. It is a section designed to stretch the imagination and capacity of the reader beyond current models. Both disturbing and contradictory, the selections in this section focus the reader's attention on the magnitude and difficulty of coming to terms with madness.

Section III offers research along a half-dozen different lines of investigation, with primary emphasis on the physiological and perceptual correlates of abnormal experience. Research strategies examined here include hypnosis, genetics, biochemistry, sensory deprivation, biorhythms, and the effects of perceptual styles. In the search for ever more sophisticated models of madness, new research methodologies grapple with the old-time question of the relationship between mind and body.

This book is specifically designed to supplement texts in abnormal psychology or psychopathology; however, any reader will find the selections exciting and provocative.

We'd like to acknowledge our reviewers, who helped guide this book through its various stages. The criticisms and suggestions of James Butcher of the University of Minnesota, William Coe of California State University at Fresno, Barry Crown of the University of Miami, George Greaves of Kitchener-Waterloo Hospital, Joel Greenspoon of Temple Buell College, Ernest Keen of Bucknell University, Edward Walker of the University of Michigan, Jack Strange of Southern Methodist University, and Robert Ornstein of the Langley Porter Neuropsychiatric Institute were important in the final structuring and choices presented here. Special thanks go to Virginia Beahrs and Paddy Moriarty, who turned our prose back into English. Finally, we wish to thank our editors, Jack Thornton and Terry Hendrix, who implemented our changes and dealt with our problems with ever-increasing flexibility and consideration.

James Fadiman

Donald Kewman

Contents

Introduction

The Reality
of Madness

Mental illness is generally understood to be a difficult, unhappy, frightening, and debilitating experience. We acknowledge this general position but do not focus on it here. Our goal is to draw attention to other levels of meaning within the experience of madness, alternative theoretical views that appear valuable, and research that is changing our conception of the nature and limitations of abnormal experience. If, from time to time, we appear to overemphasize the potential benefits of madness, it is simply an attempt to re-establish an objective vantage point that has been obscured in the last fifty years by unduly grim and depressing portraits of the inner world of the mad.

Since a realistic comprehension of the meaning and value of insanity must include close examination of the experience itself, this book includes articles that describe and explore the inner world of madness. The madman's behavior is often a symbolic performance or acting out of some intense personal drama. It is difficult but necessary to pierce through the behavior to understand its relation to the turmoil in the inner world, the *Weltanshauung*. Classifying the insane into diagnostic categories simply on the basis of behavior overlooks and even denies the richness and diversity of the individual experience.

It is revealing to apprehend madness experientially, directly perceiving the forces, ideas, and patterns structuring each individual experience. Such an approach allows serious consideration of the disturbed person's unique vantage point. This empathic approach, far from precluding objective investigation, is one means of arriving at a fuller understanding. Present research on altered states of consciousness (Ludwig, 1966; Naranjo & Ornstein, 1971; Ornstein, 1972; Tart, 1969, 1971) demonstrates that scientific methodology (observation, replication, and verification by trained observers) can be successfully applied to classes of phenomena associated with abnormal experience.

In their investigation of abnormal mental processes, many current schools focus exclusively on causative factors. Neither the Freudian, the behavioristic, nor the humanistic positions deal effectively with biochemical, genetic, or perceptual variables. All have different forms of treatment that include specific value judgments based on limited cultural value systems. This is not a denigration of these positions, but a recognition of the partial nature of all presently established schools. There simply is not a unified view of madness that balances the physical, mental, emotional, perceptual, and cognitive factors. Each of the partial positions presented in this book makes different implicit assumptions. The use of these assumptions allows each author to make his position clear, but there are few, if any, presentations that are truly objective.

Several years ago, one of us posed the following problem to a class in advanced abnormal psychology: "An undeveloped country is building and staffing new mental hospitals, using methods of treatment studied both here and in Europe. The staff reports some degree of success in treating persons previously left to fend for themselves. They now want to establish certain criteria for deciding when patients are ready to be released. Briefly, they want to know who should be judged sane and who insane."

The class made long lists of criteria but then began to discard them. Problems of cultural relativity, expression of symptoms, severity of illness, nature of family, kinds of treatment used—all appeared and disappeared from the list. The frustration of the class grew until one member proposed that the idea itself was not feasible. People could be classified only as capable or incapable of maintaining themselves in their own culture. With this change in the basic assumption, a list of usable criteria quickly emerged.

The class learned that most of what we label insanity is simply behavior that is unacceptable to most people within a culture, including those who are the residing experts in treating mental illness. There are behaviors, such as murder and incest, that are unacceptable in almost every society. Our emphasis in this book is on forms of unacceptable behavior that are generally classed as psychological, as opposed to those expressed in illegal activity.

Psychological disorders are usually considered as illness; yet they are also perceived as somewhat shameful—evidence of sin, punishable defects, a lack of moral fiber. This confusion between the medical and the Calvinistic model is evident in our treatment of the insane, which has developed into a complex mixture of compassion and detention, hostility and concern.

Before it is possible to observe and understand the inner world of the insane, it is necessary to discover which aspects of their behavior are so unsettling as to cause their banishment from society. Myths about the "madman" perpetuate the discomfort, yet fascination, that surrounds insanity. The media, as well as psychiatry itself, have popularized and dramatized the violent and bizarre aspects of mental illness. An "escaped mental patient" evokes an image of a crazed, brutish person who flies into a senseless rage if crossed, frightening animals, young children, and adults alike. Fear tends to obscure the reality. Often such a person could be more accurately compared to a deer or an antelope, skittish and frightened, looking only for a place to rest and be quiet.

There is a natural and universal dread of the uncertain and unexpected. Novelty, unless clearly labeled or restricted, creates uneasiness. We watch unrealistic fear, cruelty, or comedy on film with avid fascination, but if a friend or neighbor behaves in a similar way, we retreat in panic. People whose actions challenge basic, unstated beliefs about the nature of our accustomed, comfortable reality are unsettling. To diminish our own nervousness, we give them psychiatric labels, treat their behavior as a symptom of disease, and even place them in mental institutions.

How would you react to this mental patient? Running nude into the day room, he looked suspiciously at other patients and staff members, apparently amazed and confounded by such strange behavior as being fully clothed.

"Why are you hiding in your clothes?" he asked.

Staff reaction was predictable. The nude man was led "gently but firmly" from the room. An accepted, though unwritten, regulation was thus enforced: clothes are to be worn without questioning their utility. The patient's question was seen as wholly without merit; his behavior, regressive; his concern for staff and patients, nonexistent. In simpler terms, he was crazy. He need not be taken seriously unless dangerous.

If our reflexive attitude toward such persons could be overcome, we might pay some attention to the merit of such a question. We do, indeed, use clothing to hide behind. It is a way of defining role, class, and status without words and is a psychological defense against interpersonal and sexual thoughts and feelings.

This minor example illustrates the original thinking often associated with abnormal experience. The "fool" in many cultures is seen as a man whose perception is often more incisive than that of ordinary men. Shakespeare and Dostoevsky both use the madman to deliver insightful comments about the situations created by other characters. In the United States we find it difficult to accept the possibility that the madman's mode of perception may be not only different from ours, but also, at times, clearer and more profound. Instead of granting the congruity of his internal world, we see it as only a symptom of his sickness and assume that nothing can be gained from so unusual a perspective. We invalidate his experience and coerce him, through detention, drugs, and various forms of therapy, to deny his own internal world and accept ours. While this is undoubtedly beneficial in some cases, it does not lead to understanding the world-view of the disturbed individual.

The mainstream of psychiatry, heavily influenced by Freudian and neo-Freudian traditions, tends to interpret and treat mental illness as a form of self-deception practiced by an individual upon himself (Kaplan, 1964). In spite of the enormous cultural support given this explanation, there is no substantiating evidence.

One problem raised by the Freudian approach is that the psychiatrist becomes the evaluator of another's experience; he determines which experiences are acceptable and which are not.

Szasz (1961), in more extreme terms, suggests that a major role of the psychiatrist is that of moral policeman, enforcing legal sanctions against special forms of ideas and behaviors. This removes him one step from his original function of healing. More disturbing is the way it places a premium on conformity to legal expectations instead of trying to evolve a flexible, harmonious inner self. Szasz summarizes his position in *The Manufacture of Madness* (1970): "If a person disagrees with and disobeys authority, when that authority is religious, then he is the Devil or possessed by the Devil. Likewise, if a person disagrees with and disobeys authority, when that authority is scientific, then he is insane or mad. In the last analysis, this is a matter of definition."

It has been suggested that the present form of diagnostic labeling—for example, the widely used Diagnostic and Statistical Manual II (1959)—resembles the medieval Malleus Malleficarum, the famous witch-hunter's manual. Ullman and Krasner (1969) point out: "In retrospect the Malleus represented more than a simple manual of witchcraft. It was an attempt to maintain a rigidly doctrinaire, closed political, social, and economic order."

Madness is not well catalogued or codified; diagnostic labels are poor representations of its inner world. There is ample evidence that the world of insanity has parameters significantly different from ours. Insanity is almost always characterized by changes in the usual perceptual styles. Time, space, color, duration, object constancies, and other fundamentals of perception are altered. Once perception is altered, the resulting behaviors are sensible in terms of the new system, yet appear delusional, paranoid, catatonic, or schizophrenic to us. Since diagnostic systems have proven to be of little therapeutic value, a more fruitful line of investigation might be differentiation of cognitive styles and salient perceptual characteristics.

Disengaging ourselves from psychodynamic speculation and basing our classification on perceptual styles could give us objectively verifiable and reliable categories of world-views—not mental illness, but different ways

of seeing and reacting. The upsetting and puzzling behavior that charac-
terizes insane experience might then be understood as consonant with these
different modes of perception. Further work toward understanding the
different world-views will provide the insight to clarify, understand, and
treat such experiences.

The possibility that psychotic experience—far from being a tragedy, an
illness, or a sin—may actually be a positive and uplifting experience is
argued most cogently and poetically by R. D. Laing (1967). His technique
of allowing and even encouraging a full range of inner experience presents
an entirely different set of categories and method of treatment:

> Instead of the *degradation* ceremonial of psychiatric examination, diagnosis
> and prognostication, we need, for those who are ready for it (in psychiatric
> terminology, often those who are about to go into a schizophrenic break-
> down), an *initiation* ceremonial, through which the person will be guided
> with full social encouragement and sanction into inner space and time,
> by people who have been there and back again.

Psychiatrically, this would appear as ex-patients helping future patients
go mad.

The arresting idea underlying Laing's position is that there is something
in madness that is part of our general heritage, is resistant to extinction,
and may have beneficial aspects. Why is it that some forms of mental
illness (notably schizophrenia) seem to exist in equal percentages in most
cultures? Although it does not appear to be correlated with stress, diet,
child-rearing practices, number of siblings, or comparable data, each of
these factors may contribute to its appearance. The evidence points to a
genetic component. Rosenthal (1970) states in this connection:

> [The theory] holds that it is not a particular biochemical abnormality
> that is inherited, but rather a *predisposition* to develop the illness. Environ-
> mental stresses of certain kinds may potentiate processes involving the
> predisposition, culminating in clinical schizophrenia. With a benign envi-
> ronment no overt psychopathology need become manifest and, indeed,
> the carrier may have traits that are unusual, desirable, and adaptive. Al-
> though single-gene theories could fit here, this theory best accommodates
> a polygenic mode of inheritance [p. 187].

The schizophrenic state appears to correlate with far-better-than-average
physical health on a variety of measures. Hoffer and Osmond (1966) sum-
marize this seemingly paradoxical condition:

> There are a number of tests which show that schizophrenic body fluids
> differ from those of normal people and those with other psychiatric ill-
> nesses. Schizophrenics, as a result, have desirable physical attributes
> which non-schizophrenics may well envy.
> Schizophrenics are frequently very attractive physically. They tend to

age and lose their hair color more slowly, and generally appear more youthful than their chronological age.

They are, furthermore, much freer of any of the physical complaints of man, and seem to be able to survive misfortunes which would kill other people. Dr. John Lucy found that schizophrenics can take enormous quantities of histamines, the chemical substance which is responsible for allergies in some people. This resistance to histamine explains why allergies are rare among them. . . .

This is a characteristic of the disease itself and not the patient, for patients can and do develop allergies when they are free of schizophrenia. . . .

Schizophrenics can suffer extensive burns, severe injuries, fractures and heart attacks, acute appendicitis and even self-mutilation with abnormal stoicism and detachment. While some people faint when blood is drawn, one schizophrenic patient cut his throat and bled so much that he required five pints of blood, with little sign of shock. Some have cut off fingers and hands without collapsing or appearing to be affected in any other way.

Valuing aspects of alleged psychotic or insane experience is not new. Krober (1940) reiterates that "what high cultures stigmatize as purely personal, non-real and asocial, abnormal and pathological, lower cultures treat as objective, socially useful, and conducive to special ability or at least relatively so."

In many so-called primitive cultures, the manifestation of acute psychic symptoms—such as auditory or visual hallucinations, seizures, and bizarre physical posturing—is often regarded as the onset of healing powers. The individual thus affected is encouraged to take up shamanizing professions. The Sioux medicine man Black Elk had a long and complex vision as a youth. As his life progressed and he revealed to others the details and extent of this vision, he was encouraged to crystallize it in his external life and become a medicine man (Neihardt, 1932).

It is clear, as well, that primitive cultures have folk-nosologies of psychopathology, within which social sanctions are exercised against individuals who display certain forms of antisocial behavior. This distinction seems to be based not so much on the extent of deviation from a normal state of consciousness as on a folk-typology which recognizes that some forms of abnormal experience are beneficial and others are not.

In Europe during the Middle Ages, when deviant or bizarre behavior was often heralded as a manifestation of the divine, the insane were generally treated humanely and sometimes revered. Monasteries became havens for the insane; the treatment of their disturbance involved prayer and various theological rituals (Ullman & Krasner, 1969). With the rising fear of witchcraft and evil spirits, however, medical opinion began to separate "natural" from "supernatural" causes of abnormal behavior. Extreme mental cases were either treated as physical maladies or turned over to "higher

authorities." The following report from a medieval physician, Antonio Benivieni (1443–1502), suggests the growing split.

> A new and extraordinary disease is nowadays rife which, though I
> have seen and treated it, I scarcely dare to describe. A girl in her sixteenth
> year was seized with pain in the lowest part of her belly and kept on
> trying to pluck it away with her hands. Then she broke into terrible
> screaming and her belly swelled up at the spot, so that it looked as if
> she were eight months pregnant. When her voice failed she flung herself
> about from side to side on her bed, and, sometimes touching her neck
> with the soles of her feet, would spring to her feet, then again falling
> prostrate and again springing up. She would repeat these actions in exactly
> the same manner until she gradually came to herself and was somehow
> restored. When asked, she hardly knew what had happened.
> Investigating this disorder, I concluded that it arose from the ascent
> of the womb, harmful exhalations being thus carried upwards and attack-
> ing the heart and brain.
> I employed suitable medicines, but found them of no avail. Yet it
> did not occur to me to turn aside from the beaten track until she grew
> more frenzied and, glaring round with wild eyes, was at last violently
> sick and vomited up long bent nails and brass pins together with wax
> and hair mixed in a ball, and last of all a lump of food so large that
> no one could have swallowed it whole. As I saw her go through exactly
> the same procedure many times, I decided she was possessed by an evil
> spirit who blinded the eyes of the spectators while he was doing all this.
> She was handed over to physicians of the soul and then gave proof of
> the matter by plainer signs and tokens. For I have often heard her sooth-
> saying and seen her doing other things besides, which went further than
> any violent symptoms produced by disease and even passed human power.*

By the late fifteenth century, with the writing of the Malleus Malleficarum and the resulting purges throughout Europe, the idea of aiding the
insane gave way to eliminating them. Eventually these "campaigns of terror" were superseded by the forces of "rationalism" and of scientific curiosity.

The insane, while treated humanely, were imprisoned for their behavior.
The ground swell of enthusiasm for the power of reason led to treating
both social deviance and mental illness as defects of reason. Rosen (1968)
describes the situation:

> Among the measures taken were those dealing with persons considered
> socially disruptive. Within this portmanteau category were included a
> motley group, the members of which were characterized by the fact that
> they had overstepped the limits set by family, social position, religious
> institutions, the political order, property relations, and the like. These

*From Benivieni, Antonio, *Hidden Causes of Disease*, 1954, pp. 35–37. Courtesy Charles C
Thomas, Publisher, Springfield, Illinois.

were the people who were sent to houses of correction where they might be brought to their senses. In this way the insane in late seventeenth and eighteenth century France were put into institutions with others who exhibited socially unacceptable or irrational behavior. The emphasis in this practice was on the social, not the medical aspect.

While the law proscribed severe punishment for offenses against church and state, there developed a growing trend to substitute compassion for correction when it seemed appropriate. The following passage exemplifies the attitude toward madness at the end of the eighteenth century:

> Yesterday (wrote d'Argenson) the wife of a lawyer named Bertrand was brought to the Chatelet. This woman, having become possessed of the idea that she was holy, took communion every day for more than six months without any preparation, and even after having eaten. This behavior deserved the most extreme punishment according to the law, but as it was rather a case of madness than evil intent, and besides as one cannot punish these crimes publicly without doing harm to religion, and providing occasion for the evil talk of free thinkers and dissembling protestants, it seemed more discreet to have the husband pay for the support of this woman in a convent such as it may please the King to choose. For I have no doubt that the good example of a regular community, associated with kind attention, will restore her deranged mind in a few months [McNeill & Gamer, 1938].

The 1800s saw the rise of social psychiatry, the idea that the culture itself contributed to emotional difficulties. This prepared the way for the contemporary ideas of parental influence, childhood stresses, and cultural determinants of mental illness. Freud's original and disturbing theories arose from beliefs that were tending in the same direction. His willingness to describe and discuss taboo areas of human behavior initially obscured the most important concepts with which he dealt.

Freud's subsequent popularity and the growing acceptance of his fundamental ideas arose partially from physical medicine's lack of success in treating the insane. The search for psychological causes offered new inroads into hitherto unresolvable problems. The Freudian revelation that unconscious processes could be unrealistic, emotional, bizarre, and confusing stimulated research into the social causes of specific kinds of psychological "breakdowns." There appeared to be multiple factors that played a part in the development of any single mental illness. Psychological, cultural, sociocultural, biochemical, and genetic antecedents all seemed relevant.

In spite of our desire for simple answers, it appears that all these forces can be contributing factors to abnormal experience. Similarly, dealing with almost any one of them can be helpful in treatment. Chemotherapy with tranquilizers and stimulants, vitamin therapy, insulin therapy, social and economic rehabilitation, psychotherapies (from a long formal analysis to the most dynamic and flashy of encounter structures) all seem to work. Allowing a person to act out and become as "psychotic" as possible also appears to be helpful in some cases. The confusion centers around the fact that 65 to 70 percent of neurotic patients and 35 percent of schizophrenic patients show improvement regardless of the therapeutic methodology (Kiev, 1964).

It can be argued that psychosis is a kind of acute transitional phase in the development of some personalities. Treated as a natural process, it might have a greater tendency to run its course. Its persistence may be attributed to some sort of arrest in the psychological development of many disturbed persons (not unlike the concept of fixation discussed by Freud, Jung, and Erikson). There is also the possibility that if an individual does not "recover" from the experience following the initial phases, synthesis of neural toxins may cause permanent synaptic damage (Stein & Wise, 1971). Certain aspects of chronicity may be a function of the set and setting and not an endogenous manifestation of the mental disorder itself. Similar abnormalities have been found in the brain-wave patterns of long-term inmates of state prisons and chronic mental patients (Silverman et al., 1966). Several experiments support the speculation that a radical change in the institutional atmosphere would change the "insane" individual's patterns of thought and behavior.

The best-known example of a new institutional approach is Kingsley Hall, founded in England by R. D. Laing. Laing believes that a former, "returned" psychotic is the most effective therapist, since he can fully comprehend the dimensions of another's psychotic experience. The idea of the therapist's having been there himself is in keeping with a fundamental precept of both Jungian and Freudian psychoanalysis, which requires the analyst to undergo analysis himself before being qualified to treat others.

A different kind of experiment is reported in a study of a state mental hospital in California by Julian Silverman. The experiment is specifically designed to measure the effects of drug versus nondrug therapy on acute schizophrenics in a nondemanding, supportive atmosphere. Basically, the patient is allowed to "live out" his psychotic experience and is not pressured into therapeutic relationships either with other patients or with members of the staff. Staff members have been carefully picked for their sensitivity to, and experience with, the inner world of insanity. Early results indicate that this environment is beneficial.

Soteria, a center for first-admission schizophrenics, was opened recently in a house in San Jose, California. According to the principal investigator, Leonard Goevia, the purpose of the program is "to demonstrate the effectiveness of a new form of treatment: developmental crisis therapy. Within this concept, the patient is considered to be suffering not a disease but an emotional crisis which he needs help to resolve. Under close supervision of specially trained personnel, it is hoped he will be able to reintegrate himself without hospitalization (Goevia, 1971).

Changes are occurring in other localities as conceptions of madness and treatment change. In their book *Methods of Madness: The Mental Hospital as a Last Resort*, Braginsky and his co-authors (1969) look ahead to the development of cooperative retreats:

> The co-operative retreat will be an experiment in living for those who come there. It will be for many people a chance to be a member, if only for a short while, of a small, stable, and democratic community where one is free to choose for himself what he would like to do, free to explore the limits of his potentials in order to live a more personally satisfying life.

A recent report on schizophrenia research sponsored by the National Institute of Mental Health contains data from several unpublished studies that discuss novel approaches to treatment in mental health and emphasize the positive results that can be obtained by paying closer attention to the set and setting. One study used nonprofessional "live-in enablers," who took chronic patients into their own homes, and "visiting enablers," who visited patients in their apartments and supervised their daily activities. At follow-up one year later, patients treated by either live-in or visiting enablers were compared with outpatients who had been treated directly by professional staff. Based on this comparison, it seemed to make little difference whether therapeutic services had been delivered by professional personnel or paraprofessional enablers. Another project mentioned in the report is a program whereby chronic patients live with families in a small Midwestern community. The report concludes: "Current innovations in the treatment of schizophrenia seem more to reflect a return to techniques developed long ago: close person-to-person contact, warmth and understanding without the paternalism inherent in so many doctor-patient relationships, the development of family-like groups, community orientation and involvement, etc."

In this book we try to capture a perspective that conveys to the reader the possibility of new approaches in the examination, evaluation, and treatment of abnormal experience. Many of the professionals who have contributed to this volume are considered mavericks in their fields. We have been cautioned by some of our reviewers that the very diversity of our material will puzzle and confound the student; that it would be more sensible if we defined madness and clarified and condensed some of the divergent thinking represented here. There is no easy way to come to terms with madness if one acknowledges all the available data. But we believe that their viewpoints present serious challenges to the prevailing trend of psychiatric thought and merit careful consideration and evaluation by the student of abnormal psychology. If we cease to degrade those who may truly see "the world in a grain of sand . . . and eternity in an hour," they may stop responding with confusion and fear to their perceptions. Furthermore, if we begin to listen, we may gain untold insight in dimensions of reality still to be explored and understood.

REFERENCES

Benivieni, A. *The hidden causes of disease.* (Translated by C. Singer) Springfield, Ill.: Charles C. Thomas, 1954.

Braginsky, B. M., Braginsky, D. D. & Ring, K. *Methods of madness: The mental hospital as a last resort.* New York: Holt, Rinehart and Winston, 1969.

Diagnostic and Statistical Manual of Mental Disorders (DSM-II). Washington, D.C.: American Psychiatric Association, 1968.

Goevia, R. In *Newsletter.* Santa Clara County, California: Mental Health Association, 1971.

Hoffer, A. & Osmond, H. *How to live with schizophrenia.* New Hyde Park, New York: University Books, 1966.

Kaplan, B. (Ed.) *The inner world of mental illness.* New York: Harper and Row, 1964.

Kiev, A. The study of folk psychiatry. In A. Kiev (Ed.), *Magic, faith and healing.* New York: The Free Press, 1964.

Krober, A. L. Psychosis or social sanction. *Character and Personality,* 1940, **8**, 204–215.

Laing, R. D. *The politics of experience.* New York: Ballantine Books, 1967.

Ludwig, A. M. Altered states of consciousness. *Archives of General Psychiatry,* 1966, **15**, 225–234.

McNeill, J. & Gamer, H. *Medieval handbooks of penance: A translation of the principal libri poenitentiales and selections from related documents.* New York: Columbia University Press, 1938.

Naranjo, C. & Ornstein, R. *On the psychology of meditation.* New York: Viking, 1971.

Neihardt, J. G. (Flaming Rainbow). *Black Elk speaks.* Lincoln: University of Nebraska Press, 1961. (Originally published: 1932.)

Ornstein, R. *The psychology of consciousness.* San Francisco: Freeman, 1972.

Rosen, G. *Madness in society.* New York: Harper and Row, 1968.

Rosenthal, D. *Genetic theory and abnormal behavior.* New York: McGraw-Hill, 1970.

Silverman, J., Berg, S. D. & Kantor, R. Some perceptual correlates of institutionalizations. *Journal of Nervous and Mental Diseases,* 1966, **141**, 651–657.

Stein, L. & Wise, C. D. Possible etiology of schizophrenia: Progressive damage to the noradrenergic reward system by 6-hydroxydophmine. *Science*, 1971, **171**, 1032–1036.

Szasz, T. The uses of naming the origin of mental illness. *American Psychologist*, 1961, **16**, 59–65.

Szasz, T. *The manufacture of madness*. New York: Harper and Row, 1970.

Tart, C. (Ed.) *Altered states of consciousness*. New York: John Wiley and Sons, 1969.

Tart, C. Scientific foundations for the study of altered states of consciousness. *Journal of Transpersonal Psychology*, 1971, **3**, 93–124.

Ullman, L., & Krasner, L. *A psychological approach to abnormal behavior*. Englewood Cliffs, New Jersey: Prentice-Hall, 1969.

Section I

Experience

There is something attractive about madness that goes beyond natural compassion, intellectual curiosity, and psychological interest. It has a frightening, yet exciting, quality—frightening because it seems to evoke thoughts of mysterious and terrifying experiences that lurk just beyond the thin veil separating us from the world of insanity, and exciting because of the raw, brutish, uncivilized forces unleashed to purge the narrow and controlled sense of self we usually present to the world. It is the substance that makes up our dream world, the part of ourselves that expresses our fantasies, giving over to feeling, to delusion, without considering the consequences. It is the part of our consciousness in which fears and desires run most freely, the submerged aspects of being surfacing suddenly and vividly.

This collection of internal explorations of madness is a guided tour through a sometimes frightening and mysterious room of the mind as each author experienced and understood it. Some of the authors were institutionalized at the time of writing; others wrote following a period of madness. Still others dealt with madness in works of fiction. As you read, you may begin to understand how madness can exist side by side with normal consciousness.*

Other sections offer suggestions to aid in understanding and treating various kinds of experience. The selections based on personal experience should serve as a foundation for evaluating the theoretical and experimental articles that follow.

---

*Several of these selections are also found in *The Inner World of Mental Illness*, edited by Bert Kaplan (New York: Harper and Row, 1964). It is the most complete and useful book available for anyone wishing to gain a fuller understanding of madness through first-person accounts.

I Have Kept a Lone Death Watch with Madness When Reason Was Dying

Lara Jefferson

This selection, written by a young woman in a Midwest mental hospital, shows the driving force of madness, the powerful swings from one extreme of feeling to another, and the progression from violence to exhaustion to rest to violence again.

Using her own writing as a means of regaining the self-control she had prior to hospitalization, she presents a balance of personal insight, sensible and perceptive commentaries on institutionalization, and simple descriptions of her conflicted, jumbled, emotionally charged behaviors.

The power of her prose tempts one to overlook the pain and the uncertainty that riddled her life in the hospital. The clarity with which she reports typifies one of the states of awareness she experienced from time to time. Periods of poetic lucidity alternated with those marked by violent, uncontrollable behavior, during which coherent thought was impossible.

But this is getting me nowhere. If I must learn to think differently—there is nothing to do but to go about doing it with what few remaining shreds of intelligence I have. But how—is the question. . . .

Whether I had more insight than others, or whether it is a fact that the thing feared by us is the thing which befalls us, I do not know. However it got here, the fact is glaringly present that it did overtake me in the twenty-ninth year of my living. It caught me and swept me—where, I do not know. All the way through hell—and very far into heaven. Now it has whirled and left a stranger unknown to me. Sitting here in my body, I am weak, sick, and vomit much, and stagger so I can hardly walk. At the least movement, perspiration breaks out all over me—I am a fool—and I know it.

The State has adjudged me insane and I am no longer responsible for

From Lara Jefferson, *These Are My Sisters.* Tulsa; Vickers Publishing Co., 1948. Reprinted by permission of Vickers Publishing Company.

anything, so it is stupid and senseless for me to try and salvage anything out of the tangle. But since the tangle is I, I cannot let it lay as it is. Even though that would be better—still, I cannot do it. I still have a life on my hands—even though it must be lived out in an insane asylum. Though I have lost every encounter, I am still not dismissed from the conflict. If all my weapons have failed, I must find some others.

I cannot escape from the Madness by the door I came in, that is certain— nor do I want to. They are dead—past—the struggles of yesterday. Let them lay in the past where they have fallen—forgotten. I cannot go back—I shall have to go onward—even though the path leads to 'Three Building'—where the hopeless incurables walk and wail and wait for the death of their bodies.

I cannot escape it—I cannot face it—how can I endure it.

The whole thing is a dream and a nightmare. No doctor ever stood before me and told me that I would shortly be incurably insane unless I learned to think differently. Oh, I am sure it is all just a dream. Presently, I shall wake up and be oh, so relieved—to know that this has all been a dream. Then it will be only funny—and I can recall with humor the odd sensation I had on finding that a crazy woman had moved into my body. A crazy woman who had no sense at all, and who refused to be governed by reason—who acknowledged no law higher than her own whim—and who had no fear of anything. I shall shortly awake and re- member how frail my strength felt and how helpless I was in trying to budge her gross and unseemly proportions. Dreams seem quite real as you dream them, but how quickly they pass; when I awake I shall be able to laugh at this nightmare. For that is what this great skinned horse is—somebody's nightmare.

She is not real—she is not I—I never saw her before I dreamed her. I am dreaming her now. If I am not dreaming her—then someone else is. And presently they will wake up and this whole thing will dissolve into the night—where nightmares go on waking. Oh, it is all a dream—a delusion—a nightmare. Nothing is real. Everything is a wild toss of halluci- nations of one kind or another about one thing or another. All this other raving and howling going on around me—will not someone come and awaken me—so that I may go free?

If I am to be awakened—I must awaken myself—for no one else can do it. But I do not know how. There is only a shadow remaining of the person I used to be. My whole former life has fallen away so completely it might be an existence lived in the Stone Age—leaving only a few uncer- tain bones to mark its passing. If the person whom I used to be could not prevent the birth of the person I have become, there is not much chance that the latter more powerful creature will be controlled by the ghost of the person whom she succeeded. I attended the death of the first, and superintended her burial. Her casket was a strait-jacket and she was buried in a cell in an insane asylum. To others, I was only a maniac—howling—but who, by some odd quirk of nature had the canny Scotch foresight to ask for a strait-jacket before Madness claimed me.

Perhaps a relentless Recording Angel knew what was happening and was able to write it—but I did not understand it. The struggle that followed was waged above—or below—my conscious knowledge. All I could do was to feel—startlingly—nakedly—starkly—things no words can describe.

I was locked away in a cell—stark madness my only companion. The heavy brass lock confining me was nothing more than a symbol. Had I been the sole inhabitant of the most distant star, I could not have been more alone. No—it was not a brass lock which taught me what the nakedness and loneliness of living means. For I have kept a lone death watch with Madness—when Reason was dying.

As Madness attended the death of the first—he also ushered in the birth of the second. Though the nurses released the same body they tied down—the creature who moves about in it is not the same person. Let those who think they have an explanation of such things, explain it. I do not understand it. The whole thing is a dream—an illusion—a tricky arrangement—as slyly drawn lines can confuse the eye when a seemingly straight forward pattern will shift from one thing to another, and the first outline be lost in the second, even as the eye watches.

If it is an illusion—it is none the less real—and if this latter person whom I have become was concealed all the time in the self-same outline as the other—I would rather go through death, than the wild chaos of shifting back to the other. Let the first one lie dead—along with all the other things of the past. I would not call her back if I could. None can write her obituary better than I—for she was I. A pitiful creature who could not cope with life as she found it—nor could she escape it—nor adjust herself to it. So she became mad, and died in anguish—of frustration and raving.

The worst that could be truthfully said of her is that she was a fool and a coward. The best:—that she did have the foresight to see Madness coming, and make grim preparations. She took only herself to destruction. And God alone, who knows all about inner emotions, is the only one able to judge whether her end was a defeat—or a triumph.

I have learned through the grim lesson taught by my failure that my previous methods of trying to adjust to the problem of living were not the right ones. If my wrong way of thinking was the net my mind spun to entrap me, then it is certainly logic, that the same sort of spinning cannot release me now that I am entangled. I do not know what is the trouble—only that something is wrong—terribly wrong. And I do not know how to right it.

There is nothing solid to stand on—nothing beneath me but a vast treacherous quagmire of despondency—followed by periods of exultation and ecstasy; and neither condition has any foundation in logic. All my life I have been either in the throes of the one or the other; and I have an empty, sick feeling when I think of the energy wasted in trying to hold my moods down to something like reason. And now—since Reason has slipped—altogether—and I still have not solved the problem—well, there is only 'Three Building' left.—Unless—unless—I can do that, which, if it could be done—would be a miracle.

In the brain of this crazy wild woman, who was born while I lay in a jacket, a crazy idea is turning. Because she was born during madness, the idea resembles the monster who sired her, at least, it seems so to me who used to set great store by reason. She suggests very seductively that the best weapon with which to fight fire—is fire. And suggests fighting madness with madness. Perhaps she is not so insane as I think—perhaps she is saner than I was before she came to me. She presents her idea with so much logic she makes me think that instead of losing reason in madness—and finding insanity on the other side—that in reality, I will lose insanity in madness—and find a sound mind on the other side.

Whichever is right I know that I have been all the way through hell—and found the rest of myself somewhere on the other side. But the part of me that madness led into hell—could not endure it. The fierce heat of the journey consumed the stuff she was made of. She melted away to a shadow. This latter creature has thoughts of her own—and will not be controlled by a—shadow.

If the weak, fearing creature that I used to be, had ability to generate, out of her weakness and fright, such a creature as I have become—then the world must have had her all wrong. She was not an imbecile—but a genius; even though the creature that has grown out of her weakness and failure is a—monstrosity. If a colossal egotism is the mark of a maniac—then she is a maniac—and will shortly be on 'Three Building,' the prospect does not worry her in the least. She has come out of hell, and has both the odor of smoke—and scorched flesh—upon her; so she has the audacity to look at the fate stretched before her—and laugh—as she sees it. She cares nothing at all for the things that her predecessor considered of value. She mocks at the shadow of her former person—and waves a bold flag of defiance. And I still am divided. I cannot truly forsake all the old ideas as long as their memory stays with me. Neither is it at all likely that I can impose them on to the maniac I have become.

Any creature that can be governed by reason is not a maniac. And this latter creature has a method of reasoning that is not based on logic—but is more convincing. She reaches her conclusions in a streak that is naked and piercing. She does not rely on the slow process of thinking to reach a conclusion—but cuts a broad swath through the 'feelings'—like a streak of chained lightning.

I do not know what to do with her—nor how to withstand her nor to educate her and teach her some of the decencies I was taught at one time—and tried to put into practice. Oh, she will land up on 'Three Building'—there is no doubt. But she just mocks about it—and tells me that it does not matter at all whether life is lived inside an insane asylum or out of it.

She tells me that I have missed all the main issues of life—and can see nothing clearly. That I have concerned myself with the externals only, and have missed all the meanings of the great inner significance. That there is no such thing as a normal mind—or an abnormal mind; but only minds and more minds. That life is the important thing—not the classification of it. Life. To live it—and not fear it. Let it rip—let it roar—let it be destructive if it must, but live it and do not fear it.

She whispers that I became mad—not because of some inner deformity—but because of too close supervision and trying.—Trying to force the thing I was into an unnatural mold. I do not know. I doubt if she has the right idea—but if all this latter trouble that has befallen me is a result of too much restriction—then I think I see a new place to apply much restriction—then I think I see a new place to apply the abhorrence we feel for the Chinese custom of foot binding.

All this crooked philosophizing is not solving my problem. Let those who think they know the causes that lie back of disintegration set themselves to the task of evolving an effective treatment in freeing the victim. Or if that is not possible—let those wise enough to think to the root of the trouble, be also humanitarian enough to teach those not so gifted—how to cope with the problem. Finding the cause—or fixing the blame—if it ever is done, will come too late to help me. The fact is, I am already here, in an insane asylum—and in the big middle of Madness; headed straight for 'Three Building' and hopeless insanity—unless I can accomplish a miracle. I am already entangled—and if I am freed I must do it myself for none other can help me. And I have precious few weapons—and little equipment—unless Mother Wit, out of my very great need can forge me a weapon to meet the necessity.

Because I must face the problem and deal with it somehow—I evolved this paper and pencil idea. I had the pencil in my hand as the Doctor talked to me—and when he had finished and gone out and left me staring at my hands with stupefaction—the idea came to me born of illusion. I heard the noise of the others tied down in their raving—(one of them is dying and does not know that she dies)—and I felt all this tumult of madness—all this stark, lonely living which is worse than death—and the pain, futility and hopelessness of it all—and the endlessness, the eternity—

and the sound became mixed in my brain with another meaning. It was beating and sweeping around me—a flood—released from God knows where—and dashing us all to destruction.

I looked at the others—and felt an odd feeling of kinship. I looked at the strait-jackets that held them—(from my own arms the feeling of being tied has not yet departed)—and the thoughts that came to me then— are between my own God and myself—for they were madness. The flood that was swirling about me was sucking me under—and the pencil I had in my hand was a straw to be caught. It was just a straw—but I caught it—and now I have kept my head above water for a while—even if what I have written does not make sense to anyone—at least—it has helped me a little. I have been able to find a few inadequate phrases. And anything that can be whittled down to fit words—is not all madness.

It is only ideas of such colossal proportions that a symbol for them cannot be created—that are vague and intangible and brooding, incomprehensible and fearful, that produce madness.

The very fact that a thing—anything—can be fitted into a meaning built up of words—small, black words, that can be written with one hand and the stub of a pencil—means that it is not big enough to be overwhelming. It is the vast, formless, unknown and unknowable things that we fear. Anything which can be brought to a common point—a focus within our understanding—can be dealt with.

I do have a pencil and enough sheets of paper to last for awhile—and as long as this crazy woman that I have become, wants to rave—what matter if the sound of her raving falls into words on the paper—or goes off into air, and mixes with all the other tumult and uproar that goes on down here. Her thinking is wild—but I have the wilder idea that if I can force her to keep it hitched to a pencil, and hold it down to the slow rhythm of writing things out in long hand—the practice might tame her somewhat. I would rather try to tame a wild bull in a pasture. I know not how to deal with her because she is a maniac. Because she is I—and because I still have myself on my hands, even if I am a maniac, I must deal with me somehow.

The nurse just now picked up one of the sheets I have written. She read it—looked at me oddly—and asked what in the hell I thought I was doing. And because she expected an answer in keeping with my strange occupation—I did not have the heart to disappoint her. So I gave her an answer that fitted. I told her that I was Shakespeare, the reincarnation of Shakespeare trying to sidestep a strait-jacket. (I'll admit that I feel queer enough to be the reincarnation of something but I doubt if Shakespeare would claim me.) But hurray! She came back down the aisle with a whole ream of paper and said to me: "Go to it, Shakespeare."

Verily, verily, Shakespeare, I had no idea you could be called from your quiet English grave with so little effort. In my present predicament, I know of no one who could be quite such a fortunate choice for a delusion of grandeur. So welcome! I hope you will be as pleased with the arrangement as I am. Poor fellow, this is surely a come-down from your former position.

Perhaps this is a penance—an expiation—an atonement you must make for filling so many pages of drama in your former existence with madmen.

Poor Shakespeare—it is certainly a deflection on your former genius to suggest that you must stalk with me over to 'Three Building' because you are a maniac. And a still greater reflection on your taste and discrimination—if you had any choice in the matter—to think that you would come back to this world in this sort of a setting. But you did not choose me—I chose you—and you should not mind it—for here is an endless array of the theme you like best. And offering no disrespect to your very great genius—I am willing to wager that you will not find madness so intriguing when you have to be a mad person yourself—and have only those of your like to live with.

*   *   *   *

The Doctor was through again, just now. He is entirely too good looking. It is hard for a neurotic woman not to be sentimental about him—except that he is too damned wise. All these Doctors are. They have got us all analyzed and psychoanalyzed down to insignificant daubs of protoplasm—and personally, my Ego is not a bit flattered by the things they found out about it. Drat them! Life has settled into one burning obsession with me, to stir myself to the completion of their hypotheses—and convince them that if I am the exact duplicate of the twin sister of a Jack-Ass, then, they are most undeniably, very excellent—Veterinarians.

They call us insane—and in reality they are as inconsistent as we are, as flighty and changeable. This one in particular. One day he derides and ridicules me unmercifully; the next he talks to me sadly and this morning his eyes misted over with tears as he told me of the fate ahead. Damn him and all of his wisdom!

He has dinned into my ears a monotonous dirge—"Too Egotistical—too Egotistical—too Egotistical. Learn to think differently—Learn to think differently—Learn to think differently."—And how can I do it? How—how—can I do it? How the hell can I do it? I have tried to follow his suggestions but have not learned to think a bit differently. It was all wasted effort. Where has it got me?

Oh, he is a good Doctor all right. An excellent Doctor. All his conclusions are founded on excellent logic; the things he tells me are true—nauseatingly true. He is right, sickeningly right. In fact he is the very embodiment of all the virtue and wisdom in the world. For that reason, I detest him—passionately. But knowing these things does not keep me from the impulse to smack him down and that very impulse confirms the things he has told me.

I wish I could put a bell on him—so I would be aware when he starts probing around in the crooks and crannies of my crooked brain, hunting for phobias. He can do nothing with them when he finds them, so what is the use of hunting? Phobias are sensitive little critters—and it's like having a boil lanced, to have them probed into. He cannot cure them. All he does is go prowling around among them, knocking them over. When he finds an extra fine specimen he is as thrilled with his discovery as some be-spectacled bug-hunter who captures a rare type of beetle.

After he has found it, he does not know what to do with it. He cannot take it out and mount it or preserve it in alcohol. All he has in proof of his discovery is a long handled word to paste in his album. And I wish—Oh, how I wish, that I had the genius to take some of the smug self complacency out of him. He calls me Egotistical—and I am—but he suffers most bumptiously from it too. I do not see how he can fail to observe the symptoms in himself, when he can see them in others so clearly.

He stalks through here twice daily, in the pride of his lordly perfection. A great Modern Scientist inflated with wisdom, at work in his own laboratory. We who are patients here in the "Hydro" are no longer people—merely things he has in test tubes. Experiments. Some of us are not successful. I, in particular, am an experiment of his that is no good at all and presently I shall be dumped over into 'Three Building.'

I know now how rats and rabbits and guinea pigs feel when they are vivisected. Vivisection is painful—and let those who think it isn't, get themselves pronounced insane—and get their brain analyzed by a modern psychologist.

The Doctor comes to you and in his most professional manner—softened down with such kindness as his mood at the time will permit, says you are too Egotistical and are going to wind up on 'Three Building' unless you learn to think differently.

And if you really do have a bad case of infected, ingrowing Egotism—you get a pencil, the backs of old letters, sit down in the dormitory, call yourself Shakespeare and set out to tell all.

This is the Bug-house—the Bug-house—the Bug-house. Hooray for the Bug-house! It is also the Hydro—the Hydro—the Hydro. Hooray for the Hydro! The Bug-house is the place where Nuts are kept. The Hydro is the compartment where the very choice specimens are kept, watched, treated and worked on and done things to that have no more rhyme nor reason than a bath in flea soap has to a puppy. Perhaps it helps the pup—but he is not taken into the confidence of those who bathe him. He is just yanked up and plunged into the bath—and never mind his protests. So are we. Never mind our protests. All that is done for us is good for us.

It is just our hard luck that we have no comprehension. Yes—this is the Hydro—where is given all that is given to correct our abnormalities. And let me state that it is "Treatment"—and let me state that it is "Given."

The nurses are feeding one of the patients now. She would not eat. Did not want to eat. But they are pouring the food down her anyway. They have a wooden peg in her mouth and are crouched behind a sheet held up like a shield, because the woman tries to spew each mouthful upon them. She spits, howls, and curses simultaneously in one breath, she is tied down in a strait-jacket and can do nothing but spit and curse and howl. But how she is spitting and how she is cursing and how she is howling. Truly, it is a magnificent display of madness. Rage has mottled her face with a purple rash and the veins stand out on her neck from straining. Her mouth is open for cursing and one of the nurses reaches around the sheet with the feeding cup and splashes a great gulp of milk in her mouth. The other nurse catches her nose to shut off her breathing and covers her mouth with a towel. But she will not swallow and is strangling on the speech trapped in her throat. They gurgle up through the milk and curdle it but she will not swallow.

The sounds coming up through the milk can not quite carry the shape of the curses; they lost their shape in the liquid, or else were gnashed into shapelessness by the grinding clench of her teeth. But, the spirit of them escapes through the milk and as they rise they make it gurgle and bubble and fly out in mist as though it were boiling. And she is mad enough to almost bring it to a boil without the aid of the curses. She hates herself for her inability to strangle to death before she must swallow. She is mad with her impotency and helplessness so she hates the nurses with fury unbelievable. Now they are finished and are leaving her, and her rage is directed at the whole world in general and spouts out against the Hydro ceiling in a scalding geyser of fury.

It is flung with such fury it does not seem possible a human voice can make such a noise and still retain the power to shape itself into speech. But it does—and even the force with which it hits the ceiling does not shatter the shape of the curses—for they are solid and substantial things and ride high above the tumult of the other noise she makes. They are constructed by Madness, out of double-strength, re-inforced hatred, and neither the force which expels them nor the crashing impact with the ceiling makes any dent in them.

You might think the awful oaths and profanities she releases with such disruptive explosion would be shattered to splinters on hitting the ceiling. But there is nothing anemic about these curses. They are large and full-bodied and bounding with vigor, and much more capable of denting the ceiling than the ceiling is of denting them, and when they hit it, their direction is changed. Instead of continuing their rocket flight upward, until they burned a hole through the stratosphere, the ceiling deflects them and they go bounding off against the walls, and roll back and forth in the aisles—so we are still getting the repeated impacts of the first ones, long after more violent ones have left her.

Never was there such a vocabulary! She could give a sailor lessons in the art of cursing. For her ability reaches far beyond Art. It is Genius!

She used to be a large woman, weighing more than two hundred pounds. Now she is shrunken to a fraction of that and her flesh hangs in loose folds about her tall frame. Her pelvic bones stick up like the rim of a bowl around her abdomen, which is a great mass of shrivelled wrinkles. She keeps it scratched and clawed and over-turned in great red welts and ridges. She has dug so deeply into her flesh she has turned it wrong side out in many places.

But I like "Claw-belly"—for she rose up and danced on the day I was put into a jacket. She danced to my singing—a wild, whirling dance—and she was stark naked. She got tied down for her compliment to my singing. It was not beautiful singing—and I was stark mad or I would not have sung in the bug-house. And she was madder than I was, or she would not have danced to my singing. It was not beautiful dancing. You must be very beautiful indeed if you are able to get away with dancing without any clothes on and you must do it in the name of Art—and spell it with a very Capital A—or the police will interfere—or nurses will come with a strait-jacket.

There isn't the least bit of beauty in "Claw-belly's" carcass. So she got herself tied down; as did the "Camel," who danced too—but she did have the decency to drape her great hunched shoulders in a sheet, for, if possible, the "Camel" is uglier even than "Claw-belly." And because we were all stark mad and were all three tied down on neighboring beds, and because we each had to rave—(it is not possible to bear madness in silence)—we lay there and each fashioned songs to suit our own whims, and the Hydro was filled with more noise than usual. . . .

A Schizophrenic Patient Describes the Action of Intensive Psychotherapy

Malcolm L. Hayward, M. D.
J. Edward Taylor, M. D.

Here, in her own words, are the feelings and reactions of one woman receiving therapy in a hospital: "We schizophrenics say and do a lot of stuff that is unimportant, and then we mix important things in with all this to see if the doctor cares enough to see them and feel them."

She reveals that, while profoundly disturbed, she was still aware of her actions and could control them to test their effects on others. Behavior that appears to us to be "out of control" may actually be calculated and controlled, though based on different *mores*.

Critical to her progress was the way one therapist reacted to the many things she did. She tested and retested him to see whether he was actually working with her as an involved human being or merely treating her as "just another case." She constantly evaluated his capacity to distinguish true from false statements, testing his kindness, his acceptance, and his regard. Also probing for negative feelings, she pushed the therapist to express anger, rejection, even brutality, knowing that, in these areas, her own judgment could distinguish true emotion from skillful posturing. As he passed test after test, she rewarded him with improved behavior and a willingness to be helped.

This report has been written to describe some of the reactions to psychotherapy of a young woman who was recovering from a chronic schizophrenic illness, marked chiefly by catatonic and paranoid elements. Her statements were made from time to time over the period of convalescence, while she was freeing herself from the illness and the transference by clarifying all the forces of treatment and the various roles the therapist had played. The statements chosen for this paper deal mainly with her

From Malcolm L. Hayward, M.D., and J. Edward Taylor, M.D., A Schizophrenic Patient Describes the Action of Intensive Psychotherapy. *The Psychiatric Quarterly*, 1965, **30**. Reprinted by permission. The original article contained a discussion of the patient's therapy written by Hayward and Taylor. This shortened account contains the patient's full description, in the same order as the original.

impressions of the early stages of treatment, during the period of overt psychosis.

A good deal has now been written about the principles of psychotherapy in severe schizophrenia, and Eissler has pointed out the need to seek a common denominator for all these conflicting theories. It seems to the writers that the comments this patient has made can give some valuable aid in this direction. Particularly important are her descriptions of the essential elements in the doctor's relationship with his patient, factors that are chiefly non-verbal and extremely difficult to understand during the period of psychotic acting out.

HISTORY OF THE CASE

Joan is a 26-year-old white woman. Her illness first appeared early in 1947 when she was 17. In the ensuing two years, she was treated in four private hospitals with a regimen of psychotherapy, accompanied by a total of 34 electric-shock and 60 insulin treatments. Fifty comas occurred. She showed "little, if any, improvement" and was finally referred to one of the writers (M. L. H.), since she appeared to be hopelessly ill.

At the start of this writer's treatment, Joan was cold, withdrawn, seclusive, and suspicious. Visual and auditory hallucinations were active. She would enter into no hospital activities and frequently became so stuporous that it was difficult to elicit any response from her. If pressed about the need for treatment, she would become sullenly resistive or maintain angrily that she wanted to be let alone. Three suicidal attempts were made, by slashing herself with broken glass or taking an overdose of sedation. At times, she became so violently belligerent that she had to be placed on the agitated ward.

In spite of this discouraging picture, Joan responded well to a course of intensive psychotherapy that employed elements of the direct analytic therapy of Rosen and the joint fantasy experiences described by Whitaker and his group. In six months, she could be declared free of committable psychosis, and two months later she was moved successfully to an open ward. At the present time she is married and has been free of hospital restrictions since the fall of 1949.

Her later therapy approximated a psychoanalysis of the classical type, the purpose of which was to give her conscious understanding of the dynamics of her illness and to free her from the intense and complex transferences that developed during the course of the earlier therapy.

STATEMENTS BY THE PATIENT

At the start, I didn't listen to what you said most of the time but I watched like a hawk for your expression and the sound of your voice.

After the interview, I would add all this up to see if it seemed to show love. The words were nothing compared to the feelings you showed. I sensed that you felt confident I could be helped and that there was hope for the future.

It's like talking to a frightened horse or dog. They may not know your words but the calm and strength and confidence that you convey help them to feel safe again.

There was such a tremendous difference between you and your words. You seemed so wonderful, but your words were so horrible. Just to look at my problems without being sure of you was more than I could stand. If you forced your words on me, I usually went catatonic because of the horrible ideas. What you said was usually right and it made me see things, but you would leave me feeling like a leper looking at his sores. I felt hopeless over what to do about the problems. I could only go catatonic to get away. You should have helped me to understand why all my problems were there. You should have let me know that there was plenty of time to understand and change myself.

I had to tell you things by doing them instead of talking, because I didn't dare let you know things about me. I was sure you would turn things against me and use what I said to hurt me. Also, no one ever paid any attention to what I asked for, but they usually did react if I did something. I wanted terribly for you to help me, but I had to be sure I could trust you.

We schizophrenics say and do a lot of stuff that is unimportant, and then we mix important things in with all this to see if the doctor cares enough to see them and feel them.

Until you controlled me and took care of me in your own way, I kept losing sight of you and thinking you were my old mother. When you actually took care of me, I could feel the difference. I could realize that you would be a better mother and then I wanted to live.

Patients laugh and posture when they see through the doctor who says he will help but really won't or can't. Posturing, for a girl, is seductive, but it's also an effort to distract the doctor away from all her pelvic functions. The patients try to divert and distract him. They try to please the doctor but also confuse him so he won't go into anything important. When you find people who will really help, you don't need to distract them. You can act in a normal way. I can sense if the doctor not only wants to help but also can and will help. (The patient stressed this.)

(What kind of help did you need?) Well, one thing was getting down to my need to be a boy. The very first interview you said something about a prick. I was terrified but it really was a great relief, even though I felt like an old rag in a gun closet. Most of my doctors had avoided it with me. You showed that you felt it was a problem that had to be cleared up. You knew I was terrified, but I knew you would go down to the depths with me. All my other doctors sat on the edge and fished. They waited for me to say things. That's not fair. You went right ahead. You were willing to get in with me.

Patients kick and scream and fight when they aren't sure the doctor can see them. It's a most terrifying feeling to realize that the doctor can't see the real you, that he can't understand what you feel and that he's just going ahead with his own ideas. I would start to feel that I was invisible or maybe not there at all. I had to make an uproar to see if the doctor would respond to me, not just his own ideas.

I hated you when you first came. So many other doctors had tried things with me and got discouraged that I had thought that now at last I would be left alone in peace. But you just wouldn't go away so I wanted to kill you.

I couldn't trust love; that's why I kept planning ways to make you mad. You were too blank unless you were mad. That was more real and warm and genuine. I knew then you were sincere. When my parents loved me, they never saw the real me. They could only see and love what they wanted me to be. They could only love me by destroying the real me. Father wanted so much to do something nice. He tried so hard it made me want to cry. But he would only let me feel in his way of feeling. He wouldn't let me have my own feelings. That is why love and destruction were the same thing to me.

If I got mad at Mother and Father, and refused what they wanted, they would make me feel guilty by saying how hard they had tried and that I only wanted to hurt them. I just had to get away from that. Nobody seemed able to understand me. I thought I was just a hopeless mess, but somehow you made me feel that you could see and love the real me.

Hate has to come first. The patient hates the doctor for opening the wound again and hates himself for allowing himself to be touched again. The patient is sure it will just lead to more hurt. He really wants to be dead and hidden in a place where nothing can touch him and drag him back.

The doctor has to care enough to keep after the patient until he does hate. If you hate, you don't get hurt so much as if you love, but still you can be alive again—not just cold and dead. People mean something to you again.

The doctor must keep after the patient until he does hate. That is the only way to get started. But the patient must never be made to feel guilty for hating. The doctor has to feel sure he has the right to break into the illness, just as a parent knows he has the right to walk into a baby's room, no matter what the baby feels about it. The doctor has to know he's doing the right thing.

The patient is terribly afraid of his own problems, since they have destroyed him, so he feels terribly guilty for allowing the doctor to get mixed up in the problems. The patient is convinced that the doctor will be smashed too. It's not fair for the doctor to ask permission to come in. He must fight his way in; then the patient doesn't have to feel guilty. The patient can feel that he has done his best to protect the doctor; he can even feel it is O.K. to destroy the doctor. The doctor must say by his manner, "I'm coming in no matter what you feel."

The problem with schizophrenics is that they can't trust anyone. They can't put their eggs in one basket. The doctor will usually have to fight to get in no matter how much the patient objects. It is wonderful to be beaten up or killed because no one ever does that to you unless they really care and can be made very upset. A person kills because he really wants the other to be resurrected, not just lie dead.

Loving is impossible at first because it turns you into a helpless little baby. The patient can't feel safe to do this until he is absolutely sure the doctor understands what is needed and will provide it.

Hating is like shitting. If you shit, it shows you are alive but, if the doctor can't accept your shit, it means he doesn't want you to be alive. It makes him like a mother who can't accept her child's mess.

A mother is like a toilet because she takes away the child's mess. It used to terrify me to sit and watch you, to see if you could handle all my hate and shit, or whether you would be choked by it the way I was. I used to take cascara* every day to get rid of as much shit as possible before you came.

You should never have stood by and let me torture you by crucifying myself and making you watch my suffering. You should have forced me to come down or at least thrown rocks at me. If you had spanked me I could have been mad and more alive.

You were afraid that if you spanked me I would become more dead. Some people do spank to kill, but you could have spanked in order to warm me and make me more alive. It's like slapping a new-born baby to make it breathe. By sitting quietly and watching me suffer, we go in a vicious circle. You suffered because I suffered, and I felt guilty because you suffered, and the whole thing got worse and worse. Finally, the only thing left for me to do was to try to kill myself.

Some people go through life with vomit on their lips. You can feel their terrible hunger but they defy you to feed them.

*A laxative.

It's hellish misery to see the breast being offered gladly with love, but to know that getting close to it will make you hate it as you hated your mother's. It makes you feel hellish guilt because, before you can love, you have to be able to feel the hate too. The doctor has to show that he can feel the hate but can understand and not be hurt by it. It's too awful if the doctor is going to be hurt by the sickness.

It's hell to want the milk so much but to be torn by guilt for hating the breast at the same time. Consequently, the schizophrenic has to try to do three things at once. He's trying to get the breast but he's also trying to die. A third part of him is trying not to die.

You seemed to be just the kind of doctor I needed, but I couldn't believe I could depend on you. All my other doctors had seemed dependable but they would be pleasant to me and then end up by sending me away or trying to arrange plans with my family behind my back. The plans were what my parents wanted and never were good for me. Finally I decided I'd never trust anyone again. For two years I closed myself up and froze so I wouldn't feel anything. But no matter how mad I made you, you always came back and were always on time. You had to show me that you cared enough so that, if I went away, you would chase me and even beat me to make me come back.

My other doctors just tried to make me a "good girl" and patch things up between me and my parents. They tried to make me fit in with my parents. This was hopeless. They couldn't see that I was longing for new parents and a new life. None of the doctors seemed to take me seriously, to see how sick I was and what a big change I needed in life. No one seemed to realize that if I went back to my family I would be sucked back in and lose myself. It would be like the photograph of a big family group taken from far away. You can see that there are people there but you can't be sure who is who. I would just be lost in a group.

Meeting you made me feel like a traveler who's been lost in a land where no one speaks his language. Worst of all, the traveler doesn't even know where he should be going. He feels completely lost and helpless and alone. Then, suddenly, he meets a stranger who can speak English. Even if the stranger doesn't know the way to go, it feels so much better to be able to share the problem with someone, to have him understand how badly you feel. If you're not alone, you don't feel hopeless any more. Somehow it gives you life and a willingness to fight again.

Being crazy is like one of those nightmares where you try to call for help and no sound comes out. Or if you can call, no one hears or understands. You can't wake up from the nightmare unless someone does hear you and helps you to wake up.

I needed to be controlled and know what you wanted me to be. Then I'd be sure you would want me. With my parents I couldn't be a boy and they never made it clear what else they wanted me to be except that. So I tried to die by being catatonic. You should never have let me wear slacks. You even said I looked nice in them. I was sure you loved me like that and would be like my parents.

I would go into those violent rages at you, early in treatment, because of a sense of desperate frustration. I longed for you to take care of me and love me, but I was sure I wasn't lovable as a girl, and I knew I couldn't really become a boy. I felt sure you would soon realize I wasn't a boy and then you would go away. You seemed ready to feed me but then you never would.

I felt like a moving picture projected on the wall. I only existed because you wanted me to and I could only be what you wanted to see. I only felt real because of the reactions I could produce in you. If I had scratched you and you didn't feel it, then I'd be really dead.

I could only be good if you saw it in me. It was only when I looked at myself through your eyes that I could see anything good. Otherwise I only saw myself as a starving, annoying brat whom everyone hated and I hated myself for being that way. I wanted to tear out my stomach for being so hungry.

I had to have control. I had to know you could control me. It was the only way I felt safe because I couldn't control myself. I went wild when you seemed doubtful about this. That's why I slashed my wrists. I thought you didn't care about my fear of my anger or you didn't feel you could handle me, so I had to kill myself before I could harm you. After the big fight I felt much safer. I knew you were stronger than I.

I needed terribly to feel safe as a little girl so that I could rebel and still wouldn't need to punish myself. I could play at being grown up without having to be in complete self-control. Gradually I was able to lose my fear of not being able to control myself.

My interviews were the only place where I felt safe to be myself—to let out all my feelings and see what they were really like without fear that you would get upset and leave me. I needed you to be a great rock that I could push and push, and still you would never roll away and leave me. It was safe for me to be bitchy with you. With everyone else I was trying to change myself to please them.

I was terrified that day that I suggested we both sit on the floor and you agreed, because I knew if I got down I'd never be able to get up without help and I wasn't sure you could get up again. I knew I couldn't help you get up. I would only be able to crawl.

You should have made it clear that I would have to start in infancy and live my life all over again. Then I could know that eventually the past and the present would fit all right. For most people, nothing that happened before the age of six seems important. For the schizophrenic, nothing that happened after the age of six seems important.

By feeding me you gave me the strength to love or hurt you as much as I wanted, but you didn't mind. This was terribly important. I watched carefully while you nursed me to see if you got thinner. I had to be sure that I wasn't taking too much. I'll never forget the day your suit seemed tight and you agreed you were getting too fat. It made me feel so safe.

You wanted to feed me so you wanted me to live. Mother is dry, like the desert. She loves the desert. She never nursed me. With you it was the first time I ever sucked a breast.

No one seemed to understand that I couldn't go ahead and grow up until all the holes from the past were filled up. I couldn't go ahead until I had a chance to feel safe and happy as a baby. You have to go down before you can come up. When you feel sure you belong to someone, everything else works out all right. If you've once been loved, you never forget it.

You have no idea how the warmth of your body would bring me back from my crazy world. It would change my whole picture of life when you held me. I had been so sure that no one could ever give warmth to me. You made everything look different.

When my violent feelings became too strong, I would have to close down on all my feelings. I would become cold and dead. I would even lose my love for you. At these times the only thing that seemed real about you was the physical warmth of your body when you held me.

Everyone should be able to look back in their memory and be sure he had a mother who loved him, all of him; even his piss and shit. He should be sure his mother loved him just for being himself; not for what he could do. Otherwise he feels he has no right to exist. He feels he should never have been born.

No matter what happens to this person in life, no matter how much he gets hurt, he can always look back to this and feel that he is lovable. He can love himself and he cannot be broken. If he can't fall back on this, he can be broken.

You can only be broken if you're already in pieces. As long as my baby-self had never been loved then I was in pieces. By loving me as a baby, you made me whole.

If you could have given me a bath it would have helped me to accept my body much sooner. You could have been Mummy and there would have been no danger and guilt about liking my body. You could have shown that you liked my body; then I could have liked it.

I kept asking you to beat me because I was sure you could never like my bottom, but if you could beat it, at least you would be accepting it in a sort of way. Then I could accept it and make it part of me. I wouldn't have to fight to cut it off.

Being nursed was as good as an orgasm. It left me all relaxed and happy. The world looked real and pleasant. I could fall asleep comfortably. But the bottle had to be given by you with love. It wasn't just the milk that helped. It was the feeling that I had a mother who loved me.

Some mothers just screw their babies with the breast. They jam the breast into the baby's mouth to shut him up without finding out why he's crying.

By feeding me good milk you changed the shit inside me so it wasn't bad and dangerous any more. I didn't have to be so afraid of getting close to people any more. When I was crazy, I felt sure I was full of poisonous shit that had spread all through my body so that I would harm anyone who came close to me.

You opened the doors for me to grow that day when you admitted that you had doubts and uncertainties about me. I realized that you needed me to reassure you; that you could want me as a mother, not just a child. You allowed the baby and the mother in me to come together.

It was such a tremendous relief when you didn't have to be God any more. Before, I had to see you every day to be sure you were all right and still on your throne. I had to be sick so you could pretend you were wearing your long white coat. Any day that we were equal—that we gave and received equally—left me satisfied for at least a week. As soon as you could admit that you could be sick and have problems, then I could be the doctor or the mother at times. That allowed me to grow up from being your baby.

As long as you were safe, high above my suffering, I could only rage at you. When you comforted and reassured me, you seemed a thousand miles away, in a different world. As though I were in hell and you reached down and patted the top of my head. Your fear of coming down with me made me feel more dreadful and hopeless.

As soon as you openly showed weakness and uncertainty, my rage could turn to sympathy. I could feel with you. If you were God on a throne, I didn't think you could go down with me and feel what I felt. For me to go down alone into my problems just made us farther apart and made me desperate. I had to know you could go down with me into the suffering and the mess, to help me come up again, not just sit by and watch and pity me.

I had to force you to see that you felt angry and frightened more often than you admitted. When you hid your feelings under the appearance of loving and caring, it made you seem dead. I was terrified. It wasn't the real you at all. It was a mask. I had to make you mad to keep the real you from dying—to make you really you.

The first time I cried, you made a terrible mistake: you wiped away my tears with a handkerchief. You had no idea how I wanted to feel those tears roll down my face. At last I had some feelings that were on the outside. If only you could have licked my tears with your tongue, I would have been completely happy. Then you would have shared my feelings.

I never had anyone that I could love and show them that I loved them as much as I wanted. Mother always pushed me away and told me to stop pawing her. It left me all bottled up. You were strong enough to stand my love. I could hug you as hard as I wanted and you weren't upset. I could feel free to burst out and say, "I love you."

Father either ignored me or treated me like a grown woman. He would talk to me about his business problems which I didn't understand. When Mother was away he would bring me presents of candy or flowers.

In the interviews, when not pressed by a time limit, I felt finished sooner. I needed a period at the end to calm down. I needed to know I was more important than the clock. . . .

When a girl doesn't want to walk, it's because she doesn't want to realize that there is nothing swinging between her legs. She would like to be paralyzed from the waist down. If her legs are dead, then her genitals are dead too. She won't have to think of them again. I hated to walk. I could feel my thighs rubbing and that made me remember my genitals. I hated you for making me walk.

Patients dribble and smear their food or smear their B.M. in an effort to test it out. They want to get to know what is going in and coming out of them. They want to get acquainted and know what it feels like on the outside. Then they can feel safe when it's inside. It's terribly frightening not to know what may be going on inside.

I used to beg to go outdoors because I needed to be warmed by the sun. It's terrible to feel empty and cold inside. Rainy weather is very hard on the patients because it forces them to look inside themselves for warmth, but they can't find any. It helped me a lot to lie on the beach because then

I could feel that mother was holding me and giving me warmth and life.

When I was catatonic I tried to be dead and gray and motionless. I thought mother would like that. She could carry me around like a doll.

I felt as though I were in a bottle. I could feel that everything was outside and couldn't touch me.

I had to die to keep from dying. I know that sounds crazy but one time a boy hurt my feelings very much and I wanted to jump in front of a subway. Instead I went a little catatonic so I wouldn't feel anything. (I guess you had to die emotionally or your feelings would have killed you.) That's right. I guess I'd rather kill myself than harm somebody else.

I had to be able to tease you sexually so that I could be sure that I really was attractive, but before I could do this I had to be sure that nothing bad would come of it. While I lunged and wrestled with you and bit you, it was very close to intercourse. I was thinking of a stallion and a mare and how they rear and kick and bite. It would all be terribly intense and animal and beautiful. The animal part of me would rise to meet the animal part of you. That would be the only way I could have orgasm. It would be too violent to do it as people.

If you had actually screwed me it would have wrecked everything. It would have convinced me that you were only interested in pleasure with my animal body and that you didn't really care about the part that was a person. It would have meant that you were using me like a woman when I really wasn't one and needed a lot of help to grow into one. It would have meant you could only see my body and couldn't see the real me which was still a little girl. The real me would have been up on the ceiling watching you do things with my body. You would have seemed content to let the real me die. When you feed a girl, you make her feel that both her body and her self are wanted. This helps her get joined together. When you screw her she can feel that her body is separate and dead. People can screw dead bodies, but they never feed them.

It was terribly hard for me to stop being a schizophrenic. I knew I didn't want to be a Smith (her family name) because then I was nothing but old Professor Smith's granddaughter. I couldn't be sure that I could feel as though I were your child, and I wasn't sure of myself. The only thing I was sure of was being a "catatonic, paranoid schizophrenic." I had seen that written on my chart. That, at least, had substance and gave me an identity and personality.

(What led you to change?) When I was sure that you would let me feel like your child and that you would care for me lovingly. If you could like the real me, then I could, too. I could allow myself just to be me and didn't need a title.

I walked back to see the hospital recently, and for a moment I could lose myself in the feeling of the past. In there I could be left alone. The world was going by outside, but I had a whole world inside me. Nobody could get at it and disturb it. For a moment I felt a tremendous longing to be back. It had been so safe and quiet. But then I realized that I can have love and fun in the real world and I started to hate the hospital. I hated the four walls and the feeling of being locked in. I hated the memory of never being really satisfied by my fantasies.

A woman needs an excuse to feel angry. If the doctor is too kind, she feels guilty about her anger, and all the fun and life are taken out of the fight. It's important for a woman to be able to fight without guilt. It feels good to hate and to fight. People need practice in hating without guilt and fear, just as much as loving.

Later I came to realize that I could work out my problems for myself, but I was afraid to do it alone. I was afraid I would see something that was too big or too horrible. I needed you to help me realize that the problem wasn't too powerful for me or that I wasn't too awful for having things like that inside me. I could only believe that I was lovable because you loved me in spite of everything.

DISCUSSION

Hindsight shows that in this case the therapy of the period of overt psychosis fell into three principal phases. At the start, Joan presented chiefly the picture of catatonic withdrawal or of belligerent masculine identification, so that the work of therapy centered around efforts to help her control her aggression and overcome her fear of being hurt again if she established a human relationship. The therapist had to be tested at length until he proved he was dependable and would always strive to do what was necessary for her welfare.

Once Joan was sure that she could depend on the therapist, she began a process of replacing the deprivations of the original oral period through a new mother-infant experience. This she describes as the really vital relationship which enabled her to feel like a girl. She could only be a girl if she started with a mother who could love her as a girl.

The third phase, or period of growth, went on slowly and almost imperceptibly. Joan was free of overt psychosis by the time she began to use the therapist less as a mother and more as a good father who could convince her of her ability to be attractive and successful as a woman. She entered reality solidly when she could again see the therapist as a doctor and the relationship became more co-operative and adult.

But It's the Truth
Even If It Didn't Happen
Ken Kesey

Before writing *One Flew over the Cuckoo's Nest*, Ken Kesey worked in mental wards of a veterans hospital in California. This excerpt from the novel is a view of such a hospital, seen through the eyes of "Chief Broom," an American Indian who has been on the ward for years. Emotions become objects to him, ideas take on physical form, feelings distort perception, time is disjointed, and everything is permeated by a hum of fear. The ward routine and Chief Broom's ideas have blended into a total system. His perceptions are part of a control system run by those who manage the entire hospital. The head nurse, the machines, the windows, walls, and floors are all under their omnipotent control, forming a unified, consistent, and terrifying world for Chief Broom.

They're out there. Black boys in white suits up before me to commit sex acts in the hall and get it mopped up before I can catch them.

They're mopping when I come out the dorm, all three of them sulky and hating everything, the time of day, the place they're at here, the people they got to work around. When they hate like this, better if they don't see me. I creep along the wall quiet as dust in my canvas shoes, but they got special sensitive equipment detects my fear and they all look up, all three at once, eyes glittering out of the black faces like the hard glitter of radio tubes out of the back of an old radio.

"Here's the Chief. The *soo*-pah Chief, fellas. Ol' Chief Broom. Here you go, Chief Broom. . . "

Stick a mop in my hand and motion to the spot they aim for me to clean today, and I go. One swats the back of my legs with a broom handle to hurry me past.

"Haw, you look at 'im shag it? Big enough to eat apples off my head an' he mine like a baby."

They laugh and then I hear them mumbling behind me, heads close together. Hum of black machinery, humming hate and death and other

From *One Flew Over the Cuckoo's Nest* (Chapter 1) by Ken Kesey. Copyright © 1962 by Ken Kesey. All Rights Reserved. Published in the British Commonwealth by Methuen & Co. Reprinted by permission of The Viking Press, Inc., and Laurence Pollinger Ltd.

36

hospital secrets. They don't bother not talking out loud about their hate secrets when I'm nearby because they think I'm deaf and dumb. Everybody thinks so. I'm cagey enough to fool them that much. If my being half Indian ever helped me in any way in this dirty life, it helped me being cagey, helped me all these years.

I'm mopping near the ward door when a key hits it from the other side and I know it's the Big Nurse by the way the lockworks cleave to the key, soft and swift and familiar she been around locks so long. She slides through the door with a gust of cold and locks the door behind her and I see her fingers trail across the polished steel-tip of each finger the same color as her lips. Funny orange. Like the tip of a soldering iron. Color so hot or so cold if she touches you with it you can't tell which.

She's carrying her woven wicker bag like the ones the Umpqua tribe sells out along the hot August highway, a bag shape of a tool box with a hemp handle. She's had it all the years I been here. It's a loose weave and I can see inside it; there's no compact or lipstick or woman stuff, she's got that bag full of a thousand parts she aims to use in her duties today—wheels and gears, cogs polished to a hard glitter, tiny pills that gleam like porcelain, needles, forceps, watchmakers' pliers, rolls of copper wire. . .

She dips a nod at me as she goes past. I let the mop push me back to the wall and smile and try to foul her equipment up as much as possible by not letting her see my eyes—they can't tell so much about you if you got your eyes closed.

In my dark I hear her rubber heels hit the tile and the stuff in her wicker bag clash with the jar of her walking as she passes me in the hall. She walks stiff. When I open my eyes she's down the hall about to turn into the glass Nurses' Station where she'll spend the day sitting at her desk and looking out her window and making notes on what goes on out in front of her in the day room during the next eight hours. Her face looks pleased and peaceful with the thought.

Then . . . she sights those black boys. They're still down there together, mumbling to one another. They didn't hear her come on the ward. They sense she's glaring down at them now, but it's too late. They should of knew better'n to group up and mumble together when she was due on the ward.Their faces bob apart, confused. She goes into a crouch and advances on where they're trapped in a huddle at the end of the corridor. She knows what they been saying, and I can see she's furious clean out of control. She's going to tear the black bastards limb from limb, she's so furious. She's swelling up, swells till her back's splitting out the white uniform and she's let her arms section out long enough to wrap around the three of them five, six times. She looks around her with a swivel of her huge head. Nobody up to see, just old Broom Bromden the half-breed

Indian back there hiding behind his mop and can't talk to call for help. So she really lets herself go and her painted smile twists, stretches to an open snarl, and she blows up bigger and bigger, big as a tractor, so big I can smell the machinery inside the way you smell a motor pulling too big a load. I hold my breath and figure, My God this time they're gonna do it! This time they let the hate build up too high and overloaded and they're gonna tear one another to pieces before they realize what they're doing!

But just as she starts crooking those sectioned arms around the black boys and they go to ripping at her underside with the mop handles, all the patients start coming out of the dorms to check on what's the hullabaloo, and she has to change back before she's caught in the shape of her hideous real self. By the time the patients get their eyes rubbed to where they can halfway see what the racket's about, all they see is the head nurse, smiling and calm and cold as usual, telling the black boys they'd best not stand in a group gossiping when it *is* Monday morning and there *is* such a lot to get done on the first morning of the week. . . .

". . . mean old Monday morning, you know, boys. . ."

"Yeah, Miz Ratched. . ."

". . . and we have quite a number of appointments this morning, so perhaps, if your standing here in a group talking isn't *too urgent* . . ."

"Yeah, Miz Ratched . . ."

She stops and nods at some of the patients come to stand around and stare out of eyes all red and puffy with sleep. She nods once to each. Precise, automatic gesture. Her face is smooth, calculated, and precision-made, like an expensive baby doll, skin like flesh-colored enamel, blend of white and cream and baby-blue eyes, small nose, pink little nostrils— everything working together except the color on her lips and fingernails, and the size of her bosom. A mistake was made somehow in manufacturing, putting those big, womanly breasts on what would of otherwise been a perfect work, and you can see how bitter she is about it.

The men are still standing about and waiting to see what she was onto the black boys about, so she remembers seeing me and says, "And since it *is* Monday, boys, why don't we get a good head start on the week by shaving poor Mr. Bromden first this morning, before the after-breakfast rush on the shaving room, and see if we can't avoid some of the—ah—disturbance he tends to cause, don't you think?"

Before anybody can turn to look for me I duck back in the mop closet, jerk the door shut dark after me, hold my breath. Shaving before you get breakfast is the worst time. When you got something under your belt you're stronger and more wide awake, and the bastards who work for the Combine aren't so apt to slip one of their machines in on you in place of an electric shaver. But when you shave *before* breakfast like she has me do some mornings—six-thirty in the morning in a room all white walls and white basins, and long-tube lights in the ceiling making sure there aren't any shadows, and faces all round you trapped screaming behind the mirrors—then what chance you got against one of their machines?

I hide in the mop closet and listen, my heart beating in the dark, and I try to keep from getting scared, try to get my thoughts off someplace else—try to think back and remember things about the village and the big Columbia River, think about ah one time Papa and me were hunting birds in a stand of cedar trees near The Dalles. . . . But like always when I try to place my thoughts in the past and hide there, the fear close at hand seeps in through the memory. I can feel that least black boy out there coming up the hall, smelling out for my fear. He opens out his nostrils like black funnels, his outsized head bobbing this way and that as he sniffs, and he sucks in fear from all over the ward. He's smelling me now, I can hear him snort. He don't know where I'm hid, but he's smelling and he's hunting around. I try to keep still. . . .

(Papa tells me to keep still, tells me that the dog senses a bird somewheres right close. We borrowed a pointer dog from a man in The Dalles. All the village dogs are no-'count mongrels, Papa says, fish-gut eaters and no class a-tall; this here dog, he got *insteek!* I don't say anything, but I already see the bird up in a scrub cedar, hunched in a gray knot of feathers. Dog running in circles underneath, too much smell around for him to point for sure. The bird safe as long as he keeps still. He's holding out pretty good, but the dog keeps sniffing and circling, louder and closer. Then the bird breaks, feathers springing, breaks out of the cedar into the birdshot from Papa's gun.)

The least black boy and one of the bigger ones catch me before I get ten steps out of the mop closet, and drag me back to the shaving room. I don't fight or make any noise. If you yell it's just tougher on you. I hold back the yelling. I hold back till they get to my temples. I'm not sure it's one of those substitute machines and not a shaver till it gets to my temples; then I can't hold back. It's not a will-power thing any more when they get to my temples. It's a . . . *button*, pushed, says Air Raid Air Raid, turns me on so loud it's like no sound, everybody yelling at me, hands over their ears from behind a glass wall, faces working around in talk circles but no sound from the mouths. My sound soaks up all other sound. They start the fog machine again and its snowing down cold and white all over me like skim milk, so thick I might even be able to hide in it if they didn't have a hold on me. I can't see six inches in front of me through the fog and the only thing I can hear over the wail I'm making is the Big Nurse whoop and charge up the hall while she crashes patients outta her way with that wicker bag. I hear her coming but I still can't hush my hollering. I holler till she gets there. They hold me down while she jams wicker bag and all into my mouth and shoves it down with a mop handle.

(A bluetick hound bays out there in the fog, running scared and lost because he can't see. No tracks on the ground but the ones he's making, and he sniffs in every direction with his cold red-rubber nose and picks up no scent but his own fear, fear burning down into him like steam.) It's gonna burn me just that way, finally telling about all this, about the hospital, and her, and the guys—and about McMurphy. I been silent so long now it's gonna roar out of me like floodwaters and you think the guy telling this is ranting and raving my *God*; you think this is too horrible to have really happened, this is too awful to be the truth! But, please. It's still hard for me to have a clear mind thinking on it. But it's the truth even if it didn't happen.

Gates of Eden
Harold Massoon

The following selection consists of two letters written to a group re-
searching the effects of LSD on consciousness. Harold Massoon's account
of his experiences is straightforward and related with little resentment.
He is simply a member of our culture who has dealt with and recovered
from madness several times. On one occasion he spent time recovering
in a mental hospital; two other times he did not.

For Massoon, the important elements during his madness were those
positive times when he felt most alive and highly sensitized to everything
he did or thought of doing. Although fully aware that he was psychotic,
that he had delusions and hallucinations, and that he was committed to
a mental hospital against his will, he still reflects on these experiences
as having positive value.

He reports that during his second and third psychotic episodes, he
was increasingly capable of controlling his external behavior. He had
learned something about his own consciousness during the first break
with usual reality and applied what he had learned in his later encounters
with madness.

FIRST LETTER: TO INTERNATIONAL FEDERATION FOR
INTERNAL FREEDOM, CAMBRIDGE, MASS.

Gentlemen: Recently I chanced to read an article dealing with the activity
of your group. To myself it was heartening, in a sense, to read that the
LSD experiments produce sensory experiences of great beauty. I do not
believe that the average layman's concept of mental illness includes any
knowledge or recognition of the fact that the "disturbed" individual may
enter realms of such exquisite beauty as to upset his normal values and
reactions. Since the individual is clearly the victim of delusions, any such
gratifying experience may be chalked off as an escape mechanism—a psychotic dream. This may be so, yet having myself undergone a psychotic
experience, a portion of which involved sensory experience and feelings
of breathtaking beauty, it is hard for me to accept the idea that the things
which happened to me could be explained away so simply. The unconscious
mechanisms of man are doubtless of enormous complexity. Man may well

From *The Psychedelic Review*, No. 10, 1969. Reprinted by permission.

be a far more amazing creature than even his inflated conceptions of his contemporary self would indicate. The halucinogens may prove a valuable tool for the eventual creation of more enlightened populations—indeed, for a better race of men.

For what it may be worth I would like to touch on certain aspects of my own psychosis which occurred some four years ago. My experience was, at one end, a vista into a state of unparalleled beauty and peace, but at the opposite end there were experiences and thoughts of darkness and terror. My hallucinations, when they finally made their appearance, were terrifying; it was as if, at one stage, I stood at the portals of paradise and, at another, felt and experienced the dark gate of hell.

At the outset, while my experience had religious connotations, it should be mentioned that I am neither a church goer nor a Bible addict. In fact, I will acknowledge that I am a little afraid of the old book—I had an insane theory as to why this is so—and perhaps in my own instance it is just as well. A sensitive, imaginative, and evidently weak-minded person, I have had no wish to tangle with a book that has produced such a bumper crop of fanatics, zealots, and religious maniacs, recognizing that I was prime material. Nonetheless, I suppose I am, in a sense, a religious individual who sees religion as a matter of values to be lived up to; true religion should be an approach to life and a thing more to be lived, or attempted, than preached. However, I have learned quite a bit about the old book and what it contains, from readings as well as from conversations and from observing life itself. In my psychotic state—and somewhere I have read that this is a familiar pattern—the informations and observations gleaned throughout a lifetime *seemed* to fall neatly into place as if a lifetime had provided me with, so to speak, the keys to the kingdom in which I found myself. In my deluded state I believed that I was supposed to write the book, or formula, which would enable others to enter this realm—a realm of great inner beauty, of sensory awakening, and with utter abandon I dismissed all other considerations to plunge excitedly to the task. In the course of matters I made the dangerous mistake of letting my wild and disordered imagination be my guide, believing that I was being inspired by Divine sources and, oh brother, what a trip to the moon that was—culminating, as you might suspect, in a nuthouse.

No doubt there were several causative factors contributing to my particular psychosis and here again, for brevity's sake, I can only suggest the mechanisms which altered my interior chemistry and triggered my psychotic explosion. Heredity? A strong likelihood, I suppose. My father before me was in and out of mental institutions a number of times and I had opportunity to observe his strange behavior during his "spells." (What may have happened to the inner man is less of a mystery to me now.) Overwork, perhaps;—unrequited love (I was a 43-year-old bachelor at the time—unable to "break the ice"); and a very powerful and provocative book, Philip Wylie's *Generation of Vipers* which I had read before and was in the process of re-reading and which was an influential if not causative factor in my psychosis. But I have no intention to attempt diagnosis—why the hell, I've but a high school education.

It all began in a subtle way with a feeling of wellbeing and abundant good nature that was not unlike a continuous alcoholic "glow." In my work, I became tireless. Each day, ordinarily dull to a degree, became an adventure—my mind sharpened—my wit keened—a feeling of camaraderie enveloped me. With the passing days the feeling grew and I recognized that something (I supposed, wonderful) had happened to me. I was a man transformed. God, I felt marvelous.

In a world that grew more beautiful day by day I recognized one significant fact: no one—but no one—could feel as wonderful as I and wish to do anything but *live!* Here, within myself I had discerned—or been shown—the brotherhood of man, the pure true beauty of existence. A growing conviction took hold of me—this must be put into words. Thinking back I can see the egotism of it—just the shade of an idea that I, yes I, would be exalted, glorified, famous.

Well, suffice it to say I blew my job, leaving behind a few good-natured but pointed allusions to the company's greedy ways, withdrew my thousand odd from the credit union and set out to write "The Book of Life." Somebody had to write this, deriving it from the "Tree of Life" in the Garden of Eden, which I came to regard as a symbolism, a simple tale but fraught with hidden meaning. Legendary "Eden" never existed, but the story was written with a clever reversal and put at the front of the book instead of the back where it rightfully belonged, by a force representative of the dark half of man's heritage and symbolized in the figure of a man with some of the appurtenances of an animal. For if the old black book were purportedly a manual for man's guidance someone surely erred in disregarding the opposites in man's nature, not realizing that the devil himself might have had an equal hand in the assembly of the book. This must, of course, be regarded as an insane theory but some of these heresies bear mention. It may not be too far-fetched to suggest that the old book may have done a lot of harm as well as good, if hypocrisy, fanaticism, etc., are taken into consideration.

So I plunged into writing and the imagination soared and the words flowed freely. Each day was a continual joy and my ecstasy was unlimited. Nights I would sometimes leave the apartment and drive through the velvet dark, and the city was an enchanting place. Sometimes I drank—not that I desired liquor—only to be around people and where there was music. Liquor seemed to have a special effect on me—I was continuously "high." I began to experience feelings of rapture in my lower belly, exquisitely sweet feelings of pleasure, some so piercing and keen as to make me want to cry out, others soft and gentle like little fingers, constantly changing, never alike and this, during the height of my ecstatic feeling, was almost continuous.

Once on retiring I had an erection and began to experience climax after climax, some lasting for minutes and this continued for two or three hours, with no manipulation on my part. I could visualize an act of love of pure beauty and feeling, bodies joined in quiet dignity, no animal movements required. A breath-taking experience, even alone, and with a woman simi-larly attuned—oh God what it would be! I recall feeling a vast relief—so this was how it was and sex was not eliminated but here was an act of love a thousand times more beautiful. Small wonder that man's animal sex act has "dirty" connotations—I might note here that I have found pleasure in *that* as well, I image as much as anyone—but what I experienced was unbelievable.

I continued with my writing believing that when my work was done I would ultimately be led to "Eve," for what I was experiencing was meant to be shared and the prospects were exciting—well, that is a mild word for it.

I had been in this state of "Eden" for perhaps a couple of weeks or thereabouts when I had my first hallucination. Following a session of writ-ing I went into the bedroom to lie down and rest a bit. Suddenly there before my eyes there was the blackest of blacks and I saw my mother's face, crying out, imploring—as she was sucked into a black vortex. I was terrified—I almost went to the phone to place a long distance call home. What did this mean? Had my mother died? There was a feeling of malevo-lence accompanying the hallucination that was terrifying. Then I calmed. I'd met the Great Deceiver—it was all a clever trick to try and drive me out of my mind. And it came to me that no man "attains" Eden without doing battle with this jealous force. If one lost this psychic battle, the devil would have his mind and he'd end up in an asylum—a hopeless gibbering idiot. Terrifying prospect. Somehow I recalled what I knew of the Lord's Prayer—"Yea, though I walk through the valley of the shadow of death, I shall fear no evil" and I was vastly relieved. Let the clever sonofabitch bring on his bag of tricks—I wasn't going to be afraid.

My writing concluded, I drove my car out of the city late one night. I would just start out driving through the enchanted night and somewhere we would meet and I would know. Paradise. I stopped at a market to get some cigarettes, and noticing some large delicious apples there, I bought one. Amusedly I thought about it—a wedding present, the symbolic ap-ple—well, by God, I'd give it back to the faithless bitch and she would understand and we'd both laugh uproariously. For we would be free and wild and uninhibited and Eve a lovable shameless bitch.

Well, gentlemen, I'm running up the pages here and there are many things recalled but not gone into. Suffice it to say, I followed my deluded imagination to a motel alongside the highway and my imagination told me *"he"* had her there in one of the units and I went in and there he was, the fiend incarnate,—bald head, hooked nose, swarthy complexion and glittering brown eyes—a vicious looking specimen with what appeared to be two fangs for lowers. I am a slightly built fellow but I damned near tore that motel unit apart with my bare hands and it took about five state police to subdue me. Later, in the back of a police car, steel cuffs biting into my wrists, my jaw fractured—a figure walked by and it was the bald headed one only this time he was wearing a felt hat. He looked at me in the back of the police car and his face lit up with a saccharine grin of such sweetness that I had to smile back. How neatly he'd done me in—the bastard. He disappeared down the path to the cabins and shortly thereafter I smelled the unmistakable odor of sulphur in the police car—strong, penetrating—an olfactory hallucination, I suppose. There were some terrifying moments in the asylum but even so my cheerful glow continued for some time, gradually diminishing, the rapture fading. Released in about three months. There isn't a helluva lot that I can say about a state institution that is very commendable however and if LSD can help some of those poor devils—well, that's a great deal. And it may even be found some day that there are hidden resources in man's psyche which is not an economic push-button gadget but full of a vivid and beautiful life that has nothing to do with worldly goods.

Back in society and with a different company, two years ago I awoke one morning with a great feeling of indescribable joy. I tiptoed to the window to see that about ten inches of new snow had fallen during the night and somehow the whiteness, the purity, and the beauty of feeling seemed to go hand in hand. I went through another experience involving moments of great beauty and sensory delights as well as some pretty dark times. This time I subdued, with quite an effort, my inclinations to abandon my job, and somehow I made it through about four months of insanity, though I was very nearly deceived into answering auditory hallucinations during one hectic week. But I am a reticent person—thank God for that— and I pretty much kept my wild thoughts to myself, a not inconsiderable feat. Possibly the knowledge that all this had its beginning and end in the self was a help. Again I had a compulsion to write—I wanted to bring this beauty of feeling to others—and this time I guess I did some 200 odd pen-written pages. I've never been inclined to re-read them—I suppose they are a curious mixture of truths, delusions, and fantastic heresy. During this "illness," I did manage one constructive thing that it may be significant to mention. Always a heavy and compulsive cigarette smoker and never quite able to quit, I abandoned the weed with an ease that was really astonishing. Gave nearly a carton away after they lay around a couple of weeks untouched. After about three months abstinence, my psychosis faded, and like an ass I bought a pack and it seems I haven't been able to quit since. So it may just be that when these things are better understood and controlled that good may be realized out of what we know as insanity.

Since my last episode I've gotten along quite well. I have no special desire to flirt with another session in the booby hatch and I try and keep both feet on the ground and I don't, at my intelligence level, propose to know all the answers as to what happened to me. It may be that there is enough integrity within me, and that my personal values—not always coincident with those of society—are true enough that I am very close to something. There is no doubt that there is inner conflict and dis-integrity within my psyche and I suppose that is my "devil." But oh, God, if a man could capture and control the other feeling—I would want it always. And if numbers of men could find the route, I could foresee the beginnings of man's dream of peace.

Philip Wylie indicted society and science, and his writing bears scrutiny. The greater efforts of science, he declares, "have gone to implement man—not to enlighten him. Egotistical man assumes that he knows all there is to know of himself whereas he and his truth seekers actually know relatively little of inner spiritual man because so little effort has been devoted to that end." What occurred to me subjectively seemed much too profound to be designated an escape mechanism, but even if it was—take a hard look at your society and your people who flock by the millions to the bar rooms each night for a little "escape" and perhaps, in instances, a little human warmth, and I'll tell you there's just a great deal to want to "escape" from.

I have no special feelings of shame for my psychotic escapade and episode in the nut factory—as I've told friends, jokingly, well, it's not everyone gets the first hand experience. But I've made little effort to tell, as I have attempted here, of the exquisite beauty I experienced—after all I was "sick," "I didn't know what I was doing," etc. If my acts were incomprehensible, I recall pretty well what I did and the motivations at the time, and I readily acknowledge and recognize that my mental apparatus played tricks on me.

I suppose I have written because someone it seemed should hear my tale and perhaps your experiments have provided the only people with sufficient insights as to possibly appreciate it.

SECOND LETTER

Dear Doctor: In reply to your letter of April 30 may I say that I have no objection if you see fit to make use of my account of a psychotic adventure in your periodical.

I might mention that coincident with my writing of my experience to you people, possibly as the result of aroused feelings and the recalling of past adventure, I lapsed forthwith into another enraptured interval of psychosis. I did, in fact, awaken the morning after I had written the account, and the euphoria lasted many weeks though it was interposed with occasional terrifying thoughts. How very very sure was I *this* time that I had somehow discovered the essense of vivid life and, of course, how very very deluded I turned out to be. I abandoned a good job, went through a modest savings and was obliged to sell my (all paid for) late model automobile. It was a matter of some six months before I was re-employed—sadder, older and, it is to be hoped, possibly a trifle wiser. No nuthouse this time—I was smart enough to manage appearances, curb the tendency to loquaciousness, keep bills paid and exercise some restraint and actually I had quite an exhilarating experience, if an expensive one. Since I am a bachelor no one was particularly harmed and I have apparently emerged from the experience satisfactorily. Still and all I hope I am done with it for although it is a terrific adventure it is not a happy thing for an individual with some intelligence and a sensitive nature to be obliged to emerge from. At least I think I have shed some of my delusions in the process and perhaps the outlook is not unfavorable. My personal orientation has ever been inclined toward life and living as above personal gain and advancement so I can be philosophical about the matter—at least I have savored the heights and the depths of feeling and encountered a very crafty personal devil.

It Is the World of Your Own Soul That You Seek

Hermann Hesse

Freud once wrote: "One may heave a sigh at the thought that it is vouchsafed to a few with hardly an effort, to salve from the whirlpool of the emotions the deepest truths, to which we others have to force our way. . . . "

Hermann Hesse is one of those few. In this selection from *Steppenwolf* he presents an experience of madness, therapy for the experience, and a theory about it all, interwoven into a series of events taking place in the mind of Harry Haller, a lonely, pessimistic, fifty-year-old man. Hesse unravels levels of the personality, one at a time, then in combination, and finally in a unified whole. Like Lara Jefferson, Harry Haller has insight into his madness. Yet this insight does not preclude a psychological journey in search of a resolution beyond insight.

From far away came Pablo's warm voice.

"It is a pleasure to me, my dear Harry, to have the privilege of being your host in a small way on this occasion. You have often been sorely weary of your life. You were striving, were you not, for escape? You have a longing to forsake this world and its reality and to penetrate to a reality more native to you, to a world beyond time. Now I invite you to do so. You know, of course, where this other world lies hidden. It is the world of your own soul that you seek. Only within yourself exists that other reality for which you long. I can give you nothing that has not already its being within yourself. I can throw open to you no picture-gallery but your own soul. All I can give you is the opportunity, the impulse, the key. I help you to make your own world visible. That is all."

Again he put his hand into the pocket of his gorgeous jacket and drew out a round looking-glass.

"Look, it is thus that you have so far seen yourself."

He held the little glass before my eyes (a children's verse came to my mind: "Little glass, little glass in the hand") and I saw, though indistinctly and cloudily, the reflection of an uneasy, self-tormented, inwardly labouring and seething being—myself, Harry Haller. And within him again I saw the Steppenwolf, a shy, beautiful, dazed wolf with frightened eyes that smouldered now with anger, now with sadness. This shape of a wolf coursed through the other in ceaseless movement, as a tributary pours its cloudy turmoil into a river. In bitter strife, in unfulfilled longing each tried to devour the other so that his shape might prevail. How unutterably sad was the look this fluid inchoate figure of the wolf threw from his beautiful shy eyes.

"This is how you see yourself," Pablo remarked and put the mirror away in his pocket. I was thankful to close my eyes and take a sip of the elixir.

"And now," said Pablo, "we have had our rest. We have had our refreshment and a little talk. If your fatigue has passed off I will conduct you to my peep-show and show you my little theatre. Will you come?"

We got up. With a smile Pablo led. He opened a door, and drew a curtain aside and we found ourselves in the horseshoe-shaped corridor of a theatre, and exactly in the middle. On either side, the curving passage led past a large number, indeed an incredible number, of narrow doors into the boxes.

"This," explained Pablo, "is our theatre, an enjoyable theatre. I hope you'll find lots to laugh at." He laughed aloud as he spoke, a short laugh, but it went through me like a shot. It was the same bright and peculiar laugh that I had heard before from below.

"This little theatre of mine has as many doors into as many boxes as you please, ten or a hundred or a thousand, and behind each door exactly what you seek awaits you. It is a pretty cabinet of pictures, my dear friend; but it would be quite useless for you to go through it as you are. You would be checked and blinded at every turn by what you are pleased to call your personality. You have no doubt guessed long since that the conquest of time and the escape from reality, or however else it may be that you choose to describe your longing, means simply the wish to be relieved of your so-called personality. That is the prison where you lie. And if you were to enter the theatre as you are, you would see everything through the eyes of Harry and the old spectacles of the Steppenwolf. You are therefore requested to lay these spectacles aside and to be so kind as to leave your highly esteemed personality here in the cloak-room where you will find it again when you wish. The pleasant dance from which you have just come, the treatise on the Steppenwolf, and the little stimulant that we have only this moment partaken of may have sufficiently prepared you. You, Harry, after having left behind your valuable personality, will have the left side of the theatre at your disposal, Hermine the right. Once inside, you can meet each other as you please. Hermine will be so kind as to go for a moment behind the curtain. I should like to introduce Harry first."

Hermine disappeared to the right past a gigantic mirror that covered the rear wall from floor to vaulted ceiling.

"Now, Harry, come along, be as jolly as you can. To make it so and to teach you to laugh is the whole aim of this entertainment—I hope you will make it easy for me. You feel quite well, I trust? Not afraid? That's good, excellent. You will now, without fear and with unfeigned pleasure, enter our visionary world. You will introduce yourself to it by means of a trifling suicide, since this is the custom."

He took out the pocket-mirror again and held it in front of my face. Again I was confronted by the same indistinct and cloudy reflection, with the wolf's shape encircling it and coursing through it. I knew it too well and disliked it too sincerely for its destruction to cause me any sorrow.

"You will now extinguish this superfluous reflection, my dear friend. That is all that is necessary. To do so, it will suffice that you greet it, if your mood permits, with a hearty laugh. You are here in a school of humour. You are to learn to laugh. Now, true humour begins when a man ceases to take himself seriously."

I fixed my eyes on the little mirror, where the man Harry and the wolf were going through their convulsions. For a moment there was a convulsion deep within me too, a faint but painful one like remembrance, or like homesickness, or like remorse. Then the slight oppression gave way to a new feeling like that a man feels when a tooth has been extracted with cocaine, a sense of relief and of letting out a deep breath, and of wonder, at the same time, that it has not hurt in the least. And this feeling was accompanied by a buoyant exhilaration and a desire to laugh so irresistible that I was compelled to give way to it.

The mournful image in the glass gave a final convulsion and vanished. The glass itself turned grey and charred and opaque, as though it had been burnt. With a laugh Pablo threw the thing away and it went rolling down the endless corridor and disappeared.

"Well laughed, Harry," cried Pablo. "You will learn to laugh like the immortals yet. You have done with the Steppenwolf at last. It's no good with a razor. Take care that he stays dead. You'll be able to leave the farce of reality behind you directly. At our next meeting we'll drink brotherhood, dear fellow. I never liked you better than I do today. And if you still think it worth your while we can philosophise together and argue and talk about music and Mozart and Gluck and Plato and Goethe to your heart's content. You will understand now why it was so impossible before. I wish you good riddance of the Steppenwolf for today at any rate. For naturally, your suicide is not a final one. We are in a magic theatre; a world of pictures, not realities. See that you pick out beautiful and cheerful ones and show that you really are not in love with your highly questionable personality any longer. Should you still, however, have a hankering after it, you need only have another look in the mirror that I will now show you. But you know the old proverb: 'A mirror in the hand is worth two on the wall.' Ha! ha!" (again that laugh, beautiful and frightful!) "And now there only remains one little ceremony and quite a gay one. You have now to cast aside the spectacles of your personality. So come here and look in a proper looking-glass. It will give you some fun."

Laughingly with a few droll caresses he turned me about so that I faced the gigantic mirror on the wall. There I saw myself.

I saw myself for a brief instant as my usual self, except that I looked unusually good-humoured, bright and laughing. But I had scarcely had time to recognise myself before the reflection fell to pieces. A second, a third, a tenth, a twentieth figure sprang from it till the whole gigantic mirror was full of nothing but Harrys or bits of him, each of which I saw only for the instant of recognition. Some of these multitudinous Harrys were as old as I, some older, some very old. Others were young. There were youths, boys, schoolboys, scamps, children. Fifty-year-olds and twenty-year-olds played leap frog. Thirty-year-olds and five-year-olds, solemn and merry, worthy and comic, well dressed and unpresentable, and even quite naked, long-haired, and hairless, all were I and all were seen for a flash, recognised and gone. They sprang from each other in all directions, left and right and into the recesses of the mirror and clean out of it. One, an elegant young fellow, leapt laughing into Pablo's arms, embraced him and they went off together. And one who particularly pleased me, a good looking and charming boy of sixteen or seventeen years, sprang like lightning into the corridor and began reading the notices on the doors. I went after him and found him in front of a door on which was inscribed:

All Girls Are Yours.
One Quarter In The Slot.

The dear boy hurled himself forward, made a leap and, falling head first into the slot himself, disappeared behind the door.

Pablo too had vanished. So apparently had the mirror and with it all the countless figures. I realised that I was now left to myself and to the theatre, and I went with curiosity from door to door and read on each its alluring invitation. . . .

The series of inscriptions was endless. One was

Guidance In The Building-Up Of The
Personality. Success Guaranteed.

This seemed to me to be worth looking into and I went in at this door.

I found myself in a quiet twilit room where a man with something like a large chess-board in front of him sat in Eastern fashion on the floor. At the first glance I thought it was friend Pablo. He wore at any rate a similar gorgeous silk jacket and had the same dark and shining eyes.

"Are you Pablo?" I asked.

"I am not anybody," he replied amiably. "We have no names here and we are no persons. I am a chess-player. Do you wish for instruction in the building up of the personality?"

"Yes, please."

"Then be so kind as to place a few dozen of your pieces at my disposal."

"My pieces—?"

"Of the pieces into which you saw your so-called personality broken up. I can't play without pieces."

He held a glass up to me and again I saw the unity of my personality broken up into many selves whose number seemed even to have increased. The pieces were now, however, very small, about the size of chessmen. The player took a dozen or so of them in his sure and quiet fingers and placed them on the ground near the board. As he did so he began to speak in the monotonous way of one who goes through a recitation or reading that he has often gone through before.

"The mistaken and unhappy notion that a man is an enduring unity is known to you. It is also known to you that man consists of a multitude of souls, of numerous selves. The separation of the unity of the personality into these numerous pieces passes for madness. Science has invented the name Schizophrenia for it. Science is in this so far right as no multiplicity may be dealt with unless there be a series, a certain order and grouping. It is wrong in so far as it holds that only a single, binding and lifelong order is possible for the multiplicity of subordinate selves. This error of science has many unpleasant consequences, and the only advantage of simplifying the work of the state-appointed pastors and masters and saving them the labours of original thought. In consequence of this error many persons pass for normal, and indeed for highly valuable members of society, who are incurably mad; and many, on the other hand, are looked upon as mad who are geniuses. Hence it is that we supplement the imperfect psychology of science by the conception that we call the art of building up the soul. We demonstrate to anyone whose soul has fallen to pieces that he can rearrange these pieces of a previous self in what order he pleases, and so attain to an endless multiplicity of moves in the game of life. As the playwright shapes a drama from a handful of characters, so do we from the pieces of the disintegrated self build up ever new groups, with ever new interplay and suspense, and new situations that are eternally inexhaustible. Look!"

With the sure and silent touch of his clever fingers he took hold of my pieces, all the old men and young men and children and women, cheerful and sad, strong and weak, nimble and clumsy, and swiftly arranged them on his board for a game. At once they formed themselves into groups and families, games and battles, friendships and enmities, forming a little world all by themselves. For a while he let this lively and yet orderly world go through its evolutions before my enraptured eyes in play and strife, making treaties and fighting battles, wooing, marrying and multiplying. It was indeed a crowded stage, a moving breathless drama.

Then he passed his hand swiftly over the board and gently swept all the pieces into a heap; and, meditatively with an artist's skill, made up a new game of the same pieces with quite other groupings, relationships and entanglements. The second game had an affinity with the first, it was the same world built of the same material, but the key was different, the time changed, the motif was differently given out and the situations differently presented.

And in this fashion the clever architect built up one game after another out of the figures, each of which was a bit of myself, and every game had a distant resemblance to every other. Each belonged recognisably to the same world and acknowledged a common origin. Yet each was entirely new.

"This is the art of life," he said in the manner of a teacher. "You may develop the game of your life and lend it animation. You may complicate and enrich it as you please. It lies in your hands. Just as madness, in a higher sense, is the beginning of all wisdom, so is schizophrenia the beginning of all art and all fantasy. Even learned men have come to a partial recognition of this, as may be gathered, for example, from *Prince Wunderhorn*, that enchanting book, in which the industry and pains of a man of learning, with the assistance of the genius of a number of madmen and artists shut up as such, are immortalised. Here, take your little pieces away with you. The game will often give you pleasure. The piece that today grew to the proportions of an intolerable bugbear, you will degrade tomorrow to a mere lay figure. The luckless Cinderella will in the next game be the princess. I wish you much pleasure, my dear sir."

I bowed low in gratitude to the gifted chessplayer, put the little pieces in my pocket and withdrew through the narrow door.

The Doctors Don't Believe Me
Vaslav Nijinsky

In madness, the behavior that certain feelings and ideas evoke is not predictable. Here is a case in which love is the destructive focus of a man's world.

Vaslav Nijinsky was probably the greatest ballet dancer in modern history. In this excerpt from his personal diary, written before he was committed to a mental institution where he spent the last years of his life, Nijinsky is trying to understand and deal with the many levels of love that seem to overpower him. Here are distrust, fear, even willingness to kill in the name of love. Here, too, is the desire to be understood, respected, worshiped—also in the name of love. Nijinsky's madness is a kind of possession, not by an evil force, but by one so compelling that his own mind is not able to come to terms with it.

Everybody will say that Nijinsky has become insane. I do not care, I have already behaved like a madman at home. Everybody will think so, but I will not be put in an asylum, because I dance very well and give money to all those who ask me. People like an odd and peculiar man and they will leave me alone, calling me a "mad clown." I like insane people, I know how to talk to them. My brother was in the lunatic asylum.

I was fond of him and he understood me. His friends there liked me too, I was then eighteen years old. I know the life of lunatics and understood the psychology of an insane man. I never contradict them, therefore madmen like me. . . .

Life is not sex—sex is not God, God is man, who fecundates only one woman, a man who gives children to one woman. I am twenty-nine years old. I love my wife spiritually, not for begetting children. I will have children if God wishes it. Kyra is an intelligent girl. I do not want her to be clever. I will prevent her from developing her intelligence. I like simple people but not stupidity, because I see no feeling in that. Intelligence stops people from developing. I feel God and God feels me.

I want to correct my faults but I do not know whether I will be able

From Vaslav Nijinsky, *The Diary of Vaslav Nijinsky.* Copyright ©1936, by Simon & Schuster, Inc. Reprinted by permission of Simon & Schuster, Inc., and Eric Glass, Ltd.

to. The doctor's eyes were full of tears when he told me that he needed no promises, he knew that I would do everything to stop my wife from being nervous and worried. I explained to him that I was the one who wanted my wife's mother to come. I do not want my wife to be afraid; therefore I wanted my mother-in-law to live with us. I am not afraid of the Allied authorities. I do not care if they take all our money.[1] But I do not want this money to be taken on account of my family. I do not want my wife to be ruined. I gave her all I had which was very little, so that she should be able to live. I am not afraid of life and therefore I do not need money. My wife will weep if I die. I hope for her sake that she will soon forget me. My wife does not always understand or, rather, feel me. Tolstoy's wife had no feeling. Tolstoy's wife cannot forget that he had given all his money away. I want to give my wife money. I love my wife and Kyra more than anybody else; my hand is tired.

I do not like Shakespeare's Hamlet because he reasons. I am a philosopher who does not reason—a philosopher who feels. I do not like to write things that are thought out. I like Shakespeare because he loved the theater. Shakespeare understood the theater. I have understood the "living theater" also. I am not artificial. I am life. The theater is not life. I know the customs of the theater. The theater becomes a habit. Life does not. I do not like the theater with a square stage. I like a round stage. I will build a theater which will have a round shape, like an eye. I like to look closely in the mirror and I see only one eye in my forehead. Often I make drawings of one eye. I dislike polemics and therefore people can say what they like about my book; I will be silent. I have come to the conclusion that it is better to be silent than to speak. Diaghilev told me to be silent. Diaghilev is clever. Vassilli, his servant, used to say, "Diaghilev hasn't got a penny, but his intelligence is worth a fortune." I say, "I haven't got a penny and no intelligence, but I have a mind." I call mind that center which generates feeling. I am sensitive. I was stupid before because I thought that happiness depended on money—now I no longer think it. Many people think about money, I need some to carry out my plans; we all have our plans and aims, and we earn money to realize them, but our problems are different. I am God's problem, not Antichrist's. I am not Antichrist. I am Christ. I will help mankind.

I will go to Geneva to have a rest because the doctor tells me to do so. He thinks I am tired because my wife is now very nervous, high-strung. I am not, therefore I will stay at home. My wife can go alone. She has a little money. I have not got a penny. I am not bragging when I say that I have no money. I like to have money and will earn some to give

---

[1]Subjects of Allied countries were not allowed to spend money on the subjects of the enemy countries. Mme. Nijinsky's relatives were Hungarians.

to my wife and to poor people. Many will say that Nijinsky pretends to be like Christ. I do not pretend—I love His deeds. I am not afraid of being attacked. I say everything I have to.

I used to go out on the street. I deceived my wife, I had so much semen that I had to throw it away. I did not waste it on a cocotte. I threw it on the bed in order to protect myself from catching a venereal disease. I am not erotic and therefore will not deceive my wife any more. My seed I will save for another child—I hope I will some day have a son. I love my wife, I do not want anything bad to happen to her. She is sensitive. She thinks that I do everything on purpose, in order to frighten her. Everything I do is for the purpose of making her well and happy. She eats meat—that causes her nervousness; it does not matter if one eats meat—to lead a good life is important. My wife knows that it is good to lead a regular life, but she does not realize what this mode of life consists of. *"To listen to God—and obey Him—that is a good regular mode of life."* People do not understand God, and ask themselves who is this God who must be obeyed. I know God and His wishes. I love God.

I do not know what to write about, because I have suddenly thought of the doctors and my wife—who are talking in the next room. I know they do not like my actions but I will continue in the same way while God wishes it. I am not afraid of any complications. I will ask everybody to help me and will not be afraid if I am told this, for instance: "Your wife became insane because you have tortured her; for this you will be imprisoned for the rest of your life." I am not afraid of prison and there I will find life, but I will die there if I am put there for life. I do not wish my wife ill, I love her too much to harm her. I like to hide from people; I am used to living alone.

Maupassant was terrified of being lonely. The Count of Monte Cristo liked loneliness because he wanted time to prepare for his revenge. Maupassant was frightened of solitude; he loved people. I am afraid of loneliness but will not cry; God loves me and so I am not alone. If God leaves me I will die. As I do not want to, I will live like other people, in order to be understood by others. God is mankind, and does not like those who interfere with His plans. I do not; on the contrary I help him. I am the weapon of God, a man of God. I like God's people. I am not a beggar. I will take money if a rich man will leave it to me. I like a rich man. The rich man has a lot of money and I have none. When everyone finds out that I have no money, they will get frightened and turn away from me. That is why I want to get richer every hour.

I will hire a horse and will make him take me home without paying for it. My wife will pay. If she does not pay I will find a way of paying myself. I want my wife to love me and so I do all this to develop her character. Her intelligence is well developed but her feelings are not. I want to destroy her intelligence; then she can only develop in other ways. People think that without intelligence a man is either insane or a fool. An insane person is a person who cannot reason. A lunatic does not realize what he is doing. I understand my good and my bad actions. I am a man who has reason. In Tolstoy's book a lot is explained about reason. I read this book and therefore know what it means. I am not afraid of intelligent people. I am strong because I feel all that is said about me. I know that they invent all sorts of things to calm me. The doctors are good. My wife is also a good woman, but they think much too much. I am afraid for their intelligence. People went mad because they thought too much—I am afraid for them, they think too much. I do not want them to become insane: I will do everything to make them healthy.

I offended my wife without realizing it—then I asked her for forgiveness; my faults were continuously being brought up at a suitable moment. I am afraid of my wife; she does not understand me. She believes that I am insane or wicked. I am not wicked, I love her. I write about life, not death. I am not Nijinsky as they think. I am God in man. My wife is a good woman. I told her in secret all my plans, then she told the doctors everything, believing this would help me. My wife does not understand my object; I did not explain it, not wanting her to know. I will feel and she will understand. She will feel and I will understand. I do not want to think, thinking is death. I know what I am doing. *"I do not wish you ill. I want to live and therefore I will be with you. I spoke to you. I do not want intelligent speech."* The doctors speak with intelligence, so does my wife. I am afraid of them. I want them to understand my feelings. *"I know that it hurts you. Your wife is suffering because of you."* I do not want death to come and therefore I use all kinds of tricks. I will not reveal my object. *"Let them think you are an egoist. Let them put you in prison. I will release you because you belong to me. I do not like the intelligent Romola. I want her to leave you. I want you to be mine. I do not want you to love her as a man loves. I want you to love her with a sensitive love. I know how to simplify and smooth everything that has happened. I want the doctors to understand your feelings. I want to scold you because the doctors think that your wife is a nervous woman. Your cross[2] has done so much harm that you cannot disentangle it all. I know your faults because I have committed them."* I put on a cross on purpose: *"She understood you. The doctor came in order to find out what your intentions are and does not understand anything at all. He thinks and therefore it is difficult for him to understand. He feels Romola is right and that you are right too. I know how to understand."* I think better than doctors. *"I am afraid for you, because love for me is infinite; you obey my orders. I will do everything to make you understand, I love your wife and you. I wish her well. I am God in you. I will be yours when you will understand*

[2][Nijinsky wore a cross over his necktie and walked around St. Moritz, causing a sensation, described in the biography.]

me. I know what you are thinking. You are frightened. I know your habits. Your about: that he is here and is staring at you. I want him to look at you." I do not want to turn round because I can feel him looking at me. *"I want to show him your writing. He will think that you are ill because you write so much. I understand your feelings. I understand you well. I am making you write with a purpose because he will understand your feelings too. I want you to write everything I am telling you. People will understand you because you are sensitive. Your wife will understand you also. I know more than you and therefore I ask you not to turn around. I know your intentions. I want to carry out our plans but you must suffer. Everybody will feel and understand only when they see your sufferings."*

I want to write about my conversation in the dining room with my wife and the doctor. I pretended I was an egoist because I wanted to touch him. He will be offended if he finds this out but I do not care. I do not divide love. I wrote that I loved my wife better than anybody—I wanted to show how I feel about my wife. I love A. just as much. I know her tricks. She understands my feelings because she is going away in the next few days. I do not want her presence. I want my mother-in-law to come because I want to study her and help her. I do not study people's character in order to write about them. I want to write in order to explain to people their habits—which lead them to death. I call this book "Feelings." I love feeling and will write a big book about it. There will be a description of my life in it. I do not want to publish this book after my death. I want to publish it now. *"I am afraid for you because you are afraid for yourself. I want to say the truth. I do not want to hurt people. Perhaps you will be put in prison for writing this book. I will be with you because you love me. I cannot be silent. I must speak. I know you will not be put in prison; legally you have not committed an offense. If people want to judge you, you shall answer that everything you said is God's word. Then they will put you in an asylum, and you will understand insane people. I want you to be put in prison or into an asylum. Dostoyevsky went to the gallows and therefore you also can go and sit somewhere. I know people whose love is not dead and they will not allow you to be put anywhere. You will become as free as a bird when this book is published in many thousands of copies. I want to sign the name of Nijinsky—but my name is God. I love Nijinsky not as Narcissus but as God."* I love him because he gave me life. I do not want to pay any compliments. I love him. He loves me because he knows my habits. *"Nijinsky has faults, but Nijinsky must be listened to because he speaks the words of God."* I am Nijinsky. *"I do not want Nijinsky to be hurt and therefore I will protect him. I am only afraid for him because he is afraid for himself. I know his strength. He is a good man. I am a good God. I do not like Nijinsky when he is bad."* I do not like God when he is bad. I am God, Nijinsky is God. *"He is a good man and not evil. People have not understood him and will not understand him if they think. If people listened to me for several weeks there would be great results. I hope that my teachings will be understood."* All that I write is necessary to mankind. Romola is afraid of me, she feels I am a preacher.

Romola does not want her husband to be a preacher, she wants a young, handsome husband. I am handsome, young. She does not understand my beauty, I have not got regular features. Regular features are not like God. God has sensitiveness in the face, a hunchback can be Godlike. I like hunchbacks and other freaks. I am myself a freak who has feeling and sensitiveness, and I can dance like a hunchback. I am an artist who likes all shapes and all beauty. Beauty is not relative. Beauty is God, He is in beauty and feeling. Beauty is in feeling too. I love beauty. I feel it and understand it. Those people who think write nonsense about beauty. One cannot discuss it. One cannot criticize it. I am feeling beauty. I love beauty.

I do not want evil—I want love. People think that I am an evil man. I am not. I love everybody. I have written the truth. I have spoken the truth. I do not like untruthfulness and want goodness, not evil. I am love. People take me for a scarecrow because I put on a small cross which I liked. I wore it to show that I was Catholic. People thought I was insane. I was not. I wore the cross in order to be noticed by people. People like calm men. I am not. I love life. I want it. I do not like death. I want to love mankind. I want people to believe in me. I have said the truth about A., Diaghilev, and myself. I do not want war and murders. I want people to understand me. I told my wife that I would destroy the man who would touch my notebooks, but I will cry if I have to do it. I am not a murderer. I know that everyone dislikes me. They think I am ill. I am not. I am a man with intelligence.

The maid came and stood near me, thinking that I was sick. I am not. I am healthy. I am afraid for myself because I know God's wish. God wants my wife to leave me. I do not want it, I love her and will pray that she may remain with me. They are telephoning about something. I believe they want to send me to prison. I am weeping, as I love life, but I am not afraid of prison. I will live there. I have explained everything to my wife. She is no longer afraid, but she still has a nasty feeling. I spoke harshly because I wanted to see tears—but not those which have been caused by grief. Therefore I will go and kiss her. I want to kiss her to show her my love. I love her, I want her, I want her love. A. has felt that I love her too and she is remaining with us. She is not leaving. She has telephoned to sell her ticket. I do not know for certain but I feel it.

My little girl is singing: "Ah, ah, ah, ah!" I do not understand its meaning, but I feel what she wants to say. She wants to say seek Him. I am a seeker, for I can feel that everything—Ah! Ah!—is not horror but joy.

EPILOGUE

I want to cry but God orders me to go on writing. He does not want me to be idle. My wife is crying, crying. I also. I am afraid that the doctor will come and tell me that my wife is crying while I write. I will not go to her, because I am not to blame. My child sees and hears everything and I hope that she will understand me. I love Kyra. My little Kyra feels my love for her, but she thinks too that I am *ill*, for they have told her so. She asks me whether I sleep well and I tell her that I always sleep well. I do not know what to write, but God wishes me to. Soon I will go to Paris and create a great impression—the whole world will be talking about it. I do not wish people to think that I am a great writer or that I am a great artist nor even that I am a great man. I am a simple man who has suffered a lot. I believe I suffered more than Christ. I love life and want to live, to cry but cannot—I feel such a pain in my soul—a pain which frightens me. My soul is ill. My soul, not my mind. The doctors do not understand my illness. I know what I need to get well. My illness is too great to be cured quickly. I am incurable. My soul is ill, I am poor, a pauper, miserable. Everyone who reads these lines will suffer—they will understand my feelings. I know what I need. I am strong, not weak. My body is not ill—it is my soul that is ill. I suffer, I suffer. Everyone will feel and understand. I am a man, not a beast. I love everyone, I have faults, I am a man—not God. I want to be God and therefore I try to improve myself. I want to dance, to draw, to play the piano, to write verses, I want to love everybody. That is the—object of my life. I know that Socialists would understand me better—but I am not a Socialist. I am a part of God, my party is God's party. I love everybody. I *do not* want war or frontiers. The world exists. I have a home everywhere. I live everywhere. I do not want to have any property. I do not want to be rich. I want to love. I am love—not cruel. I am not a bloodthirsty animal. I am man. I am man. God is in me. I am in God. I want Him, I seek Him. I want my manuscripts to be published so that everybody can read them. I hope to improve myself. I do not know how to, but I feel that God will help all those who seek Him. I am a seeker, for I can feel God. God seeks me and therefore we will find each other.

God and Nijinsky,
Saint Moritz-Dorf,
Villa Guardamunl
February 27, 1919

Heat-Craze My Teeth
in Bitterest Anger
Hannah Green

In attempts to determine the prime aspect in madness, some writers emphasize biochemical aspects, while others stress disorganized thought patterns, sensory stresses, or bizarre overt behavior.

People who write of their own madness continually suggest that what appears to others to be disorganized, bizarre, or uncontrolled is often a shrewd and consciously construed act designed to achieve a particular goal. The phrase "inner world" refers to the experience of a different interior reality. Psychiatrists commonly label this kind of world a "delusional system."

In this selection from *I Never Promised You a Rose Garden*, Hannah Green portrays the frightening complexity of one inner world, a realm with its own morality, customs, gods, even language. Deborah, a sixteen-year-old girl locked in a mental hospital, describes the precarious relationship between her "inner" and "outer" worlds: "There was a gear all teeth, two at least world-caught. And now nothing engages the world!" Even the bizarre outburst described in this chapter seems to move Deborah toward self-understanding.

When the volcano erupted at last, there was no backfire in the matchbooks that was big enough to stave it off. Deborah had not anticipated anything more unusual than dark-mindedness and howling from the Collect when she began to feel the familiar whip of fear and hear the one-tone whine of accusation from the invisible hating ones. She had been in the tubroom behind the front bathroom by herself because all the seclusion rooms were full. (Often the nurses would unlock the door for her and let her be alone in there until someone needed the toilets up front; for half an hour after the evening wash-up, solitude was almost a certainty.) It had been evening and soon it would be bedtime. She hadn't wanted to carry her hell to bed with her, kicking the effects of dose after dose of chloral hydrate that kept growing deeper in the glasses and went down like burning celluloid.

She lay down on the cold floor and began beating her head slowly and methodically against the tiles. The black in her mind went red, swelling and growing out of her so far that before she knew it she was engulfed in the furious anger of eruption.

When her vision cleared, it was only enough to see and hear as if through a keyhole. She was aware that she was shouting and that attendants were in the room and that the walls of the room were covered with Yri words and sentences. Ranged around her were all the outpourings of hatred and anger and bitterness in a language whose metaphors used "broken" to mean "consenting" and "third rail" to mean "complying." All the words were extreme. *Uguru*, which was "dog-howling" and meant loneliness, was written in its superlative form in letters a foot high the length of one wall: U G U R U S U. The words were written in pencil and in blood, and in some places scratched with a broken button.

There was a look of horror and surprise even on the faces of a hardened D-ward staff, and it was that look which brought the full fire from her. The world's fear and hatred were like the sun, common and pervading, daily and accepted—a law of nature. Now its rays were focused in their look, waking fire. The words Deborah spoke were not loud, but they were full of hatred and they were Yri.

"Where is what you used to scratch this, Miss Blau?"

"*Recreat*," Deborah said. "*Recreat xangoran, temr e xangoranan. Naza e fango xangoranan. Inai dum. Ageai dum.*" ("Remember me. Remember me in anger, fear me in bitter anger. Heat-craze my teeth in bitterest anger. The signal glance drops. The Game"—Ageai meant the tearing of flesh with teeth as torture—"is over.")

Mrs. Forbes came then. Deborah had liked Mrs. Forbes—she remembered having liked her. The anger was rising steadily and too much of what Deborah said could not wait even for the Yri logic and frame of words, and went sailing off into gibberish with only an Yri word here and there to let Deborah know what she was saying. Mrs. Forbes asked Deborah if she could send the others away, and Deborah, grateful for her courage in offering this, showed the two open hands and tried for form in her speech that was only going further and further into meaningless sounds.

"This word here—the biggest one—I think I heard you say it. Has it a meaning?"

Deborah groped wildly for gestures, words, or sounds to convey the impact of the volcano's eruption; the word she had written in the blood from a cut finger was the third form of anger, which she had never spoken or written before and which was more extreme than black anger or red-white anger. After moving about restlessly for a while, she threw back her head in a soundless scream, wide-mouthed. The nurse looked at her.

"Is the word *fear?*" she asked. "No—not fear—*anger.*" And then looking at Deborah again: "An anger you cannot control." After a pause she said, "Come on, we'll try seclusion until you can take care of yourself."

The seclusion room was small, but the force of the volcano would not let her rest. It kept hurling her from one side of the room to the other; walls and floors pounded her head and hands and body. Now her lack of inner control matched the anarchic world with an Yr gone newly mad itself.

After a while they caught her up and put her in a pack. She fought with them, terrified of what she might do to them now that she had no law. English, Yri, and gibberish all flowed together. Gradually, the anger was overtaken by the fear, but the words to warn them that she was wild could not be framed, and she fought them with her head and her teeth while the restraints were being tied, trying, doglike, to bite, herself, her wrappings, the bed, the beings. She fought until she was exhausted and then she lay still.

After a while Deborah could feel the constriction of blood in her legs and feet that usually brought a familiar pain, but there was no pain. The burns, she knew, had had their raw surfaces ripped open under the bandages, but there was no pain from them either. How cold the wind was blowing above the law! . . . She lay shivering, although the sheets had been close for many hours and she should have been warm. Beyond even the laws and logic of Yr she breathed out in wonder: My enemy, my virulent, plague-pouring self—and now not even control of it. . . .

"*There was a gear . . .*" she cried aloud, and it came in Yri loud and mingled with strange words which were not hers. "*There was a gear all teeth, two at least world-caught. And now nothing, nothing engages with the world!*"

You are not of them, the Censor said. It was an old phrase, perhaps the oldest one in Yr, but its context changed from comfort and pity, to anger and terror, and now to the last deceit, the final move of the game which was part of the world's secret purposes and her damnation. She now knew that the death she feared might not be a physical one, that it could be a death of the will, the soul, the mind, the laws, and thus not death, but a perpetual dying. The tumor began to ache.

Furii looked at her and said, "Are you ill?" and Deborah laughed with the same ugliness that her cry had been. "I mean, is something physically the matter?"

"No." She tried to tell Furii, but the walls began bleeding and sweating, and the ceiling developed a large tumor which began to separate itself from its surface.

"Can you hear me?" Furii asked.

Deborah tried to say what she felt, but she could only gesture the Yri gesture for insanity: flattened hands thrust toward one another but unable to meet.

"Listen to me. Try to hear me," Furii said seriously. "You are afraid of your power and that you cannot control it."

When Deborah could speak at last, she could only say, "Yri . . . in the world . . . collision . . ."

"Try again. Just let it come."

"Gears uncaught . . . *n'ai naruai* . . . uncaught!"

"It is why you need a hospital. You are in a hospital and you do not need to fear the terrible forces that seem to have been opened in you. Listen hard now, and try to stay in contact with me. You must try to talk to me and tell me what is happening in your collided worlds. We will work with all our strength to keep you from the excesses of your sickness."

Some of the fear eased so that Deborah could say, "It came Yri, English, nonsense. Wild . . . hitting. Anger."

"Were you angry for all the years, in the way that anger gets when it grows old and is rotted with guilt and fear—like bad-smelling pebbles inside?"

"Much . . ."

"The suffering was not because of your anger then, was it?"

"No . . . Yri . . . on earth . . . collision. Censor . . . death penalty . . . the last . . ." She began to tremble in a cutting cold.

"Use the blanket," Furii said.

"Yri cold . . . *nacoi* . . . earth blankets . . ."

"We will see if Earth warmth helps," Furii said. She picked up the blanket and covered Deborah with it. Deborah remembered that there was no Yri word for "thank you." She had no word to give Furii her gratitude. It remained a mute weight inside her. Even the trembling did not lessen, so that Furii could see it and be glad.

"Tell me this," Furii was saying, "of the emotion you felt as you heard yourself cry out in these languages, how much was anger and how much was fear?"

"Ten," Deborah said, thinking of the emotion by letting a stroke of it come up and engulf her once again, "three anger, five fear."

"That is only eight."

"I suffer," Deborah said, helping herself with Yri hand-motions. "After you I suffer smarter. Now I never fill them. Two is for miscellaneous."

Furii laughed. "Anger some, fear quite a bit, and what are those little two miscellaneous? Relief, maybe, not to have to give everything to that wall between Yr and the world? Also, was there not something overt to remind me that I went away and left you with it all?"

Deborah felt that the last idea was only half true, but she let it sound in the judgment with the others, and she said, "Fear . . . Censor—doing the forbidden . . . destroy me . . . and . . ."

"And what is it?"

"Then . . . no. No-ness; not Yr even. Loud gibberish and just *No. No!!*"

"Not even the gods for friends," the doctor mused. She drew her chair up closer to where Deborah was huddled shivering under the blanket whose warmth stopped short of her interior climate. "You know, Deborah, you have a gift for health and strength. Before you let go for this breaking of walls, you trusted our work together and you trusted me. Before you let the anger come, you got yourself on D ward and in the sort of seclusion that was at hand, and when a nurse was on duty, mind you, whom you liked and trusted. Not so dumb for someone who is supposed to have lost her marbles. Not so bad at all, that talent for life."

Deborah's eyes began to get heavy. She was very tired.

"You are worn out," Furii said, "but no longer so very frightened, are you?"

"No."

"The anger may come again. The sickness you have built may also come and fight you perhaps, but I have faith that you will conquer it enough to get the help and control that you need. Half of your fear is that you will not be able to be stopped, and it is this fear which makes it impossible to speak so that others can understand."

Section II

Theoretical Perspectives

At times it seems that if there is any behavior that is "natural" to man, it is his almost insatiable need to group sets of experiences into categories—to conceptualize, to theorize. In many cases this has proven highly advantageous: It allows us to make predictions about the future based on the probability that similar kinds of events will have similar outcomes. It has allowed us to develop a complex technology, to send men into outer space, and to cure a wide range of organic diseases. This same kind of technology has also been used in attempts to understand man's psyche and behavior.

Some psychologists feel that research methodology stands in the way of understanding. The study of abnormal experience exemplifies this problem. The first article in this section, by Braginsky, Braginsky, and Ring, considers the difficulties inherent in present psychiatric theory and the development of a new theoretical model. The authors point out that "There are few investigators who still seriously maintain the view that the study of schizophrenia utilizes only value-free constructs. One's very conception of schizophrenia, and not merely one's treatment procedures, is bound to be indissolubly linked to the values one holds about men and their behavior."

The question of relative values is further emphasized in the next article by anthropologist Alfred L. Krober, who finds that behaviors that are considered pathological in one culture may be praised and cultivated by another. In his essay, Thomas Szasz attacks the entire assumption surrounding the current medical model of mental illness as a disease.

Subsequent articles present alternative ways of viewing the experience of madness, perspectives that differ from the mainstream of current psychological and psychiatric thought. R. D. Laing emphasizes some of the usually ignored or denigrated aspects of madness that he views as favorable experiences in the growth of the personality. Carl Jung, presenting a detailed examination of the dynamics of certain abnormal experiences, warns that there is a possibility of hindering personal growth or mental health by the undisciplined cultivation of abnormal experience. Baba Ram Dass (Richard Alpert) suggests a framework integrating aspects of Eastern and Western psychology that treat abnormal experience as an altered state of consciousness.

Wilson Van Dusen's intriguing article is the result of a clinical investigation that uncovered distinct parallels between the world of spirits described by a famous philosopher and the world of madness. Finally, Malcolm B. Bowers offers a reevaluation of abnormal experience. He proposes that far from being destructive, madness can sometimes offer the foundation for constructive personal growth.

There is merit in each position. Each article is accurate, but incomplete. The magnitude of the inner world is far greater than any one author has described. Try to juggle the ideas as you read, tossing and catching each in turn, until a pattern that is meaningful begins to emerge.

The Search for a New Paradigm
Benjamin M. Braginsky
Dorothea D. Braginsky
Kenneth Ring

A theory is a conceptual framework that is useful in assembling a group of facts. If the theory is viable, it not only accommodates the facts, but also serves as a tool for generating research ideas. If new research evidence further supports the theory, both the theory and its capacity to aid understanding are strengthened. If, however, discoveries do not fit within the original framework, the theory is eventually exchanged for a more inclusive one.

The theory that the moon, sun, and stars revolve around the earth was useful for hundreds of years. Eventually new observations didn't fit the theory, causing it to be abandoned. The theory that mental illness is caused by demons entering the body was useful until closer observation of mental disturbance revealed alternative possibilities. The theory then became constraining; it prevented objective evaluation of the newer observations, and it was discarded.

Braginsky, Braginsky, and Ring suggest reasons why the older theoretical models of mental illness should be rejected and new ones formulated. They believe that most current models of abnormal experience no longer accommodate the results of current research. The medical model of schizophrenia, for instance, postulates the existence of disease, a position that does not hold up under the weight of recent research evidence. For example, a current psychiatric characterization of the schizophrenic as a "weak, acquiescent, and ineffectual individual" is challenged by the authors, who find the opposite to be true. They also feel that part of the difficulty in discarding present theories lies in a basic prejudice against individuals who do not act or communicate in a fashion deemed appropriate by the larger community.

Braginsky, Braginsky, and Ring propose a theoretical and therapeutic approach that "opens our eyes to hitherto unsuspected possibilities and sets the stage for theoretical and research innovations," without sacrificing the essential humanity of the patient.

From *Methods of Madness: The Mental Hospital as a Last Resort* by Benjamin M. Braginsky, Dorothea D. Braginsky, and Kenneth Ring. Copyright © 1969 by Holt, Rinehart and Winston, Inc. Reprinted by permission of Holt, Rinehart and Winston, Inc.

"Once it has achieved the status of a paradigm," writes Kuhn, "a scientific theory is declared invalid only if an alternate candidate is available to take its place. No process yet disclosed by the historical study of scientific development at all resembles the methodological stereotype of falsification by direct comparison with nature. . . . The decision to reject one paradigm is always simultaneously the decision to accept another . . ." (p. 77). Scientific revolutions, then, do not occur merely because a paradigm is revealed to be seriously flawed; another paradigm must stand ready to replace it. In the present context the question now becomes "Do we currently have an alternate paradigm for schizophrenia that will allow us to come to terms with the facets of the behavior of schizophrenic patients that prove an embarrassment to the psychiatric perspective?"

We have already said that at the outset of our work we had no revolutionary intent—we were not interested in helping to overthrow one system of thought in order to supplant it with another. Our purpose was principally to discover how patients spent their time in a state mental hospital; our task, then, was in the main descriptive and theoretical. The observations we referred to earlier, however, forced us to examine closely the tenets of the psychiatric perspective simply and only because, as we have said, the behavior of patients made that perspective appear distressingly inadequate as a basis for understanding what we were witnessing. We hope we have made it clear that it was not merely that the psychiatric perspective was irrelevant to the kind of data we were collecting; we found instead that this paradigm either obscured the significance of some of these data or, if we were to take them seriously, either failed to predict them or predicted their opposite. To retain the psychiatric perspective in the face of such overwhelmingly contrary data appeared to us to be more than fatuous: It was an impossibility. Only drastically different assumptions about the "nature" of the mental patient would, we felt, permit us to make sense of our observations and experimental findings.

Gradually the outlines of what we have here called a paradigm began to crystallize. We found that, rather than regarding the schizophrenic as a qualitatively dissimilar being from the rest of us, the assumption most congruent with our data was to emphasize just how human he was. Instead of viewing his "illness" as the manifestation of some sort of recondite disease process, it appeared to us that it represented his not-altogether-irrational attempt to cope with the problems he confronted in his everyday life; to call it a "disease" seems, as we shall indicate later, merely to reflect a value judgment and retards understanding of the schizophrenic's behavior by invoking a specious, albeit widely accepted, analogy with pathological physical processes. Finally, what appeared most blatantly erroneous to us in the psychiatric conception of the schizophrenic was his portrayal as a weak, acquiescent, and ineffectual individual. Everything that we saw pointed to exactly the opposite characterization: The schizophrenics we observed were, as a rule, manipulative and resourceful individuals whose behavior was calculated to serve their primary motivations, which they were able to satisfy with surprising frequency and ease. Paradigms transform reality, and the schizophrenics we studied and that we describe in this book bear almost no resemblance to those depicted in standard psychiatric accounts. In a word, ours appear to have all the characteristics of ordinary human beings.

Just as we were by no means the first to record this kind of observation, we are not enunciating a totally new paradigm. Within the past decade views similar to ours have been propounded only to languish in obscurity or, if they were noted, to be quickly dismissed as, in effect, heretical. Scientific revolutions, however, in contrast to political ones, are never accomplished quickly, and repeated assaults upon a dominant paradigm are usually necessary before it begins to give way. To demonstrate that there are others who endorse the revolutionary paradigm we have outlined (though perhaps such a demonstration is really unnecessary), consider the independently elaborated views of Rakusin and Fierman (1963), whose conception of the schizophrenic is virtually point-by-point identical to ours:

> The chronically psychotic patient is human, not sub-human or different in quality from the people treating and managing him. No matter how bizarre his behavior, the patient is still capable of discriminating external events, including the presence of other humans.
> His behavior is purposeful, reactive, motivated, and goal directed. . . .
> The patient has personal interests, and purpose, pursues them avidly, and is distracted from them only with difficulty.
> We explicitly assert our belief that the patient is human, and qualitatively not different from ourselves, in order to take issue with "evidence" that he is somehow sub-human. . . . Our view of psychosis constitutes more a "way of life" hypothesis than a "disease" hypothesis. We assume the patient to have what he regards as good reasons for behaving the way he does—that he has in mind some purpose from which his behavior logically follows (p. 140).

The seemingly neglected work of Artiss (1959) and others also supports our contention that the schizophrenic's behavior is purposeful and is designed to get personally satisfactory outcomes from his environment. Symptoms and other deviant behavior may therefore represent a kind of tactical device that schizophrenics use to manipulate their interpersonal environment in order to attain certain goals:

> The data have demonstrated that certain schizophrenic trainee soldiers engage in a symptomatic statement, "I am weak and ineffectual," for which the anticipated reply is, "all right then, we'll release you from

your obligations—and from our group." . . . Did the young schizophrenic patients in this group behave in symptomatic ways in direct anticipation of release from the group, as part of a total goal-directed plan, as it were? We believe that the data will answer this question in the affirmative . . . (p. 19).

Of course, the most vigorous and well-known spokesman for the new paradigm is Thomas Szasz, whose writings (1958, 1961, 1963, 1965) have earned him a reputation as a polemicist of the first rank. In his most celebrated book, *The Myth of Mental Illness* (1961), whose title leaves no doubt about his revolutionary aspirations, Szasz demolished the commonly maintained assumption that the psychiatric conception of mental illness represents merely an objective and dispassionate account of psychopathology. Several years earlier, however, Szasz had already enunciated his position with characteristic elan:

More precisely, according to the common sense definition, mental health is the ability to play whatever the game of social living might consist of and play it well. Conversely, to refuse to play, or to play badly, means that the person is mentally ill. The question now may be raised as to what are the differences, if any, between social non-conformity (or deviation) and mental illness. Leaving technical psychiatric considerations aside for the moment, I shall argue that the difference between these two notions—as expressed for example by the statements "He is wrong" and "He is mentally ill"—does not necessarily lie in any observable facts to which they point, but may consist only of a difference in our attitudes toward our subject. If we take him seriously, consider him to have human rights and dignities, and look upon him as more or less our equal—we then speak of disagreements, deviations, fights, crimes, perhaps even treason. Should we feel, however, that we cannot communicate with him, that he is somehow "basically" different from us, we shall then be inclined to consider him no longer as an equal but rather as an inferior (rarely, superior) person; and we then speak of him as being crazy, mentally ill, insane, psychotic, immature and so forth (p. 188).[1]

Sarbin (for example, 1964, 1967a, 1967b, 1967c, 1967d, 1967e), employing the techniques of linguistic, logical, and historical analysis, has attacked the concept of mental illness with vigor. Concerning schizophrenia, Sarbin (1967b) states:

[1]Arieti's (1959) rebuttal is curiously flaccid: "Szasz's is probably one of the strongest attacks ever made on the Kraepelinian concept of dementia praecox (schizophrenia). Although I admit that in what we call the schizophrenic syndrome there is much that is indefinite, variable, inconstant and accessory, I *feel* [italics ours] nevertheless that there is a more or less homogeneous core which recognizes the schizophrenic person as such and leads us to some conclusions, some of which have pragmatic value. The fact that the nature of this core has not been fully or uncontroversially determined points to the incompleteness of the concept of schizophrenia but does not prove it is a fallacy" (p. 501).

The readiness to accept the concept of schizophrenia as a disease entity is perhaps the most widespread social implication of the continued uncritical reliance on the mental illness (and mental health) myths. To explode the myth one needs to present arguments to show the lack of utility of the major concepts contained within the myth, e.g. schizophrenia, hallucinations, anxiety. Support for the official structure of knowledge may be undermined when its metaphorical roots are exposed. . . . I have also argued that the concept of schizophrenia has negative utility for scientists and professionals concerned with the management and welfare of disordered persons. (In this context, I define disordered persons as those who engage in improper, silly, unpopular, perturbing, embarrassing, perplexing, or eccentric conduct, i.e., *conduct that violates propriety norms*) [Italics ours]. . . . A number of observations render questionable the continued use of the disease concept: (a) the fact that the label is currently attached to an infinite variety of behaviors; (b) that professionals cannot agree on whether or not the label should be applied to a particular person; (c) that similar behaviors in certain classes of persons are not so labeled; and (d) most important, that the label unwittingly may be used to designate profound effects of legal, police, medical, and nursing practices on the conduct of the disordered person. Notwithstanding, the weight of tradition and the bureaucratization of the legal and medical institution that give service to disordered persons continue the employment of the concept of schizophrenia (pp. 359-360).

. . . While I may be charged with unrestrained hyperbole, the historical facts are undeniable. The same culture thought model that generated the medieval demoniacal model also produced the modern mental-illness model to explain conduct that does not meet rule-following prescriptions. The rejection of such an entrenched thought model by the relevant professionals is in the nature of a scientific revolution (1967a, p. 454).

Other writers (for example, Goffman, 1961; Haley, 1965; Laing, 1967; Levinson and Gallagher, 1964; Ludwig and Farrell, 1966, 1967; Mowrer, 1960; Scheff, 1966; Towbin, 1966) could be cited who advocate (at least aspects of) the paradigm we are proposing here. However, the point that we wanted to establish is, we think, sufficiently buttressed by those whose views we have already quoted: We conclude that a new paradigm does exist, that it has won the adherence of a number of observers, and that, therefore, the time is ripe for a scientific revolution.

CONCLUSION: THE CASE FOR A PARADIGMATIC REVOLUTION

Our purpose in this chapter has been to show that the conditions necessary for a scientific revolution—inadequacy of the existing paradigm and availability of at least one alternate paradigm—are present in the domain of concern to us in this book, schizophrenia. If the analysis offered in the preceding pages is substantially correct, the *desirability* of such a revolution is apparent. Nevertheless, a number of reasons favoring a paradigmatic shift of the kind we advocate have not always been explicitly indicated and, in concluding, it may be well to spell these out.

The first of the reasons is simple and rests on the principle of parsimony. The current psychiatric perspective requires that a special set of assumptions and concepts be applied to the individuals it classifies as psychotic; the principles governing the behavior of the rest of us are apparently either not relevant or sufficient where psychotics are concerned. The new paradigm obviates the need for special principles and seeks to understand the behavior of *all* persons in terms of a common body of propositions.

The second advantage of the new paradigm is a heuristic one. A new conception of the schizophrenic, while obviously not depriving us of any previous sound and hard-won knowledge, opens our eyes to hitherto unsuspected possibilities and sets the stage for creative theoretical and research innovations. When led by a new paradigm, Kuhn (1962) says, "It is rather as if the professional community had been suddenly transported to another planet where familiar objects are seen in a different light and are joined by unfamiliar ones as well (p. 110)."

Another advantage that, though important, we need not dwell upon, has to do with the explanatory power of the new paradigm. We have already suggested that the psychiatric perspective tends to obfuscate many aspects of the behavior of schizophrenic patients by providing pseudoanswers to misconstrued questions. Although the reader must decide for himself, of course, how compelling the new paradigm is, the fact that (for us) it evolved in the course of our research insures a substantial fit between much (but not, in any logically entailed way, all) of our data and our paradigm.

Finally, we come to a question that has remained close to the surface of much of the discussion in this chapter, the question of values. We think we can take it for granted, without having to argue the point, that there are few investigators who still seriously maintain the view that the study of schizophrenia utilizes only value-free constructs. One's very conception of schizophrenia, and not merely one's treatment procedures, is bound to be indissolubly linked to the values one holds about men and their behavior. Accordingly, we should like to express here an explicit and we hope not gratuitous value judgment: In our opinion, the psychiatric perspective has not only impeded our scientific understanding of the schizophrenic but also has resulted both in his being demeaned and therapeutically mismanaged. The consequences of even such an innocuous feature of the psychiatric approach as psychiatric classification can be far-reaching as well as unjust. We share the views of Goffman (1961), Szasz (1961), and others who deplore the unintended but potent psychic brutalities that an unenlightened psychiatric paradigm makes inevitable. The new paradigm holds out the hope that, however one chooses to "treat" the schizophrenic, he will not be deprived of his essential humanity.

To argue in behalf of a new paradigm for the scientific study of schizophrenia on admittedly nonscientific grounds may seem like a stark inconsistency. The first three factors, it may be contended, are legitimate criteria for the evaluation of any paradigm; but to endorse a paradigm on the basis of the values it implies is clearly inadmissible. Our answer to this objection is simple: To be maintained, any paradigm has to satisfy the canons of science, but there are always nonscientific reasons for supporting it as well. Such factors may not in themselves be *sufficient* to induce support, but neither can they nor should they be disregarded.

In urging consideration of a new paradigm for schizophrenia, we have attempted to enunciate our position in bold, forthright, and distinctly hortatory language. It is not the custom, after all, for those who espouse revolutionary causes to speak in muted phrases or to mince their words. Our purpose in expressing our views in this fashion was, rather, primarily to achieve a certain clarity in exposition—a clarity that is enhanced through the effects of sharp contrast and unqualified assertion. Such a course becomes irresistible when one recalls the words of our foremost contemporary aphorist, Eric Hoffer, who has written (1954): "It is impossible to think clearly in understatements. Thought is a process of exaggeration. The refusal to exaggerate is not infrequently an alibi for the disinclination to think or praise."

REFERENCES

1. Arieti, S., Some aspects of the psychopathology of schizophrenia. *American Journal of Psychotherapy*, **8**:396, 1954.

2. Artiss, K., *The Symptom as Communication in Schizophrenia.* New York: Grune & Stratton, Inc., 1959.

3. Goffman, E., *Asylums.* New York: Doubleday & Company, Inc., 1961.

4. Haley, J., The art of being schizophrenic. *Voices*, **1**:133–147, 1965.

5. Hoffer, E., *The Passionate State of Mind.* New York: Harper & Row, Publishers, 1954.

6. Kuhn, T., *The Structure of Scientific Revolutions.* Chicago: University of Chicago Press, 1962.

7. Laing, R., *The Politics of Experience.* New York: Pantheon Books, Inc., 1967.

8. Levinson, D., and E. Gallagher, *Patienthood in the Mental Hospital.* Boston: Houghton-Mifflin Company, 1964.

9. Ludwig, A., and F. Farrell, The code of chronicity. *Archives of General Psychiatry*, **15**:562–568, 1966.

10. _____, The weapons of insanity. *American Journal of Psychotherapy*, **4**:737–749, 1967.

11. Mowrer, O. H., "Sin," the lesser of two evils. *American Psychologist*, **15**:301–304, 1960.

12. Rakusin, J., and L. Fierman. Five assumptions for treating chronic psychotics. *Mental Hospitals*, **14**:140–148, 1963.

13. Sarbin, T., Anxiety: The reification of a metaphor. *Archives of General Psychiatry*, **10**:630–638, 1964.

14. _____, On the futility of the proposition that some people be labeled "mentally ill." *Journal of Consulting Psychology*, **31**:447–453, 1967a.

15. _____, The concept of hallucination. *Journal of Personality*, **35**:359–380, 1967b.

16. _____, The scientific status of the mental illness concept. In S. Plog (ed.), *Determinants of Mental Illness—A Handbook*. New York: Holt, Rinehart and Winston, Inc., 1967c.

17. _____, Role theoretical analysis of schizophrenia. In J. H. Mann (ed.), *Reader in General Psychology*. Skokie, Ill.: Rand McNally & Company, 1967d.

18. _____, Notes on the transformation of social identity. In N. S. Greenfield, M. L. Miller, and L. M. Roberts (eds.), *Comprehensive Mental Health: The Challenge of Evaluation*. Madison, Wis.: University of Wisconsin Press, 1967e.

19. Scheff, T. J., *Being Mentally Ill: A Sociological Theory*. Chicago: Aldine, 1966.

20. Szasz, T., Psychiatry, ethics and the criminal law. *Columbia Law Review*, **58**:183–198, 1958.

21. _____, *The Myth of Mental Illness*. New York: Paul B. Hoeber, Inc., 1961.

22. _____, *Law, Liberty, and Psychiatry: An Inquiry into the Social Uses of Mental Health Practices*. New York: Crowell-Collier and Macmillan, Inc., 1963.

23. _____, *Psychiatric Justice*. New York: Crowell-Collier and Macmillan, Inc., 1965.

24. Towbin, A., Understanding the mentally deranged. *Journal of Existentialism*, 7:63–83, 1966.

Psychosis or Social Sanction
Alfred L. Krober

"Cultural relativism," asserting a point of view outside any given culture, implies that it is possible to look at a behavior, belief, ritual, or value without moral judgment. It is an attitude that suggests objectivity like that of the scientist, but it is broader in scope.

Using such objectivity, Krober warns that it is a fallacy to romanticize madness. Some behaviors that lead to mental hospitals in our culture lead to positions of prominence and respect in others. The tribes Krober has worked with differentiate between behaviors: some are treated as dysfunctional, destructive, and disturbing, while others are supported, encouraged, and rewarded.

The definition of acceptable or unacceptable behavior is not based on absolute criteria but on culturally relative mores. "Values are cultural facts," says Krober. He shows how certain values lead to the establishment and maintenance of cultural institutions dealing with madness.

Years after his article first appeared, Krober wrote a follow-up note (part of which is included). In it he modified and clarified some of his original positions, and his own point of view shifted. An implication of this shift is that one's personal point of view is *personal* and should not be confused with any absolute definition of the phenomenon under observation.

PSYCHOTIC FACTORS IN SHAMANISM

On a chance, I said to an old Lassik Indian woman: "I bet you are a doctor." "Well, I nearly was," she answered. "My baby died. I was sitting around the next afternoon. All at once I heard a baby cry overhead, and fell over unconscious. My sister brought me back; but from time to time I heard the crying again, and became more and more sick. I gave an old doctor twenty dollars to cure me, and he said it was my baby's shadow coming to tell me to become a doctor. But I did not want to; and when the shadow began to talk, urging me, I told him, 'No, I won't, ' and urged him to go away. So at last he left off, and I got well, and did not become a doctor."

From Alfred L. Krober, *Character and Personality*, Vol. 8. Copyright 1940 by Duke University Press, Durham, North Carolina. Reprinted by permission of the publisher. The original article has been edited for this edition.

In our civilization this happening would be diagnosed as a psychosis. It manifests recurrent hallucinations, fits of loss of contact with the sensory world, distress and worry, and a sense of illness. Twenty dollars was a considerable amount for a backwoods Indian woman to pay in a lump sixty years ago.

From the native point of view, one may at once suspect the functioning of a cultural pattern, because all through native northern California the onset of shamanistic power is marked by a seizure in which the candidate experiences a hallucination—always auditory and sometimes visual also—in which objectively he is unconscious, or unaware of his surroundings, and acutely ill. To his family and village mates he seems actually stricken with disease. But the older shaman who is consulted promptly diagnoses the disease as the onset of shamanistic power, predicts cure as soon as the patient adjusts himself to his new power, and, with other shamans, helps to "train" the novice, that is, to find the adjustment. In most cases, apparently, the novice accepts the power which has come upon him: considerable prestige attaches, in a simple society, to one who can cure or exercise other special faculties.

Usually the spirit in the hallucination appears from nature: he is a spirit of the woods or mountains, of the sky, of a pool, of an animal or monster. In the present instance the spirit was the patient's own child. Here is a superadded pattern: the appearance is that of a dead relative. That this is a genuinely social pattern in the region is shown by a Wailaki episode recorded by Loeb. A dead woman came back one night, grunted outdoors, slid into the house, put her hand on her sister's head, and said: "I love you, I have come back." In the morning the living woman was found lying covered with blood from her mouth and singing. She announced: "My sister came, but I shall not die. I shall be a doctor, I think." She did become one, with her sister as her helping spirit, who talked to her and aided her in curing.

These cases raise several theoretical points. First, in some cultures one of the most respected and rewarded statuses known to the society is acquired only by experience of a condition which in our culture we could not label anything else than psychotic. This is part of a wider situation which I have treated elsewhere, namely: that one consistent criterion of distinction between primitive or folk cultures and advanced or high ones, other than quantity of cultural content, is the fact that the folk cultures in their magic, shamanism, animistic ritual, and the like, recognize as objectively effective certain phenomena which the more sophisticated ones regard as not only subjective but as objectively unreal and therefore as more or less psychotic or deranged. In short, the limits of relation of personality and world are differently drawn. What high cultures stigmatize as purely personal, nonreal and nonsocial, abnormal and pathological, lower cultures treat as objective, socially useful, and conducive to special ability—or at least relatively so. The primary importance of this difference is perhaps for the student of culture, whom it may help to understand somewhat more clearly the "high and low" ratings which he tries to avoid, but never wholly succeeds in avoiding, when he compares cultures.

A side problem is this: If the native recognizes certain psychotic or pathological experiences as partaking of objective reality, the question arises whether we in our civilization do not do the same in certain other areas, being however as blind to the fact as the primitive is. (Logically of course the question could be turned around into an inquiry as to the nature of the limits of objectivity, the individual psychic experience being regarded as primary in reality; but this would of course be scientifically profitless because science assumes that it deals with the objective.) What, in other words, may there be in our own lives that does not participate in reality but which we accept as so participating? Reference is not to group attitudes characteristic of the uneducated or socially disadvantaged, which the so-phisticated and detached members of the same population can discern as affectively warped away from reality; but to other attitudes on the part of the sophisticates themselves, of whose nonparticipation in reality they are equally unaware. Obviously, it would be very hard to give even a tentative answer to this question. But the problem is certainly worth being kept in mind.

Next, there is the old question of deception. Probably most shamans or medicine men, the world over, help along with sleight-of-hand in curing and especially in exhibitions of power. This sleight-of-hand is sometimes deliberate; in many cases awareness is perhaps not deeper than the forecon-scious. The attitude, whether there has been repression or not, seems to be as toward a pious fraud. Field ethnographers seem quite generally con-vinced that even shamans who know that they add fraud nevertheless also believe in their powers, and especially in those of other shamans: they consult them when they themselves or their children are ill. When it comes to the cardinal experience with spirits, on which power is based, this almost always occurs in solitude, or inwardly as in dreams, so that objective dem-onstration is precluded. While consciously false claims would therefore be easier, there would also be less immediate pressure to make them. The Lassik old woman, at any rate, was genuine: she did not want to be a shaman, and she resisted the urgings of the spirit. There can be no doubt that she really heard her dead child's crying and talking and was troubled by it.

In fact, she felt herself ill in the same sense as among us a psychotic patient generally feels ill. This is the normal description by most Californian tribes of the onset of shamanistic power: The prospective shaman is not only out of his mind and behaving strangely, but also actually sick: he lies down; his relatives are afraid he will die, and call a shaman for treatment; the patient will not eat, wastes away, and remains for weeks or months in this condition. This point seems of some importance: the experience is not a merely subjective one of a moment or a day, but a profound organic disturbance. In this sense it is the more genuinely psychotic.

Two other features are typical. The first is the repetition of the experience. The hallucination, or among other tribes the dream, comes again and again. (Many tribes say definitely that their shamans "dream" their power; but their word for "dream" may include or connote much more than a normal sleep-dream.)

Second, this individual's hallucination was primarily, or perhaps wholly, auditory. Here tribal custom varies somewhat, and no doubt personal experience also; but it is clear from a mass of data gradually accumulated that among all the Indians of California and Nevada the crucial shamanistic experience is normally auditory, whether or not it is also visual or tactile. Almost always there is a song learned, or several. A shaman who did not have an individual spirit-given song would not be a shaman, in prevailing native opinion in this part of the world. Differences exist between tribes who say little about seeing while hearing, and those who give a clear account of seeing, or seeing and feeling, in addition. The Mohave of southern California are in this latter category. But their standard way is to "dream" parts of myths which are already known. And they do this dreaming mostly without seizure or illness. In fact, they profess to begin their dreaming in their mother's womb and to recall these dreams and to continue them later in life. Incidentally, it is also standard with the Mohave to assert that these dreams, or many of them, relate to the creation of the world. They project themselves backward into the beginning of time, where they insist they were really present to hear, see, and feel what was happening. This is a Mohave specialty—a somewhat unusual addition to the usual beliefs entertained. I do not know how often such an affirmed projection into the past is characteristic of our psychotics.

The difference between these primitives and ourselves may be expressed in two different ways. The first is formulated in terms of *reality*. The primitive assumes as actual and real certain phenomena which we hold to have only a mental or subjective existence, and in that sense to be unreal in the sense in which stones and houses and birds are real. Or perhaps it would be more accurate to say that the primitive is also aware of a distinction, but inverts his emphasis. To him a stone or a bird seen or heard in a certain kind of dream is far more important than a physical stone or bird which one can pick up or eat, because it is the potential source of infinitely more power and control. (Certain things which we classify as unreal are to him super-real—"surrealistic.")

The second difference is formulated in terms of *socialization* or social acceptability. To us a person that hears the dead speak, or proclaims that he sometimes turns into a bear, is socially abnormal, at best useless, and likely to be a burden or menace. To the Indians he is potentially a personality of enhanced powers, which he may indeed abuse malevolently in witchcraft but which primarily result in benefits to the community: enhanced health, food supply, triumph over enemies.

This difference of social attitude or pattern of culture is as important as the difference in attitude toward reality. It is perhaps, in fact, a cause of the latter. At first thought, indeed, one might be inclined to assume the contrary: as enlightenment increases, dreams, visions, and the voices of the dead are more and more recognized as being internal to individuals and unrelated to objective reality as defined by the everyday experience of the mass of mankind. Thereupon society withdraws recognition and prestige value from the visions; they become dubious assets, and finally stigmata and disabilities. This is how we ordinarily assume the change from primitive attitudes to our own to have come about: there is a progressive increase in our understanding of reality. However, it may be doubted whether anything so rational is the efficient cause of the change. Abstractly, it seems at least equally probable that the greater rationality or enlightenment is a by-product of the change in attitudes, and that these attitudes in turn are nonrationally social or cultural.

On this view, certain societies gradually attach fewer approval or premium values to dreams and voices, until they may come, like ourselves, to look upon them as socially useless, if not harmful—abnormal, unfortunate, and to be dreaded. The influences bringing about such a shift of values might be various: increases of the size of the social group, technological or economic factors, the growth of science, a greater sense of security. Enlightenment as such, in the sense of a better discrimination of objective reality, need not be among them. It may be, for all one knows, an effect rather than a cause—a flattering name bestowed on the change after it has occurred.

Obviously, this theoretical interpretation may not be pressed too dogmatically. But it may serve as a counterbalance to the current assumption, which is certainly also dogmatic. And there is one specific point in its favor. The primitive, as has just been pointed out, does not really fail to discriminate the objective from the subjective, the normally natural from the supernatural. He distinguishes them much as we do. He merely weights or favors the supernatural, as we disfavor and try to exclude it. The voice of the dead, the dream, and the magic act stand out for him from the run of commonplace experience of reality much as they do for us; but he endows them with a quality of special super-reality and desirability, we of unreality and undesirability. The values have changed rather than the perception. And values are cultural facts.

To put it in another form, certain of what one calls "psychotic" phenomena are socially channeled by primitives—standardized, recognized, approved, rewarded—but are regarded as wholly outside the approved sociocultural channel by ourselves.

ANIMAL IDENTIFICATIONS

An old Kato woman narrated the following as having happened before her birth: A young woman, pregnant, went with her husband and a group of fellow-initiates for a stay in the woods, presumably to cook for the party. There she saw them perform their "tricks" and performances and was made to jump a trench and was pelted with pine cones. All this apparently had some reference to bears. When her child was born, he had a tuft of hair on each shoulder. He grew up apparently stupid and sluggish, not participating much in ordinary activities. Once, when he was being teased, he grew angry, growled, turned into a bear, scattered the coals of the fire, and began to cuff people around. After this incident he was carefully let alone, except when his anger could be directed against the enemy Yuki. He continued generally peaceable but solitary, or at least aloof. He was nearly useless for hunting or ordinary work, but, if a trail was to be broken through the snow, he was sent ahead, and with his bearlike strength performed this task easily and cheerfully.

This tale, which the informant evidently believed to be true as implicitly as her parents had believed it, possesses some of the qualities of a dream among ourselves. However, it is recounted here primarily to introduce the matter of what may be called bear men—a concept similar to the European one of werewolves.

In this case we have a human being with bear nature and shape potential in him, showing only partially most of the time, but under special stimulus temporarily supplanting his human form and character. The stimulus however was everyday and realistic, even though the cause of his latent nature was evidently considered to be something magico-religious or supernatural.

An allied but distinct concept in the area is what the Uki call the *wa"shit lamshiimi*, literally, "grizzly bear doctor." (All the concepts seem to relate to the grizzly bear, much the more dangerous of the two local bear species.) The bear doctor might become so by first dreaming of bears. Then young female bears took him into the woods and lived with him; one of them might be reported as having physically carried off the future doctor's person. Other men sought bear power, swimming in forest holes, and dancing toward, clawing, and growling at a tree or stump until hair grew out of their body. The bear doctor cured bear bites and gave demonstrations of strength.

A third type of bear person was what the Yuki called *aumol*, "chewer" or "biter." He was a man trained by older *aumol* to walk about on all fours completely disguised in a bearskin, but carrying a bone dagger with which he stabbed the personal or tribal enemies he encountered, and then disemboweled and scattered their bodies. No doubt his community stood in awe of the *aumol*, but they also considered him valuable for the damage he could singlehanded inflict on their enemies without exposing them to the reprisals of open warfare. It is much to be doubted whether going out to murder from ambush encased in a clumsy bearskin would be physically possible; but the Indians elaborate the tale, speaking of strings of shell beads worn around the body to afford an armor inside the bear hide; of baskets worn in it containing a stone or water to simulate growling or the rumbling of the viscera; and so on. It looks very much as if the whole thing were only an elaborated fantasy never actually acted out. But it was certainly believed in as a reality by the overwhelming majority of the members of a whole series of tribes. Quite likely some men let it be known that they were *aumol*, and perhaps kept a bearskin and some of the accessory paraphernalia. What is of interest is the elaborateness of the physical apparatus insisted on.[1]

A fourth type of person associated with bears was the initiated dancer, who, wearing a bearhide, performed as a bear at gatherings, just as other dancers impersonated spirits, ghosts of the dead, or eagles. For this office one was trained, and while it had much of the esoteric and dangerous about it, the community knew who the recognized bear dancer or dancers were.

These then are the varieties of men resembling bears. They can be arranged in the following order, according to the degree of their participation in the supernatural: (1) the true bear shaman who, in virtue of power personally received from bears in his manhood, can turn himself into a bear; (2) the man who, as a result of prenatal influencing, occasionally and involuntarily turns into a bear; (3) the man who secretly disguises himself as a bear but manifests preternatural strength, endurance, and ferocity; and (4) the bear dancer, who holds the religious office of impersonating a bear as one part of a cult system magically serving the public welfare. Occurring side by side in a limited area—the southerly part of the northern Coast Ranges of California—there can be no doubt that the four beliefs

---

[1]Margaret Mead (in *Psyche*, VIII [1928], 72-77) has pointed out a similar difference between Samoans and other Polynesians. "Contacts with the supernatural were accidental, trivial, uninstitutionalized" in Samoa. Religious and unstable individuals were "given no accepted place in a pattern."

or practices are historically associated. It is however of interest that the four variations on the one theme differ so much in strength of supernatural participation. In other words, mystic and rational, emotional and objective, expressions coexist in one pattern. Or again, it might be said that suggestion and autosuggestion ranged from a maximum in type 1 to a minimum in type 4. The Pomo and the Patwin, whose culture was on the whole slightly the most elaborate and systematized in the region, adhered to types 3 and 4; the Yuki, poorer backwoodsmen, to 1 and 3; type 2, along with 3, is recorded from the Kato, who are more or less transitional.

There are similar gradations in regard to the method of curing supernaturally. (There was also curing with household remedies of roots or herbs, for headaches, constipation, bruises, and other minor ills; but these hardly count in the present connection because in any serious or alarming illness only the specialist in the supernatural could help.) The Yuki distinguished three kinds of treatment of disease. Perhaps the most generally effective was by the *lamshiimi*, the shaman or doctor proper, who had in his own person received power from some kind of spiritual being, and after "going into a trance," sucked out the disease (*ha^nchmi*). He used no rattle, sang little, if any, and in modern Indian vernacular is a "sucking doctor." The "singing doctor" was called *moli* by the Yuki, and held a public office: he was caretaker and firetender of the religious assembly house. In addition however, he sang with a rattle, and thereby was able to see and diagnose illness. He "investigated and prophesied." The third type of treatment was named *hilyulit* and used cult ritual. Songs pertaining to the various spirits impersonated by the cult initiates—the Creator and the ghosts—were sung until the patient trembled violently. Thereby it was known which kind of spirit had "frightened" him into illness. Then the cure was arranged by having the corresponding spirit impersonation—singing, dancing, and touching—made for him. This worked homeopathically.

The Pomo cure in two ways. The *madu* corresponds to the first Yuki type: he has himself dreamed or encountered spirits, and he sucks. However he is, in contrast with the Yuki, considered the less powerful practitioner. Grave illness comes from *k'o'o*, "poison," that is, bewitching, and is handled by the *k'o'o-bakiyahale*, or performer for the poisoned. This type of doctor operated by means of a sack of fetishes, which he used with elaborate rattling, singing, and ritual motions. These paraphernalia and the knowledge associated with them he mostly did not claim to have been given to him by spirits or supernatural beings in a dream or trance, but to have received, with careful teaching, from a previous shaman, ordinarily an older relative. Again the Pomo differ from the Yuki in giving a higher valuation to the more rational (or pseudorational), orderly, tangible, formal procedure, whereas the Yuki pin their faith in the person who has had a powerful abnormal experience and more or less repeats it in curing.

Since the general culture of the tribes is closely similar, this variation of predilection toward and away from "psychopathological" manifestations, within the primitive level, is of some interest.

SUGGESTIBILITY

Through all these practices and beliefs there evidently runs a very strong strain of suggestion and autosuggestion. My own conviction is that this factor is decidedly more important than the deliberate deception which undoubtedly also occurs. The audience certainly does not deceive, and it does see miracles. The shamans may know that they deceive, but many of them certainly believe that other shamans do real miracles. Beyond that, we do not know how far, in performing, they use deception consciously or under autosuggestion. When shamans recount how they received their powers, experienced ethnologists pretty unanimously feel that the overwhelming majority of them believe sincerely that they have really had such an experience. Moreover, this experience is of a kind which in our civilization would often be diagnosed as psychotic. I do not wish to rule out the question of "deception," which undoubtedly occurs and is relevant. But of more cardinal importance to an understanding of the shamanism of primitives are the two factors of psychosis-like symptoms and of suggestion. When psychologists as a whole return seriously to the problem of suggestion and suggestibility, striking at aspects of it that go deeper than conscious propaganda, salesmanship, and advertising, it is likely that anthropologists may be better able to interpret shamanistic performances.

SUMMARY

Among many unsophisticated people, socially sanctioned and distinguished individuals who exercise special powers, especially of curing, acquire their capacity through experiences which in our culture would be stigmatized as psychotic. How far the hallucinations and other symptoms are simulated, autosuggested, or compulsive is not clear; but it is certain that deception will not account for all of them. This means that manifestations which are pathological, or at any rate are so regarded by us, are accepted and socially channeled in many primitive societies. At the same time, societies of nearly the same general cultural level may differ considerably in the degree to which they rationalize or ceremonialize their curing or other shamanistic practices away from the psychotic or induced psychotic experience: some put a premium on certain frankly abnormal experiences, others on more nearly normal ones. The situation thus is far from simple; but it evidences the strong bearing which cultural patterns have on the problem of the nature of psychosis.

Postscript 1951: I am now ready to admit a qualification to my previous position, as well as to make an extension of it. The qualification is this: In general the psychopathologies that get rewarded among primitives are only the mild or transient ones. A markedly deteriorative psychosis, even a persistent and pointless delusion, such as a man's acting out the belief that he was a tree, would be rated and deplored by them much as by us. It is the lighter aberrations from objective reality that can win social approval: neurotic symptoms of the hysteric type, involving suggestibility or half-conscious volition. This means that primitives also recognize psychopathology, and that they discriminate the degrees and kinds of it to which they allocate tolerance or esteem. Thus, so far as I know, they do not grant social rewards to compulsion neuroses. The rewards seem to be reserved for individuals who can claim abnormal powers and controls, not for those who are controlled. This qualification is illuminating, but it does limit somewhat my original contention.

The new extension is this. Not only shamans—the professionally possessed or entranced or fraudulent—are involved in psychopathology, but often also the whole lay public of primitive societies. This is so when suspicion of potential witchcraft becomes widespread or omnipresent and may or may not lead to a constant flow of revenge killings. Here we might well recognize something akin to a specially channeled paranoia, low-grade and diffuse, but persistent and nearly unanimous through the community. It will be noted that the element of suggestibility is again strong.

The Myth of Mental Illness
Thomas Szasz

Once we are labeled or label ourselves, we prove tenacious in keeping the label in spite of strong pressures to modify or dispose of it. A story goes that a man who thought he was dead was sent by his alarmed relatives to see his doctor. The doctor argued with him, but it was no use. Finally, the doctor asked, "Do dead men bleed?"

"Of course not, doctor, everybody knows that.." The doctor took the man's thumb and jabbed it with a needle. It began to bleed. The man looked at the blood dripping down his finger. "Hey, Doc. Dead men *do* bleed!"

Thomas Szasz warns of the dangers in labeling others' behavior. He argues that the use of the concept mental illness "has already outlived whatever cognitive usefulness it might have had and (that) it now functions as a myth." The myth, according to Szasz, is based on the fundamental errors that mental illness is a disease and that bizarre behavior is a function of abnormal neurological conditions. Szasz views our treatment of the insane as a tool of social repression, and he suggests that current psychiatric nosologies be revised to reflect different behaviors as "expressions of man's struggle with the problem of how he should live"—not as illness.

Szasz views the contemporary model primarily from a social rather than an interpsychic perspective. He does not pay attention to the unusual states of awareness that most of the writers in this book emphasize. His position is that consideration of social influences is pivotal in effecting changes in how therapists and patients treat altered states of consciousness.

At the core of virtually all contemporary psychiatric theories and practices lies the concept of mental illness. A critical examination of this concept is therefore indispensable for understanding the ideas, institutions, and interventions of psychiatrists.

My aim in this essay is to ask if there is such a thing as mental illness, and to argue that there is *not*. Of course, mental illness is not a thing

Adapted from an article by Thomas Szasz, "The Myth of Mental Illness," *The American Psychologist*, Feb., 1960, pp. 113–118. Copyright 1960 by the American Psychological Association, and reproduced by permission. This version appeared as Chapter Two in *Ideology and Insanity* by Thomas Szasz, Doubleday, 1970.

or physical object; hence it can exist only in the same sort of way as do other theoretical concepts. Yet, to those who believe in them, familiar theories are likely to appear, sooner or later, as "objective truths" or "facts." During certain historical periods, explanatory concepts such as deities, witches, and instincts appeared not only as theories but as *self-evident causes* of a vast number of events. Today mental illness is widely regarded in a similar fashion, that is, as the cause of innumerable diverse happenings.

As an antidote to the complacent use of the notion of mental illness—as a self-evident phenomenon, theory, or cause—let us ask: What is meant when it is asserted that someone is mentally ill? In this essay I shall describe the main uses of the concept of mental illness, and I shall argue that this notion has outlived whatever cognitive usefulness it might have had and that it now functions as a myth.

II

The notion of mental illness derives its main support from such phenomena as syphilis of the brain or delirious conditions—intoxications, for instance—in which persons may manifest certain disorders of thinking and behavior. Correctly speaking, however, these are diseases of the brain, not of the mind. According to one school of thought, *all* so-called mental illness is of this type. The assumption is made that some neurological defect, perhaps a very subtle one, will ultimately be found to explain all the disorders of thinking and behavior. Many contemporary physicians, psychiatrists, and other scientists hold this view, which implies that people's troubles cannot be caused by conflicting personal needs, opinions, social aspirations, values, and so forth. These difficulties—which I think we may simply call *problems in living*—are thus attributed to physiochemical processes that in due time will be discovered (and no doubt corrected) by medical research.

Mental illnesses are thus regarded as basically similar to other diseases. The only difference, in this view, between mental and bodily disease is that the former, affecting the brain, manifests itself by means of mental symptoms; whereas the latter, affecting other organ systems—for example, the skin, liver, and so on—manifests itself by means of symptoms referable to those parts of the body.

In my opinion, this view is based on two fundamental errors. In the first place, a disease of the brain, analogous to a disease of the skin or bone, is a neurological defect, not a problem in living. For example, a *defect* in a person's visual field may be explained by correlating it with certain lesions in the nervous system. On the other hand, a person's *belief*—whether it be in Christianity, in Communism, or in the idea that his internal organs are rotting and that his body is already dead—cannot be explained by a defect or disease of the nervous system. Explanations of this sort of occurrence—assuming that one is interested in the belief itself and does not regard it simply as a symptom or expression of something else that is more interesting—must be sought along different lines.

The second error is epistemological. It consists of interpreting communications about ourselves and the world around us as symptoms of neurological functioning. This is an error not in observation or reasoning, but rather in the organization and expression of knowledge. In the present case, the error lies in making a dualism between mental and physical symptoms, a dualism that is a habit of speech and not the result of known observations. Let us see if this is so.

In medical practice, when we speak of physical disturbances we mean either signs (for example, fever) or symptoms (for example, pain). We speak of mental symptoms, on the other hand, when we refer to a patient's communications about himself, others, and the world about him. The patient might assert that he is Napoleon or that he is being persecuted by the Communists. These would be considered mental symptoms only if the observer believed that the patient was *not* Napoleon or that he was *not* being persecuted by the Communists. This makes it apparent that the statement "X is a mental symptom" involves rendering a judgment that entails a covert comparison between the patient's ideas, concepts, or beliefs and those of the observer and the society in which they live. The notion of mental symptom is therefore inextricably tied to the social, and particularly the ethical, context in which it is made, just as the notion of bodily symptom is tied to an anatomical and genetic context.[1]

To sum up: For those who regard mental symptoms as signs of brain disease, the concept of mental illness is unnecessary and misleading. If they mean that people so labeled suffer from diseases of the brain, it would seem better, for the sake of clarity, to say that and not something else.

III

The term "mental illness" is also widely used to describe something quite different from a disease of the brain. Many people today take it for granted that living is an arduous affair. Its hardship for modern man derives, moreover, not so much from a struggle for biological survival as from the stresses and strains inherent in the social intercourse of complex human personalities. In this context, the notion of mental illness is used to identify or describe some feature of an individual's so-called personality. Mental illness—as a deformity of the personality, so to speak—is then

[1]See Szasz, T. S.: *Pain and Pleasure: A Study of Bodily Feelings* (New York: Basic Books, 1957), especially pp. 70-81; "The problem of psychiatric nosology." *Amer. J. Psychiatry*, 114:405-13 (Nov.), 1957.

regarded as the cause of human disharmony. It is implicit in this view that social intercourse between people is regarded as something inherently harmonious, its disturbance being due solely to the presence of "mental illness" in many people. Clearly, this is faulty reasoning, for it makes the abstraction "mental illness" into a cause of, even though this abstraction was originally created to serve only as a shorthand expression for, certain types of human behavior. It now becomes necessary to ask: What kinds of behavior are regarded as indicative of mental illness, and by whom?

The concept of illness, whether bodily or mental, implies deviation from some clearly defined norm. In the case of physical illness, the norm is the structural and functional integrity of the human body. Thus, although the desirability of physical health, as such, is an ethical value, what health is can be stated in anatomical and physiological terms. What is the norm, deviation from which is regarded as mental illness? This question cannot be easily answered. But whatever this norm may be, we can be certain of only one thing: namely, that it must be stated in terms of psychosocial, ethical, and legal concepts. For example, notions such as "excessive repression" and "acting out an unconscious impulse" illustrate the use of psychological concepts for judging so-called mental health and illness. The idea that chronic hostility, vengefulness, or divorce are indicative of mental illness is an illustration of the use of ethical norms (that is, the desirability of love, kindness, and a stable marriage relationship). Finally, the widespread psychiatric opinion that only a mentally ill person would commit homicide illustrates the use of a legal concept as a norm of mental health. In short, when one speaks of mental illness, the norm from which deviation is measured is a *psychosocial and ethical* standard. Yet, the remedy is sought in terms of *medical* measures that—it is hoped and assumed—are free from wide differences of ethical value. The definition of the disorder and the terms in which its remedy is sought are therefore at serious odds with one another. The practical significance of this covert conflict between the alleged nature of the defect and the actual remedy can hardly be exaggerated.

Having identified the norms used for measuring deviations in cases of mental illness, we shall now turn to the question, Who defines the norms and hence the deviation? Two basic answers may be offered: First, it may be the person himself—that is, the patient—who decides that he deviates from a norm; for example, an artist may believe that he suffers from a work inhibition; and he may implement this conclusion by seeking help *for himself* from a psychotherapist. Second, it may be someone other than the "patient" who decides that the latter is deviant—for example, relatives, physicians, legal authorities, society generally; a psychiatrist may then be hired by persons other than the "patient" to do something *to him* in order to correct the deviation.

These considerations underscore the importance of asking the question, Whose agent is the psychiatrist? and of giving a candid answer to it. The psychiatrist (or non-medical mental health worker) may be the agent of the patient, the relatives, the school, the military services, a business organization, a court of law, and so forth. In speaking of the psychiatrist as the agent of these persons or organizations, it is not implied that his moral values, or his ideas and aims concerning the proper nature of remedial action, must coincide exactly with those of his employer. For example, a patient in individual psychotherapy may believe that his salvation lies in a new marriage; his psychotherapist need not share this hypothesis. As the patient's agent, however, he must not resort to social or legal force to prevent the patient from putting his beliefs into action. If his _contract is with the patient_, the psychiatrist (psychotherapist) may disagree with him or stop his treatment, but he cannot engage others to obstruct the patient's aspirations.[2] Similarly, if a psychiatrist is retained by a court to determine the sanity of an offender, he need not fully share the legal authorities' values and intentions in regard to the criminal, nor the means deemed appropriate for dealing with him; such a psychiatrist cannot testify, however, that the accused is not insane, but that the legislators are—for passing the law that decrees the offender's actions illegal.[3] This sort of opinion could be voiced, of course—but not in a courtroom, and not by a psychiatrist who is there to assist the court in performing its daily work.

To recapitulate: In contemporary social usage, the finding of mental illness is made by establishing a deviance in behavior from certain psychosocial, ethical, or legal norms. The judgment may be made, as in medicine, by the patient, the physician (psychiatrist), or others. Remedial action, finally, tends to be sought in a therapeutic—or covertly medical— framework. This creates a situation in which it is claimed that psychosocial, ethical, and legal deviations can be corrected by medical action. Since medical interventions are designed to remedy only medical problems, it is logically absurd to expect that they will help solve problems whose very existence has been defined and established on non-medical grounds.

IV

Anything that people _do_—in contrast to things that _happen_ to them[4]— takes place in a context of value. Hence, no human activity is devoid of moral implications. When the values underlying certain activities are widely

[2]See Szasz, T. S.: _The Ethics of Psychoanalysis: The Theory and Method of Autonomous Psychotherapy_ (New York: Basic Books, 1965).

[3]See Szasz, T. S.: _Law, Liberty, and Psychiatry: An Inquiry into the Social Uses of Mental Health Practices_ (New York: Macmillan, 1963).

[4]Peters, R. S.: _The Concept of Motivation_ (London: Routledge & Kegan Paul, 1958), especially pp. 12–15.

shared, those who participate in their pursuit often lose sight of them altogether. The discipline of medicine—both as a pure science (for example, research) and as an applied science or technology (for example, therapy)—contains many ethical considerations and judgments. Unfortunately, these are often denied, minimized, or obscured, for the ideal of the medical profession as well as of the people whom it serves is to have an ostensibly value-free system of medical care. This sentimental notion is expressed by such things as the doctor's willingness to treat patients regardless of their religious or political beliefs. But such claims only serve to obscure the fact that ethical considerations encompass a vast range of human affairs. Making medical practice neutral with respect to some specific issues of moral value (such as race or sex) need not mean, and indeed does not mean, that it can be kept free from others (such as control over pregnancy or regulation of sex relations). Thus, birth control, abortion, homosexuality, suicide, and euthanasia continue to pose major problems in medical ethics.

Psychiatry is much more intimately related to problems of ethics than is medicine in general. I use the word "psychiatry" here to refer to the contemporary discipline concerned with problems in living, and not with diseases of the brain, which belong to neurology. Difficulties in human relations can be analyzed, interpreted, and given meaning only within specific social and ethical contexts. Accordingly, the psychiatrist's socioethical orientations will influence his ideas on what is wrong with the patient, on what deserves comment or interpretation, in what directions change might be desirable, and so forth. Even in medicine proper, these factors play a role, as illustrated by the divergent orientations that physicians, depending on their religious affiliations, have toward such things as birth control and therapeutic abortion. Can anyone really believe that a psychotherapist's ideas on religion, politics, and related issues play no role in his practical work? If, on the other hand, they do matter, what are we to infer from it? Does it not seem reasonable that perhaps we ought to have different psychiatric therapies—each recognized for the ethical positions that it embodies—for, say, Catholics and Jews, religious persons and atheists, democrats and Communists, white supremacists and Negroes, and so on? Indeed, if we look at the way psychiatry is actually practiced today, especially in the United States, we find that the psychiatric interventions people seek and receive depend more on their socioeconomic status and moral beliefs than on the "mental illnesses" from which they ostensibly suffer.[5] This fact should occasion no greater surprise than that practicing Catholics rarely frequent birth-control clinics, or that Christian Scientists rarely consult psychoanalysts.

[5]Hollingshead, A. B. and Redlich, F. C.: *Social Class and Mental Illness* (New York: Wiley, 1958).

V

The position outlined above, according to which contemporary psycho-therapists deal with problems in living, not with mental illnesses and their cures, stands in sharp opposition to the currently prevalent position, accor-ding to which psychiatrists treat mental diseases, which are just as "real" and "objective" as bodily diseases. I submit that the holders of the latter view have no evidence whatever to justify their claim, which is actually a kind of psychiatric propaganda: their aim is to create in the popular mind a confident belief that mental illness is some sort of disease entity, like an infection or a malignancy. If this were true, one could *catch* or *get* a mental illness, one might *have* or *harbor* it, one might *transmit* it to others, and finally one could *get rid* of it. Not only is there not a shred of evidence to support this idea, but, on the contrary, all the evidence is the other way and supports the view that what people now call mental illnesses are, for the most part, *communications* expressing unacceptable ideas, often framed in an unusual idiom.

This is not the place to consider in detail the similarities and differences between bodily and mental illnesses. It should suffice to emphasize that whereas the term "bodily illness" refers to physicochemical occurrences that are not affected by being made public, the term "mental illness" refers to sociopsychological events that are crucially affected by being made pub-lic. The psychiatrist thus cannot, and does not, stand apart from the person he observes, as the pathologist can and often does. The psychiatrist is committed to some picture of what he considers reality, and to what he thinks society considers reality, and he observes and judges the patient's behavior in the light of these beliefs. The very notion of "mental symptom" or "mental illness" thus implies a covert comparison, and often conflict, between observer and observed, psychiatrist and patient. Though obvious, this fact needs to be re-emphasized, if one wishes, as I do here, to counter the prevailing tendency to deny the moral aspects of psychiatry and to substitute for them allegedly value-free medical concepts and interventions.

Psychotherapy is thus widely practiced as though it entailed nothing other than restoring the patient from a state of mental sickness to one of mental health. While it is generally accepted that mental illness has something to do with man's social or interpersonal relations, it is paradox-ically maintained that problems of values—that is, of ethics—do not arise in this process. Freud himself went so far as to assert: "I consider ethics to be taken for granted. Actually I have never done a mean thing."[6] This is an astounding thing to say, especially for someone who had studied

---

[6]Quoted in Jones, E.: *The Life and Work of Sigmund Freud* (New York: Basic Books, 1957), Vol. III, p. 247.

man as a social being as deeply as Freud had. I mention it here to show how the notion of "illness"—in the case of psychoanalysis, "psychopathology," or "mental illness"—was used by Freud, and by most of his followers, as a means of classifying certain types of human behavior as falling within the scope of medicine, and hence, by fiat, outside that of ethics. Nevertheless, the stubborn fact remains that, in a sense, much of psychotherapy revolves around nothing other than the elucidation and weighing of goals and values—many of which may be mutually contradictory—and the means whereby they might best be harmonized, realized, or relinquished.

Because the range of human values and of the methods by which they may be attained is so vast, and because many such ends and means are persistently unacknowledged, conflicts among values are the main source of conflicts in human relations. Indeed, to say that human relations at all levels—from mother to child, through husband and wife, to nation and nation—are fraught with stress, strain, and disharmony is, once again, to make the obvious explicit. Yet, what may be obvious may be also poorly understood. This, I think, is the case here. For it seems to me that in our scientific theories of behavior we have failed to accept the simple fact that human relations are inherently fraught with difficulties, and to make them even relatively harmonious requires much patience and hard work. I submit that the idea of mental illness is now being put to work to obscure certain difficulties that at present may be inherent—not that they need to be unmodifiable—in the social intercourse of persons. If this is true, the concept functions as a disguise: instead of calling attention to conflicting human needs, aspirations, and values, the concept of mental illness provides an amoral and impersonal "thing" an "illness"—as an explanation for problems in living. We may recall in this connection that not so long ago it was devils and witches that were held responsible for man's problems in living. The belief in mental illness, as something other than man's trouble in getting along with his fellow man, is the proper heir to the belief in demonology and witchcraft. Mental illness thus exists or is "real" in exactly the same sense in which witches existed or were "real."

VI

While I maintain that mental illnesses do not exist, I obviously do not imply or mean that the social and psychological occurrences to which this label is attached also do not exist. Like the personal and social troubles that people had in the Middle Ages, contemporary human problems are real enough. It is the labels we give them that concern me, and, having labeled them, what we do about them. The demonologic concept of problems in living gave rise to therapy along theological lines. Today, a belief in mental illness implies—nay, requires—therapy along medical or psycho-therapeutic lines.

I do not here propose to offer a new conception of "psychiatric illness" or a new form of "therapy." My aim is more modest and yet also more ambitious. It is to suggest that the phenomena now called mental illnesses be looked at afresh and more simply, that they be removed from the category of illnesses, and that they be regarded as the expressions of man's struggle with *the problem of how he should live.* This problem is obviously a vast one, its enormity reflecting not only man's inability to cope with his environment, but even more his increasing self-reflectiveness.

By problems in living, then, I refer to that explosive chain reaction that began with man's fall from divine grace by partaking of the fruit of the tree of knowledge. Man's awareness of himself and of the world about him seems to be a steadily expanding one, bringing in its wake an ever larger *burden of understanding.*[7] This burden is to be expected and must not be misinterpreted. Our only rational means for easing it is more under-standing, and appropriate action based on such understanding. The main alternative lies in acting as though the burden were not what in fact we perceive it to be, and taking refuge in an outmoded theological view of man. In such a view, man does not fashion his life and much of his world about him, but merely lives out his fate in a world created by superior beings. This may logically lead to pleading non-responsibility in the face of seemingly unfathomable problems and insurmountable difficulties. Yet, if man fails to take increasing responsibility for his actions, individually as well as collectively, it seems unlikely that some higher power or being would assume this task and carry this burden for him. Moreover, this seems hardly a propitious time in human history for obscuring the issue of man's responsibility for his actions by hiding it behind the skirt of an all-explaining conception of mental illness.

VII

I have tried to show that the notion of mental illness has outlived whatev-er usefulness it may have had and that it now functions as a myth. As such, it is a true heir to religious myths in general, and to the belief in witchcraft in particular. It was the function of these belief-systems to act as social tranquilizers, fostering hope that mastery of certain problems may be achieved by means of substitutive, symbolic-magical, operations. The concept of mental illness thus serves mainly to obscure the everyday fact

[7]In this connection, see Langer, S. K.: *Philosophy in a New Key* [1942] (New York: Mentor Books, 1953), especially Chap. 5 and 10.

that life for most people is a continuous struggle, not for biological survival, but for a "place in the sun," "peace of mind," or some other meaning or value. Once the needs of preserving the body, and perhaps of the race, are satisfied, man faces the problem of personal significance: What should he do with himself? For what should he live? Sustained adherence to the myth of mental illness allows people to avoid facing this problem, believing that mental health, conceived as the absence of mental illness, automatically insures the making of right and safe choices in the conduct of life. But the facts are all the other way. It is the making of wise choices in life that people regard, retrospectively, as evidence of good mental health!

When I assert that mental illness is a myth, I am not saying that personal unhappiness and socially deviant behavior do not exist; what I am saying is that we categorize them as diseases at our own peril.

The expression "mental illness" is a metaphor that we have come to mistake for a fact. We call people physically ill when their body-functioning violates certain anatomical and physiological norms; similarly, we call people mentally ill when their personal conduct violates certain ethical, political, and social norms. This explains why many historical figures, from Jesus to Castro, and from Job to Hitler, have been diagnosed as suffering from this or that psychiatric malady.

Finally, the myth of mental illness encourages us to believe in its logical corollary: that social intercourse would be harmonious, satisfying, and the secure basis of a good life were it not for the disrupting influences of mental illness, or psychopathology. However, universal human happiness, in this form at least, is but another example of a wishful fantasy. I believe that human happiness, or well-being, is possible—not just for a select few, but on a scale hitherto unimaginable. But this can be achieved only if many men, not just a few, are willing and able to confront frankly, and tackle courageously, their ethical, personal, and social conflicts. This means having the courage and integrity to forego waging battles on false fronts, finding solutions for substitute problems—for instance, fighting the battle of stomach acid and chronic fatigue instead of facing up to a marital conflict.

Our adversaries are not demons, witches, fate, or mental illness. We have no enemy that we can fight, exorcise, or dispel by "cure." What we do have are problems in living—whether these be biologic, economic, political, sociopsychological. In this essay I was concerned only with problems belonging in the last-mentioned category, and within this group mainly with those pertaining to moral values. The field to which modern psychiatry addresses itself is vast, and I made no effort to encompass it all. My argument was limited to the proposition that mental illness is a myth, whose function it is to disguise and thus render more palatable the bitter pill of moral conflicts in human relations.

Transcendental Experience in Relation to Religion and Psychosis
R. D. Laing

Pretend that you are shipwrecked, and your raft beaches on a tropical island, leaving you with a fine radio transmitter and the tools and extra parts to maintain it. You try to use the radio, but you find it has been damaged in the shipwreck. Exhausted and hungry, you are working on it when the local population finds you. They know nothing of machinery or radios, and it is hard to convince the natives that you need the equipment. The local shaman instructs the natives to take away your tools and parts and eventually your radio, in order to prevent you from indulging in the fantasy that you can contact unseen and powerful forces in ways that cannot be functionally explained with totems. You become extremely upset and "difficult" because your questions about your radio are politely but pointedly ignored. Instead, helpful natives instruct you in fishing and basket-weaving in hopes that, through these sensible, constructive activities, you will tire of your dreamworld and eventually become a useful member of their society.

In moving, poetic prose, Laing suggests that this is exactly the predicament of certain persons in mental institutions. He indicates that they deserve a different kind of help from that which they often receive. His position is that it is something less than human to consider ourselves sane and therefore all-wise, whereas the madman, not being sane, must consequently be a fool. This is another way of coming to terms with madness—a respectful way, suggesting that in our ignorance we should move more carefully. He further suggests that for those whose experiences are in another psychological or spiritual realm, conventional treatment can be both disruptive and ultimately destructive. Like the castaway's radio, the "radio" certain patients attempt to use may be as real as the tools of the doctors.

Laing's own treatment center uses "returned" psychotics as guides for persons having psychotic-like experiences. It is not entirely clear whether the positive results he reports are due to the effectiveness of the guides or to the care and consideration his patients receive. His position is a direct attack on conventional treatment, and, as a respected rebel, Laing has forced many treatment programs to re-evaluate their goals and methods.

We must remember that we are living in an age in which the ground is shifting and the foundations are shaking. I cannot answer for other times and places. Perhaps it has always been so. We know it is true today.

In these circumstances, we have all reason to be insecure. When the ultimate basis of our world is in question, we run to different holes in the ground; we scurry into roles, statuses, identities, interpersonal relations. We attempt to live in castles that can only be in the air, because there is no firm ground in the social cosmos on which to build. Priest and physician are both witness to this state of affairs. Each sometimes sees the same fragment of the whole situation differently; often our concern is with different presentations of the original catastrophe.

In this paper I wish to relate the transcendental experiences that *sometimes* break through in psychosis, to those experiences of the divine that are the Living Fount of all religion.

Elsewhere I have outlined the way in which some psychiatrists are beginning to dissolve their clinical-medical categories of understanding madness. I believe that if we can begin to understand sanity and madness in existential social terms, we, as priests and physicians, will be enabled to see more clearly the extent to which we confront common problems and share common dilemmas.

The main clinical terms for madness, where no organic lesion has so far been found, are schizophrenia, manic-depressive psychosis and involutional depression. From a social point of view, they characterize different forms of behavior, regarded in our society as deviant. People behave in such ways because their experience of themselves is different. It is on the existential meaning of such unusual experience that I wish to focus.

Experience is mad when it steps beyond the horizons of our common, that is, our communal sense.

What regions of experience does this lead to? It entails a loss of the usual foundations of the 'sense' of the world that we share with one another. Old purposes no longer seem viable. Old meanings are senseless; the distinctions between imagination, dream, external perceptions often seem no longer to apply in the old way. External events may seem magically conjured up. Dreams may seem direct communications from others: imagination may seem to be objective reality.

But most radically of all, the very ontological foundations are shaken. The being of phenomena shifts, and the phenomenon of being may no longer present itself to us as before. The person is plunged into a void of non-being in which he founders. There are no supports, nothing to cling to, except perhaps some fragments from the wreck, a few memories, names, sounds, one or two objects, that retain a link with a world long

Reprinted by permission from *The Psychedelic Review*, No. 6, 1965, 7-15.

lost. This void may not be empty. It may be peopled by visions and voices, ghosts, strange shapes and apparitions. No one who has not experienced how insubstantial the pageant of external reality can be, how it may fade, can fully realize the sublime and grotesque presences that can replace it, or exist alongside it.

When a person goes mad, a profound transposition of his position in relation to all domains of being occurs. His center of experience moves from ego to Self. Mundane time becomes merely anecdotal, only the Eternal matters. The madman is, however, confused. He muddles ego with self, inner with outer, natural and supernatural. Nevertheless, he often can be to us, even through his profound wretchedness and disintegration, the hierophant of the sacred. An exile from the scene of being as we know it, he is an alien, a stranger, signalling to us from the void in which he is foundering. This void may be peopled by presences that we do not even dream of. They used to be called demons and spirits, that were known and named. He has lost his sense of self, his feelings, his place in the world as we know it. He tells us he is dead. But we are distracted from our cozy security by this mad ghost that haunts us with his visions and voices that seem so senseless and of which we feel impelled to rid him, cleanse him, cure him.

Madness need not be all break*down*. It is also break*through*. It is potentially liberation and renewal, as well as enslavement and existential death.

There are now a growing number of accounts by people who have been through the experience of madness.[1] I want to quote at some length from one of the earlier contemporary accounts, as recorded by Karl Jaspers in his *General Psychopathology*.[2]

> I believe I caused the illness myself. In my attempt to penetrate the other world I met its natural guardians, the embodiment of my own weaknesses and faults. I first thought these demons were lowly inhabitants of the other world who could play me like a ball because I went into these regions unprepared and lost my way. Later I thought they were split-off parts of my own mind (passions) which existed near me in free space and thrived on my feelings. I believed everyone else had these too but did not perceive them, thanks to the protective and successful deceit of the feeling of personal existence. I thought the latter was an artifact of memory, thought-complexes, etc., a doll that was nice enough to look at from outside but nothing real inside it.
>
> In my case the personal self had grown porous because of my dimmed consciousness. Through it I wanted to bring myself closer to the higher sources of life. I should have prepared myself for this over a long period

[1] See, for example, the anthology, *The Inner World of Mental Illness:* A Series of First-Person Accounts of What It Was Like. Ed. Bert Kaplan. N.Y.: Harper and Row, 1964.

[2] Manchester University Press, 1962, pp. 417-18. (Also from Univ. of Chicago and Univ. of Toronto Presses.)

by invoking in me a higher, impersonal self, since "nectar" is not for mortal lips. It acted destructively on the animal-human self, split it up into its parts. These gradually disintegrated, the doll was really broken and the body damaged. I had forced untimely access to the "source of life," the curse of the "gods" descended on me. I recognized too late that murky elements had taken a hand. I got to know them after they had already too much power. There was no way back. I now had the world of spirits I had wanted to see. The demons came up from the abyss, as guardian Cerberi, denying admission to the unauthorized. I decided to take up the life-and-death struggle. This meant for me in the end a decision to die, since I had to put aside everything that maintained the enemy, but this was also everything that maintained life. I wanted to enter death without going mad and stood before the Sphinx: either thou into the abyss or I!

Then came illumination. I fasted and so penetrated into the true nature of my seducers. They were pimps and deceivers of my dear personal self which seemed as much a thing of naught as they. A larger and more comprehensive self emerged and I could abandon the previous personality with its entire entourage. I saw this earlier personality could never enter transcendental realms. I felt as a result a terrible pain, like an annihilating blow, but I was rescued, the demons shrivelled, vanished and perished. A new life began for me and from now on I felt different from other people. A self that consisted of conventional lies, shams, self-deceptions, memory-images, a self just like that of other people, grew in me again but behind and above it stood a greater and more comprehensive self which impressed me with something of what is eternal, unchanging, immortal and inviolable and which ever since that time has been my protector and refuge. I believe it would be good for many if they were acquainted with such a higher self and that there are people who have attained this goal in fact by kinder means.

Jaspers comments:

"Such self-interpretations are obviously made under the influence of delusion-like tendencies and deep psychic forces. They originate from profound experiences and the wealth of such schizophrenic experience calls on the observer as well as on the reflective patient not to take all this merely as a chaotic jumble of contents. Mind and spirit are present in the morbid psychic life as well as in the healthy. But interpretations of this sort must be divested of any causal importance. All they can do is to throw light on content and bring it into some sort of context."

I would rather say that this patient has described with a lucidity I could not improve upon, a Quest, with its pitfalls and dangers, which he eventually appears to have transcended. Even Jaspers still speaks of this experience as morbid, and discounts the patient's own construction. Both the experience and construction seem to me valid in their own terms.

I should make it clear that I am speaking of certain *transcendental experiences* that seem to me to be the original well-spring of all religions. Some psychotic people have transcendental experiences. Often (to the best of their recollection) they have never had such experiences before, and frequently they will never have them again. I am not saying, however, that psychotic experience necessarily contains this element more manifestly than sane experience.

The person who is transported into such domains is likely to act curiously. In other places, I have described in some detail the circumstances that seem to occasion this transportation, at least in certain instances, and the gross mystification that the language and thinking of the medical clinic perpetrates when it is brought to bear on the phenomena of madness, both as a social fact and as an existential experience.

The schizophrenic may indeed be mad. He is mad. He is not ill.

I have been told by people who have been through the mad experience how what was then revealed to them was veritable manna from Heaven. The person's whole life may be changed, but it is difficult not to doubt the validity of such vision. Also, not everyone comes back to us again.

Are these experiences simply the effulgence of a pathological process, or of a particular alienation? I do not think they are.

When all has been said against the different schools of psychoanalysis and depth psychology, one of their great merits is that they recognize explicitly the crucial relevance of each person's experience to his or her outward behavior, especially the so-called "unconscious."

There is a view, still current, that there is some correlation between being sane and being unconscious, or at least not too conscious of the "unconscious," and that some forms of psychosis are the behavioral disruption caused by being overwhelmed by the "unconscious."

What both Freud and Jung called "the unconscious" is simply what we, in our historically conditioned estrangement, are unconscious of. It is not necessarily or essentially unconscious.

I am not merely spinning senseless paradoxes when I say that we, the sane ones, are out of our minds. The mind is what the ego is unconscious of. We are unconscious of our minds. Our minds are not unconscious. Our minds are conscious of us. Ask yourself who and what it is that dreams our dreams. Our unconscious minds? The Dreamer who dreams our dreams knows far more of us than we know of it. It is only from a remarkable position of alienation that the source of life, the Fountain of Life, is experienced as the It. The mind of which we are unaware, is aware of us. It is we who are out of our minds. We need not be unaware of the inner world.

We do not realize its existence most of the time.

But many people enter it—unfortunately without guides, confusing outer with inner realities, and inner with outer—and generally lose their capacity to function competently in ordinary relations.

This need not be so. The process of entering into *the other* world from this world, and returning to *this* world from the other world, is as "natural" as death and childbirth or being born. But in our present world, that is both so terrified and so unconscious of the other world, it is not surprising that, when "reality," the fabric of this world, bursts, and a person enters the other world, he is completely lost and terrified, and meets only incomprehension in others.

In certain cases, a man blind from birth may have an operation performed which gives him his sight. The result: frequently misery, confusion, disorientation. The light that illumines the madman is an unearthly light, but I do not believe it is a projection, an emanation from his mundane ego. He is irradiated by a light that is more than he. It may burn him out.

This "other" world is not essentially a battlefield wherein psychological forces, derived or diverted, displaced or sublimated from their original object-cathexes, are engaged in an illusionary fight—although such forces may obscure these realities, just as they may obscure so-called external realities. When Ivan, in the *Brothers Karamazov*, says, "If God does not exist, everything is permissible," he is *not* saying: "If my superego, in projected form, can be abolished, I can do anything with a good conscience." He *is* saying: "If there is *only* my conscience, then there is no ultimate validity for my will."

The proper task of the physician (psychotherapist, analyst) should be, in select instances, to educt the person from this world and induct him to the other. To guide him in it: and to lead him back again.

One enters the other world by breaking a shell: or through a door: through a partition: the curtains part or rise: a veil is lifted. It is not the same as a dream. It is "real" in a different way from dream, imagination, perception or fantasy. Seven veils: seven seals, seven heavens.

The "ego" is the instrument for living in *this* world. If "the ego" is broken up, or destroyed (by the insurmountable contradictions of certain life situations, by toxins, chemical changes, etc.), then the person may be exposed to this other world.

The world that one enters, one's capacity to experience it, seems to be partly conditional on the state of one's "ego."

Our time has been distinguished, more than by anything else, by a mastery, a control, of the external world, and by an almost total forgetfulness of the internal world. If one estimates human evolution from the point of view of knowledge of the external world, then we are in many respects progressing.

If our estimate is from the point of view of the internal world, and of oneness of internal and external, then the judgment must be very different.

Phenomenologically the terms "internal" and "external" have little validity. But in this whole realm one is reduced to mere verbal expedients—words are simply the finger pointing to the moon. One of the difficul-

ties of talking in the present day of these matters is that the very existence
of inner realities is now called into question.

By "inner" I mean all those realities that have usually no "external,"
"objective" presence—the realities of imagination, dreams, fantasies,
trances, the realities of contemplative and meditative states: realities that
modern man, for the most part, has not the slightest direct awareness of.

Nowhere in the Bible, for example, is there any argument about the
existence of gods, demons, angels. People did not first "believe in" God:
they experienced His Presence, as was true of other spiritual agencies. The
question was not whether God existed, but whether this particular God
was the greatest God of all, or the only god; and what was the relation
of the various spiritual agencies to each other. Today, there is a public
debate, not as to the trustworthiness of God, the particular place in the
spiritual hierarchy of different spirits, etc., but whether God or such spirits
even exist, or ever have existed.

Sanity today appears to rest very largely on a capacity to adapt to the
external world—the interpersonal world, and the realm of human collectivi-
ties.

As this external human world is almost completely and totally estranged
from the inner, any personal direct awareness of the inner world already
entails grave risks.

But since society, without knowing it, is *starving* for the inner, the demands on people to evoke its presence in a "safe" way, in a way that
need not be taken seriously, etc., is tremendous—while the ambivalence
is equally intense. Small wonder that the list of artists in, say, the last
150 years, who have become shipwrecked on these reefs is so long—Höl-
derlin, John Clare, Rimbaud, Van Gogh, Nietzsche, Antonin Artaud, Strind-
berg, Munch, Bartok, Schumann, Büchner, Ezra Pound . . .

Those who survived have had exceptional qualities—a capacity for se-
crecy, slyness, cunning—a thoroughly realistic appraisal of the risks they
run, not only from the spiritual realms that they frequent, but from the
hatred of their fellows for any one engaged in this pursuit.

Let us *cure* them. The poet who mistakes a real woman for his Muse
and acts accordingly . . . The young man who sets off in a yacht in search
of God . . .

The outer divorced from any illumination from the inner is in a state
of darkness. We are in an age of darkness. The state of outer darkness
is a state of sin—i.e., alienation or estrangement from the Inner Light.
Certain actions lead to greater estrangement; certain others help one not
to be so far removed. The former are bad; the latter are good.

The ways of losing one's way are legion. Madness is certainly not the
least unambiguous. The counter-madness of Kraepelinian psychiatry is the
exact counterpart of "official" psychosis. Literally, and absolutely seriously,

it is as *mad*, if by madness we mean any radical estrangement from the subjective or objective truth. Remember Kierkegaard's objective madness.

As we experience the world, so we act. We conduct ourselves in the light of our view of what is the case and what is not the case. That is, each person is a more or less naive ontologist. Each person has views of what is, and what is not.

There is no doubt, it seems to me, that there have been profound changes in the experience of man in the last thousand years. In some ways this is more evident than changes in the patterns of his behavior. There is everything to suggest that man experienced God. Faith was never a matter of believing He existed, but of trusting in the Presence that was experienced and known to exist as a self-validating datum. It seems likely that far more people in our time neither experience the Presence of God, nor the Presence of His absence, but the absence of His Presence.

We require a history of phenomena—not simply more phenomena of history.

As it is, the secular psychotherapist is often in the role of the blind leading the half-blind.

The fountain has not played itself out, the Flame still shines, the River still flows, the Spring still bubbles forth, the Light has not faded. But between *us* and It, there is a veil which is more like fifty feet of solid concrete. *Deus absconditus.* Or we have absconded.

Already everything in our time is directed to categorizing and segregating this reality from objective facts. This is precisely the concrete wall. Intellectually, emotionally, interpersonally, organizationally, intuitively, theoretically, we have to blast our way through the solid wall, even if at the risk of chaos, madness and death. For from *this* side of the wall, this is the risk. There are no assurances, no guarantees.

Many people are prepared to have faith in the sense of scientifically indefensible belief in an untested hypothesis. Few have trust enough to test it. Many people make-believe what they experience. Few are made to believe by their experience. Paul of Tarsus was picked up by the scruff of the neck, thrown to the ground and blinded for three days. This direct experience was self-validating.

We live in a secular world. To adapt to this world the child abdicates its ecstacy. (*L'enfant abdique son extase.*—Mallarmé.) Having lost our experience of the Spirit, we are expected to have faith. But this faith comes to be a belief in a reality which is not evident. There is a prophecy in Amos that there will be a time when there will be a famine in the land, "not a famine for bread, nor a thirst for water, but of *hearing* the words of the Lord." That time has now come to pass. It is the present age.

From the alienated starting point of our pseudo-sanity, everything is equivocal. Our sanity is not "true" sanity. Their madness is not "true" madness. The madness of our patients is an artifact of the destruction wreaked on them by us, and by them on themselves. Let no one suppose that we meet any more "true" madness than that we are truly sane. The madness that we encounter in "patients" is a gross travesty, a mockery, a grotesque caricature of what the natural healing of that estranged integration we call sanity might be. True sanity entails in one way or another the dissolution of the normal ego, that false self competently adjusted to our alienated social reality: the emergence of the "inner" archetypal mediators of divine power, and through this death a rebirth, and the eventual re-establishment of a new kind of ego-functioning, the ego now being the servant of the Divine, no longer its betrayer.

The Disintegration of Consciousness

C. G. Jung

Carl Gustav Jung's somewhat unsettling article presents our Western models in a larger context. Drawing from Chinese and Tibetan sources, he formulates a viewpoint that includes more variations than the simple two-fold dichotomy of illness or health. The older, more inclusive systems are as concerned with methods of changing from one state of consciousness to another as our system is on maintaining one state of consciousness. The end goal of these systems is not only to be able to alter one's state at will, but to go beyond all states of consciousness and operate at an entirely different level. Facilitating and developing the capacity for changes of consciousness allows a flexibility in defining consciousness not open to the Western psychotherapist.

The selection is part of Jung's introduction to a Chinese text that contains directions for meditation from both Buddhist and Taoist sources. The Tibetan Book of the Dead, to which he refers, is a manual for experiencing various levels of consciousness. Traditionally, it is to be read to a dying man so that he may remember how to function between his death in one body and his rebirth or reincarnation in another.

Perhaps what appealed to Jung in the Chinese book was the idea expressed that the unconscious is connected to more than the single personality. This concept, called by Jung "The Collective Unconscious," is critical to his own theory of mental functioning, and provides a key that may unlock some of the deeper mysteries of the world of madness.

Whenever the narrowly delimited, but intensely clear, individual consciousness meets the immense expansion of the collective unconscious, there is danger because the latter has a definitely disintegrating effect on consciousness. Indeed, according to the exposition of the *Hui Ming Ching,* this effect belongs to the peculiar phenomena of Chinese yoga practice. It is said there: "Every separate thought takes shape and becomes visible in colour and form. The total spiritual power unfolds its traces. . . ."[1] One of the illustrations accompanying the book shows a sage sunk in contempla-

From "The Commentary" by C. G. Jung in Wilhelm: *The Secret of the Golden Flower,* English translation by Cary F. Baynes. Reprinted by permission of Harcourt Brace Jovanovich, Inc., and Routledge & Kegan Paul, Ltd.

[1] Cf. the recurrent memories of earlier incarnations that arise during contemplation.

tion, his head surrounded by tongues of fire, out of which five human figures emerge; these five split up again into twenty-five smaller figures. This would be a schizophrenic process if it were to become a permanent state. Therefore the instructions, as though warning the adept, say: "The shapes formed by the spirit-fire are only empty colours and forms. / The light of human nature [*hsing*] shines back on the primordial, the true."

Thus it is understandable that the text returns to the protecting figure of the "enclosing circle." It is intended to prevent "outflowing" and to protect the unity of consciousness from being split apart by the unconscious. Moreover, the Chinese concept points a way towards lessening the disintegrating effect of the unconscious; it describes the "thought-figures" or "separate thoughts" as "empty colours and shapes," and thus depotentiates them as much as possible. This idea runs through the whole of Buddhism (especially the Mahayana form), and, in the instructions to the dead in the Tibetan Book of the Dead, it is even pushed to the point of explaining favourable as well as unfavourable gods as illusions still to be overcome. It certainly is not within the competence of the psychologist to establish the metaphysical truth or falsity of this idea; he must be content to determine wherever possible what has psychic effect. In doing this, he need not bother himself as to whether the shape in question is a transcendental illusion or not, since faith, not science, has to decide this point. We are working here in a field which for a long time has seemed to be outside the domain of science, and which has therefore been looked upon as wholly illusory. But there is no scientific justification for such an assumption, for the substantiality of these things is not a scientific problem since in any case it would lie beyond the range of human perception and judgement, and therefore beyond any possibility of proof. The psychologist is not concerned with the substance of these complexes, but with the psychic experience. Without a doubt they are psychic contents which can be experienced, and which have an indisputable autonomy. They are fragmentary psychic systems which either appear spontaneously in ecstatic states and, under certain circumstances, elicit powerful impressions and effects, or else become fixed as mental disturbances in the form of delusions and hallucinations, thus destroying the unity of the personality.

The psychiatrist is prone to believe in toxins and the like, and to explain schizophrenia (splitting of the mind in a psychosis) in these terms, and hence to put no emphasis on the psychic contents. On the other hand, in psychogenic disturbances (hysteria, compulsion neurosis, etc.), where toxic effects and cell degeneration are out of the question, spontaneous split-off complexes are to be found, as, for example, in somnambulistic states. Freud, it is true, would like to explain these as due to unconscious repression of sexuality, but this explanation is by no means valid for all cases, because contents which the conscious cannot assimilate can evolve spontaneously out of the unconscious, and the repression hypothesis is inadequate in such instances. Moreover, the essential autonomy of these elements can be observed in the affects of daily life which obstinately obtrude themselves against our wills, and then, in spite of our earnest efforts to repress them, overwhelm the ego and force it under their control. No wonder that the primitive either sees in these moods a state of possession or sets them down to a loss of soul. Our colloquial speech reflects the same thing when we say: "I don't know what has got into him to-day"; "He is possessed of the devil"; "He is beside himself"; "He behaves as if possessed." Even legal practice recognizes a degree of diminished responsibility in a state of affect. Autonomic psychic contents thus are quite common experiences for us. Such contents have a disintegrating effect on the conscious mood.

But besides the ordinary, familiar affects, there are subtler, more complex emotional states which can no longer be described as affects pure and simple but which are complicated fragmentary psychic systems. The more complicated they are, the more they have the character of personalities. As constituent factors of the psychic personality, they necessarily have the character of "persons." Such fragmentary systems appear especially in mental diseases, in cases of psychogenic splitting of the personality (double personality), and of course in mediumistic phenomena. They are also encountered in religious phenomena. Many of the earlier gods have evolved out of "persons" into personified ideas, and finally into abstract ideas, for activated unconscious contents always appear first as projections upon the outside world. In the course of mental development, consciousness gradually assimilates them as projections in space and reshapes them into conscious ideas which then forfeit their originally autonomous and personal character. As we know, some of the old gods have become mere descriptive attributes via astrology (martial, jovial, saturnine, erotic, logical, lunatic, and so on).

The instructions of the Tibetan Book of the Dead in particular enable us to see how greatly the conscious is threatened with disintegration through these figures. Again and again, the dead are instructed not to take these shapes for truth, and not to confuse their murky appearance with the pure white light of *Dharmakaya* ("the divine body of truth"). The meaning is that they are not to project the one light of highest consciousness into concretized figures, and in such a way dissolve it into a plurality of autonomous fragmentary systems. If there were no danger of this, and if these systems did not represent menacingly autonomous and divergent tendencies, such urgent instructions would not be necessary. If we consider the simpler, polytheistically oriented attitude of the Eastern mind, these instructions would almost be the equivalent of warnings to a Christian not to let himself be blinded by the illusion of a personal God, not to mention a Trinity and innumerable angels and saints.

If tendencies towards disassociation were not inherent in the human psyche, parts never would have been split off; in other words, neither spirits nor gods would ever have come to exist. That is the reason, too, that our time is so utterly godless and profane, for we lack knowledge of the unconscious psyche and pursue the cult of consciousness to the exclusion of all else. Our true religion is a monotheism of consciousness, a possession by it, coupled with a fanatical denial that there are parts of the psyche which are autonomous. But we differ from the Buddhist yoga doctrine in that we even deny that such autonomous parts are experienceable. A great psychic danger arises here, because the parts then behave like any other repressed contents: they necessarily induce wrong attitudes, for the repressed material appears again in consciousness in a spurious form. This fact, which is so striking in every case of neurosis, holds true also for collective psychic phenomena. In this respect our time is caught in a fatal error: we believe we can criticize religious facts intellectually; we think, for instance, like Laplace, that God is a hypothesis which can be subjected to intellectual treatment, to affirmation or denial. It is completely forgotten that the reason mankind believes in the "daemon" has nothing whatever to do with outside factors, but is due to simple perception of the powerful inner effect of the autonomous fragmentary systems. This effect is not nullified by criticizing its name intellectually, nor by describing it as false. The effect is collectively always present; the autonomous systems are always at work, because the fundamental structure of the unconscious is not touched by the fluctuations of a transitory consciousness.

If we deny the existence of the autonomous systems, imagining that we have got rid of them by a critique of the name, then their effect which nevertheless continues cannot be understood, and they can no longer be assimilated to consciousness. They become an inexplicable factor of disturbance which we finally assume must exist somewhere or other outside of ourselves. In this way, a projection of the autonomous fragmentary systems results, and at the same time a dangerous situation is created, because the disturbing effects are now attributed to bad will outside ourselves which of course is not to be found anywhere but at our neighbour's—de l'autre côté de la rivière. This leads to collective delusions, "incidents," war, and revolution, in a word, to destructive mass psychoses.

Insanity is possession by an unconscious content which, as such, is not assimilated to consciousness; nor can it be assimilated, since the conscious mind has denied the existence of such contents. Expressed in terms of religion, the attitude is equivalent to saying: "We no longer have any fear of God and believe that everything is to be judged by human standards."

This *hybris*, that is, this narrowness of consciousness, is always the shortest way to the insane asylum. I recommend the excellent presentation of this problem in H. G. Wells' novel *Christina Alberta's Father*, and Schreber's *Denkwürdigkeiten eines Nervenkranken.*[2]

The enlightened European is likely to be relieved when it is said in the *Hui Ming Ching* that the "shapes formed by the spirit-fire are only empty colours and forms." That sounds quite European and seems to suit our reason excellently. Indeed, we think we can flatter ourselves at having already reached these heights of clarity because we imagine we have left such phantoms of gods far behind. But what we have outgrown are only the word-ghosts, not the psychic facts which were responsible for the birth of the gods. We are still as possessed by our autonomous psychic contents as if they were gods. To-day they are called phobias, compulsions, and so forth, or in a word, neurotic symptoms. The gods have become diseases; Zeus no longer rules Olympus but the solar plexus, and creates specimens for the physician's consulting room, or disturbs the brains of the politicians and journalists who then unwittingly unleash mental epidemics.

So it is better for Western man if at the start he does not know too much about the secret insight of Eastern wise men, for it would be a case of the "right means in the hands of the wrong man." Instead of allowing himself to be convinced once more that the daemon is an illusion, the Westerner ought again to experience the reality of this illusion. He ought to learn to recognize these psychic forces again, and not wait until his moods, nervous states, and hallucinations make clear to him in the most painful way possible that he is not the only master in his house. The products of the disassociation tendencies are actual psychic personalities of relative reality. They are real when they are not recognized as such and are therefore projected; relatively real when they are related to the conscious (in religious terms, when a cult exists); but they are unreal to the extent that consciousness has begun to detach itself from its contents. However, this last is the case only when life has been lived so exhaustively, and with such devotedness, that no more unfulfilled obligations to life exist, when, therefore, no desires that cannot be sacrificed unhesitatingly stand in the way of inner detachment from the world. It is futile to lie to ourselves about this. Wherever we are still attached, we are still possessed; and when one is possessed, it means the existence of something stronger than oneself. ("Truly from thence thou wilt ne'er come forth until thou hast paid the last farthing.") It is not a matter of indifference whether one calls something a "mania" or a "god." To serve a mania is detestable and undignified, but to serve a god is decidedly more meaningful and

[2]Mutze, Leipzig.

more productive because it means an act of submission to a higher, spiritual being. The personification enables one to see the relative reality of the autonomous psychic fragmentary system, and thus makes its assimilation possible and depotentiates the forces of fate. Where the god is not acknowledged, ego-mania develops, and out of this mania comes illness.

The teaching of yoga takes acknowledgement of the gods for granted. Its secret instruction is therefore intended only for him whose light of consciousness is on the point of disentangling itself from the powers of fate, in order to enter into the ultimate undivided unity, into the "centre of emptiness," where "dwells the god of utmost emptiness and life," as our text says. "To hear such a teaching is difficult to attain in thousands of aeons." Clearly the veil of maya cannot be lifted by a mere decision of reason, but demands the most thoroughgoing and persevering preparation consisting in the full payment of all debts to life. For as long as unconditional attachment through *cupiditas* exists, the veil is not lifted and the heights of a consciousness free of contents and free of illusion are not reached; nor can any trick nor any deceit bring this about. It is an ideal that can be completely realized only in death. Until then there are real and relatively real figures of the unconscious.

Psychosis: A Framework for an Alternate Possibility
Baba Ram Dass

Baba Ram Dass (Richard Alpert, Ph.D.) brings together widely disparate ideas in his selection, part of a question-and-answer session following a talk given at the Menninger Clinic in Topeka, Kansas. Trained in Western psychotherapeutic techniques himself (including five years of personal psychoanalysis), he is sensitive to how our culture deals with madness.

Prior to his talk, Ram Dass had been in India for a year, working with a teacher whose theories of personality, behavior, and altered states of consciousness had practically nothing in common with those of Ram Dass' former teachers and colleagues at Stanford and Harvard. In his address to Western therapists, he deliberately and deftly exposed the unwritten rules of the Western model, concentrating upon the contrast between his brother, locked up in a mental hospital, and himself, lecturing to an audience of therapists.

If all states of consciousness are given equal credence, if normal waking reality receives no more respect than psychosis, if both are seen as delusions—then how does one determine what is real? Although this issue is at the core of many Eastern systems, it has not commonly been dealt with in Western thought. In this presentation it is used to illustrate that the way we treat people with unorthodox belief systems is a result of our own assumptions about the nature of consciousness.

Ram Dass, more explicitly than Krober, looks at the Western model of understanding as only one among many possible models. Different approaches lead to differing forms of therapeutic intervention. Even more important, the outcomes are valued differently. A successful intervention from a Hindu standpoint might be seen by our culture as an intensification of the delusional system. Conversely, the psychotic who has come to the conclusion that his experiences were insane and who adjusts to living without them may be viewed in the Hindu framework as having intensified and elaborated his delusional system.

PERCEPTUAL VANTAGE POINTS AND PSYCHOSIS

Audience: Would you say a word about insanity or psychosis?

Ram Dass: I feel the resonance of all the past words that have been said about that in this room. I'm sure I could find something in here to resonate with. We live at a plane of reality which we share . . . it would seem . . . in which we all agree that certain things are the way they are. And when somebody disagrees with that and disagrees with it with deep faith, under certain conditions we characterize that as psychosis. I would now reinterpret that and say that what has happened is, that the person— and this is not yet saying anything more, it's merely giving us a framework to see an alternative possibility—has moved from one perceptual vantage point to another. A person through something which might be a chemical change, could be a trauma of some sort, it might be ingested, or psychically induced, psychogenic in nature—but through some trauma to the system— moves from one perceptual vantage point to another one, and then gets as attached to that one as we are to the one we're in. Right? He is attached to that and from our point of view he is psychotic. From his point of view, we are. That is because we don't see reality as he sees it. He's seeing another reality. In any kind of a Hindu system this would be called merely an astral plane. He's in another astral plane.

ON DIFFERENT WAYS OF BEING "STUCK"

This morning I was talking with one of the psychiatrists here on the staff, and I was telling him about my brother who has been in a mental hospital, who has been considered psychotic, who thinks of himself as the Messiah, and with whom I have spent a great deal of time, since I have as much a karmic link to him as to my father and whatever this consciousness is all about, it must have something to do with my brother, too. And my relation to him was to be as much "here and now" as I could be just as I had been with my father. To realize that he is stuck in a reality, just like my father is, just like I get stuck, and that any reality you're stuck in is just as bad as any other reality you're stuck in. And so, one of the things I do is I go into the reality he's stuck in with him. I look around, enjoy it with him, look at the world from that place with him, and then show him that from my point of view, you have to be able to go in and out of all of them, that any one you get stuck in is the wrong one. And if one guy's stuck in one who may be a psychiatrist, he is trying to cure somebody else stuck in another and is, in one sense, just substituting one stuckness for another stuckness. The journey of consciousness is to go to the place where you see that all of them are really relative realities and these are merely perceptual vantage points for looking at it all. When one looks at the universe from within the spirit, which is the . . . another "take," one sees that the entire universe all makes absolutely exquisite sense, but it's all slightly different because you're looking at it from an entirely different perceptual vantage point.

LIMITATIONS OF CURRENT CATEGORIES OF PSYCHOSIS

There are some beings that we call psychotic who in India would be called "God-Intoxicants." They are people who are primarily preoccupied with the fifth chakra at this moment. That is, they are beings who have experienced compassion outwardly and then their entire energy turns inward to inner states that they are experiencing. We see them as catatonic. That would be usually the category we would see them in. Because we are not getting an elicited response out of them, we project into them a cerain kind of psychological state. Now in India they project another kind of interpretation into that, surround the person with another environment, which changes the nature of his experience, because of their models of what it is that's happening to him, you see? So that a God-Intoxicant is treated with great reverence and respect. Ramakrishna, a very famous mystic in India, was often God-Intoxicant. I would say that probably most catatonics are not God-Intoxicants, but there are some that we're confusing, and we've got them in the same category because we don't have these differentiations at this point.

ANOTHER KARMIC RELATIONSHIP

My further understanding is that there is no being at any state of consciousness that one cannot make contact with, if one is himself free of attachment to any specific plane of consciousness. That is, I think that all of us are available at all times. There is a place in all of us that is available at all times, and our inability to make contact with another human being is our own inability to get out of the place we are stuck in. There is much to say for the flexibility of the consciousness of the . . . the behavior change agent . . . to be able to make contact with another human being where he is, without themselves getting stuck in where he's stuck. That's the work on one's self. It is my . . . from dealing with my brother . . . he was producing voluminous amounts of material, reading Greek, which he had never been able to read before. He was doing a number of phenomenal things which the doctors saw as pathological—his agitation, his . . . the fact that he could steal, lie, and cheat and tell that he was Christ. He escaped from the hospital a number of times, a very creative fellow. My reading of his materials showed me that he was tuned in on some of the greatest truths in the world that have ever been enunciated by some of the highest beings. He was experiencing these directly, but he was caught in a feeling that this was happening only to him. In other words, he had taken an ego with him into this other state of consciousness and he was experiencing it as unique to himself. And, therefore, he got into a messy predicament of saying, "I've been given this, and you haven't," you see. As we decided to share time and space, he noted that everything he said on this level I understood, and we could talk at this level together, although the psychiatrist sitting in the room was having a very difficult time dealing with this visitor who was obviously crazier than the patient, you know. And my brother often said to me, "I don't know," he says, "I'm a lawyer, I'm a decent citizen, I've got a tie and a jacket, and I go to church, and I'm a good person, and I read the Bible. Me they've got in a mental hospital; you, you walk barefoot, you've got a beard, you've got a funny name, you really wear . . . you, you're out, free. How do you explain that?" And I say, "Well, I'll show you how." I said, "Do you think you're Christ? the Christ . . . in pure consciousness?" He says, "Yes." I say, "Well, I think I am too." And he looks at me and he says, "No, you don't understand." I say, "That's why they lock you up," you see. Because the minute you tell somebody else they're not Christ, they lock you up. The minute you say, "I am and you're not," then you gotta go. It's very clear. That's the way the game is played. As far as I'm concerned, we're all God. Here we all are. Now I don't go around forcing you to say "You are God, aren't you?" Because you only come to somebody else when you are caught in an ego drama, when you are caught having to "do" something. I said, "Leonard, if you didn't have to do anything to anybody else, nobody would put you away." The funny play . . . the reason they put him away, which was just so cosmically humorous, was that my father, a Republican, conservative . . . came into my brother's apartment and found him sitting there naked, surrounded by five or six elderly ladies who were worshipping him. And he was sitting there burning his money and his credit cards. In a Jewish middle-class family you can do everything, but you don't burn the money, I'll tell you . . . so that anybody could see that he was obviously crazy.

Now if you happen to be a very deeply religious student you would understand exactly what was going on on quite another level, you see, and the humor of it is very far out . . . and the compassion and the poignancy and the predicament. Now, I don't feel pity for Leonard. I just see his karma unfolding. I feel great compassion. I certainly don't want him to suffer. I realize that I can reduce his suffering by not getting caught in his suffering with him, by being with him at the highest level of consciousness we can meet at, at all times. Therefore, I can help him by working on myself, and all summer long I would go to the Veterans Hospital one day a week and I would sit with him for many hours, just being as conscious as I could be. We would share this space. And all that time he became extraordinarily right here and now, because there wasn't anybody surrounding him that said, "You're nuts," because I don't think he's nuts. I just think he's living on another plane. That plane is a plane, just like this plane is a plane. And he and I would sit around and we'd look at the psychiatrist and we'd say, "Do you think he knows he's God?" And the psychiatrist would say, "They are wondering whether I think I'm God?" A beautiful flip-over predicament we created there, you see. And that reinforcement of my brother's position . . . he is out of the hospital now, by the way, and he's studying . . . it's very strange . . . he's studying Yoga and he's studying meditation. It's not all pure, by any means: He's perhaps just waiting for the day he can go back to being the Christ again, you know. And maybe he's just cooling it so he won't get locked up. I don't know the level at which he's playing the game.

COMPASSION WITHOUT PITY

I have worked for ten years under the model that there was nobody that I couldn't make contact with if I could purify myself enough, you see. That was the model I worked under. And I have dealt with many, many emergency situations when I was a therapist and LSD guide with people calling up in terrible states. And generally what I deal with is I go immediately to the place where I feel compassion for their predicament, but no pity, and I don't get caught in a symbiotic role to the dance they're presenting to me. I center, that's what I do on myself, so that somebody calls up and says, "This is horrible and I'm going to commit suicide." I say, "Well, then don't let me keep you. If you've got to go do that, you do whatever you need to do. But I just want you to know I'm here, if you want to hang out for a while before you commit suicide. Since you're going to do it anyway, you know what you've got to do, but if you'd like to hang out, here we are." And I always am right here. A girl calls me in the middle of the night and she says, "I've taken LSD and my mind is falling apart," and she's crying hysterically. She calls from California to New York. And I say, "Well, who called me?" She says, "Well, I did." I say, "Well, who dialed the number?" She says, "I did." Well, I say, "Would you put whoever it was that dialed the number on, because whoever dialed seven digits plus an area code in the middle of the night to find me, that person I can talk to. You, you're a raving maniac." That is, I am perfectly convinced that always in another human being there is that place, if I can just cut through to that place, which is my own ability to not get caught in the melodrama each time. Now often it becomes an ego struggle and all I do is center because a person does what he can do. And I never, at any time, get involved. I just do what I do. If the person can make the contact, fine. If he can't, there are often times when custodial care is required for a person, because he is doing work. You see, I'm very far out and I'm somewhat scary from a societal point of view, because I'm not sure I can tell you that two years in a mental hospital isn't much more advantageous in one's growth as a being than four years of a college education. And that maybe six months in prison could be comparable to a post-graduate education in education.

NEED FOR SOCIALLY SANCTIONED MORATORIUM CENTERS

I'm not sure I can look at total-care institutions as other than total-care institutions that do a certain kind of training and provide you with a certain kind of psychological environment. And I do see that there are points in the transformations in beings where they "can't keep it all together." That is, where more is happening to them than they fit . . . so that they can't keep all the planes together at any one moment. So they get stuck in one plane or another. A schizophrenic goes into one and then flips back into the other, and flips back and forth. Somebody that's totally psychotic stays in another plane. Somebody that is a total anxiety neurotic is afraid to leave this plane. You know, there are all these deep, different gradations. And it seems to me that we must introduce into our society the concept that there are socially sanctioned moratorium centers, there are places where a person can have a total-care environment, where they can go through the changes they need to go through with respect for the fact that they are doing work on themselves. I would say now that a good 40 percent of my friends have been through mental hospitals because they didn't see the world like the psychiatric community saw the world. And I would say that they are now out and that they are some of the highest beings in our culture, and they are functioning optimally and effectively and quite beautifully as human beings. And I think that they did their work often with the help of very hip psychiatrists, and often in spite of the psychiatrist. I think that many of them just needed that kind of total environmental protection while they did the work. And the psychiatrist needed the security that he was doing something, so he met with the patient so many times and he did his thing. The patient humored him, and then kept doing the work he needed to do on himself. I only guide patients, and I say, "Cool it, Baby, so they won't, you know, shoot you up with stuff or shoot your brain full of electric current, or stuff like that. Just cool it enough so that doesn't happen, and then just use it as a moratorium center. It's a groovy ashram. It'll protect you. It's cool." I guess that's what I have to say about psychosis. How far out it all is.

The Presence of Spirits
in Madness
Wilson Van Dusen

Wilson Van Dusen, describing the world of madness as filled with spirits, offers evidence based on clinical research that appears to verify the formulations of the Swedish scholar Emanuel Swedenborg. Van Dusen and Swedenborg both differentiate between "higher" and "lower" order spirits that are present in madness. The lower order are characterized as predominantly persecutory; the rarer, higher order spirits "act in the direction of the individual's own higher, unconscious, unused potentialities."

Particularly striking is the style of Van Dusen's presentation, which does not use standard psychological terminology. Instead, Van Dusen uses terms that are more typical of madmen and "primitive" curers. However, his basic theory is similar to that of other researchers. Jung, for instance, describes autonomous forces of the unconscious that implode into consciousness during a psychotic break. Other researchers including Grof (1973), Monroe (1971), and Masters and Houston (1966), present similar findings.

Van Dusen's article suggests that it is possible, with training or guidance, to become aware of spirit forces without being disturbed by them. A normal individual can train himself to experience these psychotic places in consciousness, without the manifestation of bizarre behavior, through the voluntary evocation and exploration of the hypnogogic state. Jung makes a similar inference.

The relationship between the manifestation of voices and the concept of madness in Van Dusen's theory is not clear. He implies two possibilities: madness may simply be the intrusion of "voices" or spirits into an "unreceptive" consciousness, or there may be some requisite state (that is, madness) that allows the entrance of spirits into a vulnerable consciousness. Neither possibility fits within our present paradigm of symptoms associated with madness, but both give credence to the idea that the "voices" have an identity independent of the person hearing them.

INTRODUCTION

I will compare the detailed accounts of patients' hallucinations to Emanuel Swedenborg's descriptions of the world of spirits. So few know of

Swedenborg's work that he needs some introduction. Emanuel Swedenborg, who lived from 1688–1772, was one of the last men to have encompassed practically all of human knowledge. Just as a sample, he was fluent in nine languages, wrote 150 works in 17 sciences, was expert in at least seven crafts, was a musician, member of parliament, and a mining engineer. Among many scientific accomplishments he first propounded the nebular hypothesis, did the first exhaustive works on metallurgy, wrote on algebra and calculus, found the function of several areas of the brain and ductless glands, suggested the particle structure of magnets, designed a glider and an undersea boat, engineered the world's largest drydock, etc., etc. In a way he outdid himself. Had he stopped with these little accomplishments he would have been remembered. But having mastered all of the physical sciences he then took on psychology and religion. His findings here were so rich and incredible that it cast a shadow over his name. He probably explored the hypnogogic state more than any other man has ever done before or since. In this region he broke through into the spiritual world. While living a productive and successful life in the world he had daily intercourse with spirits, which he candidly described in one of his 32 religious volumes titled *Heaven and Hell* (Swedenborg Foundation, 139 East 23 St., NYC). There were a number of miracles, such as the time he reported in detail a fire in Stockholm when he was hundreds of miles away, or when he would talk to departed relatives and friends and bring back accurate information which shocked the living. He delved into the symbolic language of the Bible and, for instance, wrote 12 volumes on the psychological meanings buried in Genesis and Exodus. This later work is so rich I've reserved my later years for understanding it. He had gone too far. He estranged the religious by not supporting any one religion while talking of the root values which underlie all religions. He was tried as a heretic and his works banned in his native Sweden. He was criticized for not going to church regularly. He didn't because he found church shallow and boring. He gradually became relatively unknown except for a small group of followers in many countries who continue to study his works.

One amusing anecdote occurred when Swedenborg wrote John Wesley, the founder of Methodism, that he had learned in the world of spirits that Wesley strongly wanted to see him. Wesley, surprised, acknowledged this and set an appointment months in the future because he was to go on a journey. Swedenborg wrote back he was sorry but he could not then see Wesley for he was due to die on a given date, which, of course, he did!

Reprinted by permission of the Swedenborg Foundation, 139 East 23rd Street, New York, N.Y. 10010.

SPIRITS AND MADNESS

By an extraordinary series of circumstances a confirmation appears to have been found for one of Emanuel Swedenborg's most unusual doctrines—that man's life depends on his relationship to a hierarchy of spirits. Out of my professional role as a clinical psychologist in a state mental hospital and my own personal interest, I set out to describe as faithfully as possible mental patients' experiences of hallucinations. A discovery four years ago helped me to get a relatively rich and consistent picture of the patients' experience. Though I noticed similarities with Swedenborg's description of the relationships of man to spirits it was only three years after all the major findings on hallucinations had been made that the striking similarity between what Twentieth-Century patients describe and Swedenborg's Eighteenth-Century accounts became apparent to me. I then collected as many details as possible of his description. I found that Swedenborg's system not only is an almost perfect fit with patients' experiences, but even more impressively, accounts for otherwise quite puzzling aspects of hallucinations. I will first describe how I worked and my findings, and then relate this to Swedenborg's work.

All the people involved hallucinated. They included chronic schizophrenics, alcoholics, brain-damaged and senile persons. The subjects of this study came to the attention of friends of the public because of unusual behavior. The average layman's picture of the mentally ill as raving lunatics is far from reality. Most of these people have become entangled in inner processes and simply fail to manage their lives well. In the hospital most have freedom of the grounds and the average visitor is impressed that, aside from occasional odd bits of behavior, the patients have most of their powers and appear like almost everyone else. Many return home in a month or two never to need mental hospitalization again. Some become so enmeshed in inner processes that they slip to lower levels of mental disorder. The most severe disorder is usually that of a person who sits all day involved in inner processes, who obediently obeys the request of hospital staff to dress, eat, bathe, and sleep in the hospital routine.

The people described here range from a few months in the hospital to twenty years. Most would be like the patients on the hospital grounds who strike the visitor as not unlike themselves. A conversation with one of these patients might indicate to the visitor that the patient has an unusual set of beliefs—for instance, that he is kept in the hospital by a gang of thieves, or that ordinary clouds are radiation pollution. In many, even unusual beliefs would not be apparent. Most conceal that they hear and see things because they are wise enough to know the visitor doesn't and wouldn't understand. Their adjustment within the hospital is relatively good. Many do productive work ten to thirty hours a week. It is when they return to the relatively complex and demanding outside world that their adjustment often worsens. None of the patients at the most severe level of mental disorders could be included in this study because they couldn't describe their hallucinations well enough.

After dealing with hundreds of such patients, I discovered about four years ago that it was possible to speak to their hallucinations. To do so I looked for patients who could distinguish between their own thoughts and the things they heard and saw in the world of hallucinations. The patient was told that I simply wanted to get as accurate a description of their experiences as possible. I held out no hope for recovery or special reward. It soon became apparent that many were embarrassed by what they saw and heard and hence they concealed it from others. Also they knew their experiences were not shared by others, and some were even concerned that their reputations would suffer if they revealed the obscene nature of their voices. It took some care to make the patients comfortable enough to reveal their experience honestly. A further complication was that the voices were sometimes frightened of me and themselves needed reassurance. I struck up a relationship with both the patient and the persons he saw and heard. I would question these other persons directly, and instructed the patient to give a word-for-word account of what the voices answered or what was seen. In this way I could hold long dialogues with a patient's hallucinations and record both my questions and their answers. My method is that of phenomenology. My only purpose was to come to as accurate a description as possible of the patient's experiences. The reader may notice I treat the hallucinations as realities because that is what they are to the patient. I would work with a patient for as little as one hour or up to several months of inquiry where the hallucinated world was complex enough.

Some may wonder why one should believe what these patients report. The patients cooperated with me only because I was honestly trying to learn of their experiences. They were not paid or even promised recovery or release from the hospital. Most of my subjects seemed fairly sensible except for the fact of hallucinations which invaded and interfered with their lives. On several occasions I held conversation with hallucinations that the patient himself did not really understand. This was especially true when I dealt with what will be described as the higher order hallucinations which can be symbolically rich beyond the patient's own understanding. There was great consistency in what was reported independently by different patients. I have no reason to doubt they were reporting real experiences. They seemed to be honest people as puzzled as I was to explain what was happening to them. The differences among the experiences of schizophrenics, alcoholics, the brain damaged and senile were not as striking as the similarities; so I will describe these hallucinated worlds in general.

One consistent finding was that patients felt they had contact with an-other world or order of beings. Most thought these other persons were living persons. All objected to the term hallucination. Each coined his own term such as The Other Order, the Eavesdroppers, etc.

For most individuals the hallucinations came on suddenly. One woman was working in a garden when an unseen man addressed her. Another man described sudden loud noises and voices he heard while riding in a bus. Most were frightened, and adjusted with difficulty to this new experi-ence. All patients describe voices as having the quality of a real voice sometimes louder, sometimes softer, than normal voices. The experience they describe is quite unlike thoughts or fantasies. When things are seen they appear fully real. For instance a patient described being awakened one night by Air Force officers calling him to the service of his country. He got up and was dressing when he noticed their insignia wasn't quite right; then their faces altered. With this he knew they were of The Other Order and struck one hard in the face. He hit the wall and injured his hand. He could not distinguish them from reality until he noticed the insignia. Most patients soon realize that they are having experiences that others do not share, and for this reason learn to keep quiet about them. Many suffer insults, threats and attacks for years from voices with no one around them aware of it. Women have reported hearing such vile things they felt it would reflect on them should they even be mentioned.

In my dialogues with patients I learned of two orders of experience, borrowing from the voices themselves, called the higher and the lower order. Lower order voices are as though one is dealing with drunken bums at a bar who like to tease and torment just for the fun of it. They will suggest lewd acts and then scold the patient for considering them. They find a weak point of conscience and work on it interminably. For instance one man heard voices teasing him for three years over a ten-cent debt he had already paid. They call the patient every conceivable name, suggest every lewd act, steal memories or ideas right out of consciousness, threaten death, and work on the patient's credibility in every way. For instance they will brag that they will produce some disaster on the morrow and then claim honor for one in the daily paper. They suggest foolish acts (such as: Raise your right hand in the air and stay that way) and tease if he does it and threaten him if he doesn't. The lower order can work for a long time to possess some part of the patient's body. Several worked on the ear and the patient seemed to grow deafer. One voice worked two years to capture a patient's eye which visibly went out of alignment. Many patients have heard loud and clear voices plotting their death for weeks on end, an apparently nerve-wracking experience. One patient saw a noose around his neck which tied to "I don't know what" while voices plotted his death by hanging. They threaten pain and can cause felt pain as a way of enforcing their power. The most devastating experience of all is to be shouted at constantly by dozens of voices. When this occurred the patient had to be sedated. The vocabulary and range of ideas of the lower order is limited, but they have a persistent will to destroy. They invade every nook and cranny of privacy, work on every weakness and credibility, claim awesome powers, lie, make promises and then undermine the patients' will. They never have a personal identity though they accept most names or identities given them. They either conceal or have no awareness of personal memories. Though they claim to be separate identities they will reveal no detail which might help to trace them as separate individuals. Their voice quality can change or shift, leaving the patient quite confused as to whom might be speaking. When identified as some friend known to the patient they can assume this voice quality perfectly. For convenience many patients call them by nicknames, such as "Fred," "The Doctor," or "The Old Timer." I've heard it said by the higher order that the purpose of the lower order is to illuminate all of the person's weaknesses. They do that admirably and with infinite patience. To make matters worse they hold out promises to patients and even give helpful sounding advice only to catch the patient in some weakness. Even with the patient's help I found the lower order difficult to relate to because of their disdain for me as well as the patient.

The limited vocabulary and range of ideas of the lower order is striking. A few ideas can be repeated endlessly. One voice just said "hey" for months while the patient tried to figure out what "hey" or "hay" meant. Even when I was supposedly speaking to an engineer that a woman heard, the engineer was unable to do any more arithmetic than simple sums and multiplication the woman had memorized. The lower order seems incapable of sequential reasoning. Though they often claim to be in some distant city they cannot report more than the patient sees, hears, or remembers. They seem imprisoned in the lowest level of the patient's mind, giving no real evidence of a personal world or any higher order thinking or experiencing.

All of the lower order are irreligious or anti-religious. Some actively interfered with the patients' religious practices. Most considered them to be ordinary living people, though once they appeared as conventional devils and referred to themselves as demons. In a few instances they referred to themselves as from hell. Occasionally they would speak through the patient so that the patient's voice and speech would be directly those of the voices. Sometimes they acted through the patient. One of my female patients was found going out the hospital gate arguing loudly with her male voice that she didn't want to leave, but he was insisting. Like many, this particular hallucination claimed to be Jesus Christ, but his bragging and argumentativeness rather gave him away as of the lower order. Sometimes the lower order is embedded in physical concerns, such as a lady who was tormented by "experimenters" painfully treating her joints to prevent arthritis. She held out hope they were helping her, though it was apparent to any onlooker they had all but destroyed her life as a free and intelligent person.

In direct contrast stands the rarer higher order hallucinations. In quantity they make up perhaps a fifth or less of the patient's experiences. The contrast may be illustrated by the experience of one man. He had heard the lower order arguing a long while how they would murder him. He also had a light come to him at night like the sun. He knew it was a different order because the light respected his freedom and would withdraw if it frightened him. In contrast, the lower order worked against his will and would attack if it could see fear in him. This rarer higher order seldom speaks, whereas the lower order can talk endlessly. The higher order is much more likely to be symbolic, religious, supportive, genuinely instructive, and communicate directly with the inner feelings of the patient. I've learned to help the patient approach the higher order because of its great power to broaden the individual's values. When the man was encouraged to approach his friendly sun he entered a world of powerful numinous experiences, in some ways more frightening than the murderers who plotted his death. In one scene he found himself at the bottom of a long corridor with doors at the end behind which raged the powers of hell. He was about to let out these powers when a very powerful and impressive Christ-like figure appeared and by direct mind-to-mind communication counseled him to leave the doors closed and follow him into other experiences which were therapeutic to him. In another instance the higher order appeared to a man as a lovely woman who entertained him while showing him thousands of symbols. Though the patient was a high-school educated gas-pipe fitter, his female vision showed a knowledge of religion and myth far beyond the patient's comprehension. At the end of a very rich dialogue with her (the patient reporting her symbols and responses) the patient asked for just a clue as to what she and I were talking about. Another example is that of a Negro who gave up being useful and lived as a drunken thief. In his weeks of hallucinations the higher order carefully instructed him on the trials of all minority groups and left him with the feeling he would like to do something for minorities.

In general the higher order is richer than the patient's normal experience, respectful of his freedom, helpful, instructive, supportive, highly symbolic and religious. It looks most like Carl Jung's archetypes, whereas the lower order looks like Freud's id. In contrast to the lower order it thinks in something like universal ideas in ways that are richer and more complex than the patient's own mode of thought. It can be very powerful emotionally and carry with it an almost inexpressible ring of truth. The higher order tends to enlarge a patient's values, something like a very wise and considerate instructor. Some patients experience both the higher and lower orders at various times and feel caught between a private heaven and hell. Many only know the attacks of the lower order. The higher order claims power over the lower order and indeed shows it at times, but not enough to give peace of mind to most patients. The higher order itself had indicated that the usefulness of the lower order is to illustrate and make conscious the patients' weaknesses and faults.

Though I could say much more on what the patients reported, and quote extensively from dialogues with hallucinations, this is the substance of my findings. I was very early impressed by the over-all similarities of what patients reported even though they had no contact with each other. After twenty patients there wasn't much more to be learned. I was also impressed by the similarity to the relatively little shown in the Biblical accounts of possession. These patients might well be going through experiences quite similar to what others experienced centuries ago.

Several things stood out as curious and puzzling. The lower order seemed strangely prevalent and limited. In the face of their claim of separate identity, their concealing or not knowing any fact (birthplace, schooling, name, personal history) which would set them apart was unusual. Their malevolence and persistence in undermining the patient was striking. And why would they consistently be unreligious or anti-religious? Just the mention of religion provokes anger or derision from them. In contrast, the higher order appeared strangely gifted, sensitive, wise and religious. They did not conceal identity but rather would have an identity above the human. For instance, a lady of the higher order was described as "an emanation of the feminine aspect of the Divine." When I implied she was Divine she took offense. She herself was not divine but she was an emanation of the Divine. I couldn't help but begin to feel I was dealing with some kind of contrasting polarity of good and evil. The patients' accounts of voices trying to seize for their own some part of the body such as eye, ear or tongue had a strangely ancient ring to it. Some people might suspect that my manner of questioning fed back to the patients what I wanted to hear, but after I addressed on hallucinations an audience including patients many warmly commended me for capturing their own experiences too. As incredible as it may seem, I'm inclined to believe the above is a roughly accurate account of many patients' hallucinatory experiences.

I read and admired Swedenborg's work for some while, primarily because his religious experiences fit with my own and partly because of his immense knowledge of the hypnogogic state and the inner structure of the psyche. His doctrine regarding spirits I could neither affirm nor deny from my own experience, though it seemed a little incredible. As I describe Swedenborg's doctrine in this matter the similarity with my own findings will become apparent.

Swedenborg describes all of life as a hierarchy of beings representing essentially different orders and yet acting in correspondence with each other. The Lord acts through celestial angels, who in turn correspond on a lower level to spiritual angels, who in turn correspond to a third lower heaven—all of which corresponds to and acts into man. On the opposite side there are three levels of hell acting out of direct contact into man. Man is the free space and meeting ground of these great hierarchies. In effect, good and its opposite evil rule through this hierarchy of beings down to man who stands in the free space between them. Out of his experiences and choices he identifies with either or both sides. These influences coming from both sides are the very life of man. The man who takes pride in his own powers tends toward the evil side. The man who acknowledges that he is the receptacle of all that is good, even the power to think and to feel, tends toward the good side. In the extreme of evil, spirits claim power over all things and seek to subjugate others. In the extreme of good, angels feel themselves free in that the good of the Lord acts freely through them. Swedenborg's doctrine of the effect of spirits with man is simply the lower aspect of a whole cosmology of the structure of existence.

> Such is the equilibrium of all in the universal heaven that one is moved by another, thinks from another, as if in a chain; so that not the least thing can [occur from itself]: thus the universe is ruled by the Lord, and, indeed, with no trouble (SD 2466).* From this order of creation it may appear, that such is the binding chain of connection from firsts to lasts that all things together make one, in which the prior cannot be separated from the posterior (just as a cause cannot be separated from its effect); and that thus the spiritual world cannot be separated from the natural, nor the natural world from the spiritual; thence neither the angelic heaven from the human race, nor the human race from the angelic heaven. Wherefore it is so provided by the Lord, that each shall afford a mutual assistance to the other. . . . Hence it is, that the angelic mansions are indeed in heaven, and to appearance separate from the mansions where men are; and yet they are with man in his affections of good and truth (LJ 9).

Each, man or spirit, is given to feel he is free and rules. Yet all are ruled (SD 3633). Even the world of matter is created and sustained by the Lord through the spiritual world (DP 3). It is normal that man does not feel himself to be the subject of a spiritual world. Swedenborg repeated-

---

*All references here are to books by Emanuel Swedenborg. Full titles are listed in the references at the end of the article.

ly enjoins that one is not even to attempt to become aware of the world of spirits because it is dangerous (HH 249, AC 5863). In the normal man spirits are adjoined to the man's spirit (AC 5862) or, what is the same, to more unconscious levels of his mind so that man is not aware of them. They flow into his feelings or into the matrix of thought (AE 1182). Spirits think spiritually and man naturally so that the two correspond to each other. In modern terms one would say spirits are in the unconscious and there live out their desires in what is to man the origin of his thoughts and feelings. In the normal situation man is not aware of their action, taking it to be his own thought and feeling. They, too, do not feel themselves to be in the life of a man. To all of man's experiences they have corresponding spiritual experiences. They do not see or hear the man's world. The spirits adjoined to man have dispositions similar to the man's. As Swedenborg says, with a bit of humor, enthusiastic spirits are with the enthusiastic (AE 1182). Thus they act together. Man is free to act, but by this relation to a hierarchy of spirits his tendencies are conditioned (AC 5850). His identification with good or evil tendencies, by his acts, further the conditioning in one direction or another. Good spirits or angels dwell in the most interior aspects of man's mind—in his loves, affections or ends (AC 5851). They think by generals or universals (AC 2472), or as modern psychology would put it, they think more abstractly. One of their thoughts would cover thousands of a natural man's thoughts. The soul, spirit or interior man are the same thing (AC 6059).

> . . . being thus supereminent, spiritual ideas or thoughts, relatively to natural, are ideas of ideas, thoughts of thoughts; that by them, therefore, are expressed qualities of qualities and affections of affections; and, consequently, that spiritual thoughts are the beginnings and origins of natural thoughts (CL 326:7).

Evil spirits reside in a lower but still unconscious area of mind, the personal memory. Those like the man are joined to him and they take on the memory of the man and neither the man nor they know that they are separate. They are in what Swedenborg calls his scientifics, or the facts and tendencies stored in the memory.

To some this whole conception of Swedenborg's sounds strange and even highly improbable. Scientifically it appears beyond any real test. If man cannot know these spirits, nor do they even know they are with man, the matter is like the worst speculation and not open to examination. In Swedenborg's personal diary and other works he tells how he felt gifted by the Lord with the experience both of heaven and hell and could examine over a period of many years their exact relationship to man. To learn of the powers and tendencies of evil spirits he was attacked by them as though he were a man possessed, yet it was not permitted that he be injured by them. In this respect his account sounds very much like madness with hallucinations and delusions. Yet the many documents that have been gathered[1] testify to his normal and even prosperous life as a nobleman, respected scientist and man of the world. Apparently he was a gifted man who was allowed to explore experiences that other less gifted persons are caught within.

The diagnosis of schizophrenia did not exist in his day, it having been first clearly delineated in 1911 by Eugen Bleuler. He did speculate on the nature of madness, sometimes describing it as being too involved in one's own fantasies (SD 172), and sometimes ascribing it to pride in one's own powers (spiritual madness) (AC 10227:3). He gave much description of possession by spirits and what they did. Present day psychosis always involves some degree of self pride (spiritual madness) but the hallucinated aspect looks most like what Swedenborg described under the general headings of obsessions (to be caught in false ideas) and possession (to have alien spirits acting into one's thought, feelings, or even into one's bodily acts (HH 257). He indicates that normally there is a barrier between these spiritual entities and man's own consciousness. He also makes quite clear that if this barrier of awareness were penetrated the man would be in grave danger for his mental health and even for his life (HH 249).

If evil spirits knew they were with man they would do all sorts of things to torment him and destroy his life. What he describes looks remarkably like my own findings on the lower order hallucinations. Let us consider lower order hallucinations and possession by evil spirits together. You will recall that I said lower order hallucinations act against the patient's will, and are extremely verbal, persistent, attacking, and malevolent. They use trickery to deceive the patient as to their own powers, threaten, cajole, entreat, and undermine in every conceivable way. These are all characteristic of possession by evil spirits which takes place when the spirits are no longer unconscious, but have some awareness of themselves as separate entities and act into consciousness.

It is not clear how the awareness barrier between spirits and man is broken. In Swedenborg's case he had a way of minimal breathing and concentrating inwardly for most of his life—a practice that resembles the yogic Pranayama and Pratyahara, which is calculated to awaken inner awareness. In the context of his whole system of thought one would surmise this inner barrier of awareness is penetrated when the person habitually withdraws from social usefulness into inner fantasy and pride. This would conform to contemporary social withdrawal which is the earliest aspect of schizophrenia. I am relatively certain that religious faith alone doesn't

[1]R. L. Tafel, *Documents Concerning Swedenborg*, 3 Vols., Swedenborg Society, London, 1890.
A. Action, *Letters and Memorials of Emanuel Swedenborg*, 2 Vols., Swedenborg Scientific Association, Bryn Athyn, Pa., 1948.
G. Trobridge, *Swedenborg, Life and Teaching*, Swedenborg Society, London, 1945.

prevent hallucinations because many patients try to save themselves by their faith. Observation would suggest useful social acts (charity) would come closer to preventing schizophrenia.

All of Swedenborg's observations on the effect of evil spirits entering man's consciousness conform to my findings. The most fundamental is that they attempt to destroy him (AC 6192, 4227). They can cause anxiety or pain (AC 6202). They speak in man's own native tongue (CL 326, DP 135). (The only instances I could find where hallucinations seemed to know a language other than the patient's were from the higher order.) They seek to destroy conscience (AC 1983) and seem to be against every higher value. For instance they interfere with reading or religious practices. They suggest acts against the patient's conscience and if refused, threaten, make them seem plausible, or do anything to overcome the patient's resistance. Swedenborg says these spirits can impersonate and deceive (SD 2687). This accounts for one puzzling aspect. Patients say voices can shift and identify as they speak, making it impossible to identify them. Or if a patient treats them as some known individual they will act like them. They lie (SD 1622). Most patients who have experienced voices for any length of time come to recognize this. They tell a patient he will die tomorrow and yet he lives. They claim to be anyone including the Holy Spirit (HH 249). It took some while for a woman patient to come to realize the male voice in her probably was not Jesus Christ as he claimed. She considered him sick and proceeded to counsel this voice, which improved and left her! He claimed he could read my mind, but I showed her by a simple experiment that he couldn't.

> When spirits begin to speak with man, he must beware lest he believe them in anything; for they say almost anything; things are fabricated by them, and they lie; for if they were permitted to relate what heaven is, and how things are in the heavens, they would tell so many lies, and indeed with a solemn affirmation, that man would be astonished; . . . They are extremely fond of fabricating: and whenever any subject of discourse is proposed, they think that they know it, and give their opinions one after another, one in one way, and another in another, altogether as if they knew; and if a man listens and believes, they press on, and deceive, and seduce in diverse ways (SD 1622).

Though most patients tend to recognize this, most still put faith in their voices and remain caught by them. For instance, one lady felt a group of scientists including a physician and engineer were doing important but painful experiments on the ends of her bones. Even though I couldn't find a trace of medical knowledge in the physician or any mathematical ability above simple sums in the engineer, she continued to believe in them.

Many voices have indicated they will take over the world, or have already done so, which bit of bragging Swedenborg noticed too (SD 4476). They can suggest and try to enforce strange acts in the patient and then condemn him for compliance (AC 761). They draw attention to things sexual or simply filthy (SD 2852) and then proceed to condemn the person for noticing them. They often refer to the person as just an automaton or machine (SD 3633), a common delusional idea that many schizophrenics adopt. In the normal condition these spirits cannot see and hear the world of man (AC 1880), but in mental illness they can (SD 3963). For instance I was able to give the Rorschach Ink Blot Test to a patient's voices separately from the patient's own responses. Since I could talk with them through the patient's hearing they could hear what the patient heard. Though they seem to have the same sensory experience as the patient I could find no evidence they could see or hear things remote from the patient's senses as they often claimed.

There are a number of peculiar traits of the lower order hallucinations on which Swedenborg throws light. If voices are merely the patient's unconscious coming forth I would have no reason to expect them to be particularly for or against religion. Yet the lower order can be counted on to give its most scurrilous comments to any suggestion of religion. They either totally deny any afterlife or oppose God and all religious practices (AC 6197). Once I asked if they were spirits and they answered, "the only spirits around here are in bottles" (followed by raucous laughter). To Swedenborg it is their opposition to God, religion, and all that it implies that makes them what they are.

Another peculiar finding is that the lower order hallucinations were somehow bound to and limited within the patient's own experiences (AC 7961). The lower order could not reason sequentially or think abstractly as could the higher order. Also it seemed limited within the patient's own memory. For instance, one group of voices could attack the patient only for things he had recalled since they invaded him; and they were most anxious to get any dirt to use against the patient. Swedenborg throws light on this when he indicates evil spirits invade man's memory and scientific (the facts he has learned). This accounts for their memory limitation, their lack of sequential and abstract reasoning, and their extreme repentiveness. As I indicated earlier, it is not uncommon for voices to attack a person for years over a single past guilt. It also accounts for the very verbal quality of the lower order as against the higher order's frequent inability to speak at all (AC 5977).

Swedenborg indicates the possibility of spirits acting through the subject (AC 5990), which is to possess him. This I have occasionally seen. For instance the man who thought he was Christ within a woman sometimes spoke through her, at which times her voice was unnaturally rough and deep. She also had trouble with him dressing at the same time she was because she would be caught in the incongruities of doing two different acts at once.

Another peculiar finding which Swedenborg unintentionally explained is my consistent experience that lower order hallucinations act as though they are separate individuals and yet they can in no way reveal even a trace of personal identity, nor even a name. Nor can they produce anything more than was in the patient's memory. Most patients have the impression they are other beings. They will take on any identity suggested, but they seem to have none of their own. This strange but consistent finding is clarified by Swedenborg's account. These lower order spirits enter the man's memory and lose all personal memory. The personal memory was taken off at their death leaving their more interior aspects. That they discover they are other than the man allows obsession and possession to take place and accounts for their claiming separate identity and convincing the patient of this. But their actual lack of personal memory comes from their taking on the patient's memory.

It may be that in the deeper degree of schizophrenia the spirits have taken on more of their own memory. Swedenborg says this would lead man to believe he had done what he had not done (AC 2478, HH 256). For instance delusional ideas are a belief in what has not occurred. Some patients speak of themselves as dead and buried and their present identity as of another person. "For were spirits to retain their corporeal memory, they would so far obsess man, that he would have no more self-control or be in the enjoyment of his life, than one actually obsessed" (SD 3783). I am just guessing at this point that the most serious of the mental disorders, where a person is totally out of contact and jabbers to himself and gesticulates strangely, are instances where these spirits have more memory and act more thoroughly through the person. It is then symbolically accurate that they are dead and someone else lives.

I deliberately looked for some discrepancy between my patients' present experiences and what Swedenborg described. It appeared I had found it in the number of spirits who were with one patient. They may have three or four most frequent voices but they can experience a number of different people. Swedenborg says there usually are only two good and two evil spirits with a person (AC 904, 5470, 6189). He also gives instances where spirits come in clouds of people at a time (SD 4546). I later learned that where there is a split between the internal and external experience of a person, as in schizophrenia, there can be many spirits with a person (SD 160). Also as patients' voices themselves have described the situation, one spirit can be the subject or voice of many (HH 601). This was the case with the lady who had a team of researchers working on her bones. They themselves were in a kind of hierarchy and represented many. Only the lowest few members of the hierarchy became known to the patient and myself. Swedenborg refers to such spirits as the subjects of many.

Both Swedenborg and the medieval literature speak of the aim of spirits to possess and control some part of a patient's body (SD 1751, 2656, 4910, 5569). Parts involved in my observations have been the ear, eye, tongue, and genitals. The medieval literature speaks of intercourse between a person and his or her possessing spirit, giving these spirits the names of incubi and succubi depending on their sex.[2] One female patient described her sexual relations with her male spirit as both more pleasurable and more inward than normal intercourse. Swedenborg makes clear that those who enter the affections or emotions enter thereby into all things of the body. These more subtle possessions are more powerful than simply having voices talking to one, and can easily account for affective psychoses where there is a serious mood change (AC 6212, SD 5981). One older German woman was depressed by tiny devils who tormented her in the genital region and made her feel the horror of hell. There are many impressive similarities between the patients' experiences of lower order hallucinations and Swedenborg's obsession and possession by evil spirits.

The higher order hallucinations are quite a bit rarer, do not oppose the patient's will, but rather are helpful guides, and are far more abstract, symbolic and creative than lower order hallucinations. In Swedenborg's terms the higher order would be angels who come to assist the person. As Swedenborg describes it, they reside in the interior mind which does not think in words but in universals which comprise many particulars (AC 5614). The higher order in one patient visually showed him hundreds of universal symbols in the space of one hour. Though he found them entertaining he couldn't understand their meaning. Many of the higher order are purely visual and use no words at all, while the lower order talk endlessly. One patient described a higher order spirit who appeared all in white, radiant, very powerful in his presence and communicated directly with the spirit of the patient to guide him out of his hell. Swedenborg describes how the influx of angels gently leads to good and leaves the person in freedom (AC 6205). I've described the incident where the patient recognized good forces first as a sun which withdrew from him when he was frightened whereas all his experiences of the lower order had been attacking. It was this simple respect for his freedom that led the patient to believe this was another order.

Swedenborg indicates that good spirits have some degree of control over the evil ones (AC 592, 6308; SD 3525). Higher order hallucinations have made the same comment—that they can control lower order ones, but it is seldom to the degree the patient would desire. In some respects they overcome the evil insofar as the patient identifies with them. In one case I encouraged the patient to become acquainted with these helpful forces that tended to frighten him. When he did so their values merged into

---

[2]See Domoniality; or, Incubi and Succubi (17th Century), London, 1927.

him and the evil plotters, who had been saying for months they would kill him, disappeared. I seem to see some kind of control of the higher order over the lower, though the nature and conditions of this control are not yet clear. Again, precisely in agreement with Swedenborg. I found evil spirits cannot see the good but the good can the evil (HH 583). The lower order may know of the presence of the higher order but they cannot see them.

It remained a considerable puzzle to me for over a year why the higher order hallucinations were rarer since they were far more interesting to the patient and myself and potentially more therapeutic. Again, Swedenborg has an explanation that fits beautifully with my findings. I have noticed the higher order tends to be non-verbal and highly symbolic. He indicates angels possess the very interior of man. Their influx is tacit. It does not stir up material ideals or memories but is directed to man's ends or inner motives (AC 5854, 6193, 6209). It is for this reason not so apparent and hence rarer in the patients' reports.

CONCLUSION

There are a number of points which make the similarity of Swedenborg's accounts and my own findings impressive. My patients acted independently of each other and yet gave similar accounts. They also agreed on every particular I could find with Swedenborg's account. My own findings were established years before I really examined Swedenborg's position in this matter. I'm inclined to believe Swedenborg and I are dealing with the same matter. It seems remarkable to me that, over two centuries of time, men of very different cultures working under entirely different circumstances on quite different people could come to such similar findings. Normally such a separation in time, cultures and persons should have led to greater differences. Because of this I am inclined to speculate that we are looking at a process which transcends cultures and remains stable over time.

Then I wonder whether hallucinations, often thought of as detached pieces of the unconscious, and hallucinations as spiritual possession might not simply be two ways of describing the same process. Are they really spirits or pieces of one's own unconscious? If the hallucinations came up with confirmably separate histories it would tend to confirm the spiritual hypothesis. We have already touched on their singular absence of a personal history and how this fits into the spirit model. In a way there are too many aspects of the matter that do not explain as well by the unconscious model as by the spiritual—consider for instance the gifts of the higher order spirits. The difference between the unconscious and spirit models grows darker when one considers that lower order spirits can only get in if they have tendencies like the person's own unconscious. Conversely

I think higher order spirits only act in the direction of the individual's own higher, unconscious, unused potentialities. If this is so, it makes it difficult to separate them out as other than the person's own. One way of checking this occurs if the hypothesis of spirits leads to successful treatments fundamentally unlike what would occur from the hypothesis of a personal unconscious. I would hope that further work might settle the matter for spirits or for a personal unconscious. But it might be that it is not either/or. If these two views should be the same thing then my brothers may be my keeper and I theirs simultaneously.

There are many unsettled matters beyond that of spirit possession. For instance the experiences Swedenborg described can be awakened in normal individuals by a study of the hypnogogic state. With the experience of alien forces in this state one comes to recognize their operation on impulsive thoughts in normal consciousness. One could also ask how possessing spirits might be removed. The several ways this can be accomplished is another study in itself.

It is curious to reflect that, as Swedenborg has indicated, our lives may be the little free space at the confluence of giant higher and lower spiritual hierarchies. It may well be this confluence is normal and only seems abnormal, as in hallucinations, when we become aware of being met by these forces. There is some kind of lesson in this—man freely poised between good and evil, under the influence of cosmic forces he usually doesn't know exist. Man, thinking he chooses, may be the resultant of other forces.

REFERENCES

AC — Arcana Celestia, 12 volumes
AE — Apocalypse Explained, 6 volumes
CL — Conjugal Love
DP — Divine Providence
HH — Heaven and Hell
LJ — Last Judgment
SD — Spiritual Diary, 5 volumes
These works are inexpensively available from:
The Swedenborg Foundation
139 East 23rd Street
New York, New York 10010

Psychosis and Human Growth
Malcolm B. Bowers, Jr.

It is not enough to understand the state we call madness. Understanding is only the prelude to helping others cope with the state, seeing its shadows within ourselves, and using this understanding as a touchstone for further work. In research, theory, therapy, counseling, teaching, and simply being in the world, it is our own theoretical perspective that shapes—and in some cases conditions—our attitudes and actions.

It is appropriate to end this section with an article that looks less at the dynamics of psychosis than at the possibilities for growth. The beauty of Malcolm Bowers' article is his straightforward presentation. Bowers examines the aftereffects of psychosis, suggesting that therapists might work differently, without changing their models, if they were more aware of the healthful potential within such personal implosions.

I. INTRODUCTION

At least two ideas seem to be crystallizing from much of the current clinical research dealing with psychotic states.[1] First is the notion that current terminology is in great need of revision. Much of our Kraepelinian and Bleulerian heritage has been tested and found wanting.[2] Experience suggests that current diagnostic labels in psychosis have neither test-retest reliability nor predictive value. Rare studies of the natural history of psychosis demonstrate that intra-individual diagnostic variation over a period of years can span the list of most conventional subtypes.[3] Currently we are only beginning to attempt to account for the *course* of psychotic illness rather than to utilize static categories.

The other emerging (more properly, re-emerging) observation is that some psychotic patients recover and go on to progress psychologically and

From *The Human Context*, Volume 3, Number 1, 1971, pp. 134–145. Reprinted by permission.

[1]Through this paper we will not distinguish between the major "functional psychoses." It is our opinion that although prototypes can be found, more commonly no firm line can presently be drawn between those conditions commonly designated as manic depressive, schizoaffective, and schizophrenic states.

[2]R. W. Payne and R. B. Sloane, "Can Schizophrenia be Defined?" *Dis. of the Nervous System,* Vol. 29, 1968, Supplement.

[3]G. E. Vaillant, "Natural History of the Remitting Schizophrenias," *Amer. J. Psychiatry,* Vol. 120, 1963.

socially; that is, continue to grow. Recent workers have attempted to explain this fact by emphasizing various pre-morbid social factors which appear related to level of cognitive and perceptual functioning and to prognosis.[4] Such studies imply that the psychosis, an ill-fated event falling across the path of human growth and development, is essentially unrelated to the essence of maturation, and that(prognosis is determined by the state of social development achieved prior to the psychotic episode.)

That some psychotics continue to grow as human beings is not a new observation and it is startling to recall that some workers emphasized this fact prior to the advent of the major somatic therapies. Sullivan, for instance, focusing on the significance of the patient's experience of psychosis, accounts for outcome in the following manner.

> If the conservative reorganization of complexes and sentiments, which appears to underlie a goodly share of the early schizophrenic phenomenology, leads the patient to a foreconscious belief that he can circumvent or rise above environmental handicaps, and if this belief is the presenting feature of a comprehensive mental integration, his recovery proceeds. If no such reconstruction is accomplished, the patient does not recover.[5]

Similarly, Mayer-Gross attempted to account for the "course of the acute psychoses" by categorizing the possible outcomes.[6] He too felt that the way in which the psychotic episode was assimilated by the individual determined prognosis. The least favorable outcome he characterized by total denial of the entire event, the most favorable by a kind of "integration" of the experience into the ongoing life of the individual in such a way that the "challenge of continuity" was preserved. For Mayer-Gross "continuity" could be achieved with or without growth or "melting" of the experience with the core or existence values of the patient. Continuity without growth would include such outcomes as total denial of the psychosis, hopeless despair, or substitution of chronic physical complaints in the aftermath of the psychotic experience. With growth one might achieve a genuine continuity, without exclusion of the experience. Whether or not we can accurately paraphrase Mayer-Gross in the language of ego psychology, the comparison seems clear enough. We might say that the acute psychosis, among other altered states, sets up a "search for synthesis" and that synthesis may be achieved in ways that may or may not promote ego develop-

---

[4]R. E. Kantor and W. G. Herron, *Process and Reactive Schizophrenia.* Science and Behavior Books, Inc., Palo Alto, 1966.

[5]H. S. Sullivan, *Schizophrenia as a Human Process.* W. W. Norton and Co., Inc., New York, 1962.

[6]W. Mayer-Gross, "Über die Stellungnahme zur Abgelaufenen Akuten Psychose." *Zeitschrift für die gesamte Neurologie und Psychiatrie, Vol. 60,* 1920.

ment.[7] Recently, retrospective evidence has been obtained which shows that those individuals who are able to integrate their psychotic experience (in the sense that Mayer-Gross used the term) do in fact have better post-hospital adjustments.[8] The suggestion here is not only that social competence at the time of the illness can affect outcome but that, in addition, the psychotic episode itself can be seen as a growth struggle whose ultimate intrapsychic representation has much to do with subsequent adjustment. We will trace some of the evidence in support of this argument and point to some criteria from which to view growth possibilities latent in the acute psychosis.

II. ACCOUNTS FROM PATIENTS

Many patients regard their psychotic experience in retrospect as one which involved a struggle for growth and maturation. We found that a significant number of our patients, when interviewed in a follow-up study, characterized their psychotic experience in this fashion.[8] Individuals who have written about their psychotic experience have made similar claims. Commenting upon his psychotic episode Krim states:

> I needed an excuse to force some sort of balance between my bulging inner life and my timid outer behavior. . . . We can be grateful that the human soul is so constructed that it ultimately bursts concepts once held as true out of this terrible need to live and creates the world anew just in order to breathe in it.[9]

A very sensitive anonymous author lists some of the personality changes that occurred in the course of several psychotic episodes as including loss of a chronic premorbid anxiety, a shift from a masochistic to a non-masochistic emotional orientation, loss of excessive dependency on others, a greater capacity for warmth and interest in people, a deeper sense of human equality, improvement in sexual function, freer use of intellectual capacities and a capacity for religious experience.[9] Norma McDonald (pseudonym), a recovered schizophrenic, wrote:

> living with schizophrenia can be living in hell . . . but seen from another angle it can be really living, for it seems to thrive on art and education, it seems to lead to a deeper understanding of people and living for people. . . . [9]

---

[7]M. B. Bowers, Jr. and D. X. Freedman, " 'Psychedelic' Experiences in Acute Psychoses." *Arch. Gen. Psych.*, Vol. 15, 1966.
[8]D. Soskis and M. B. Bowers, Jr., "The Schizophrenic Experience: A Follow-up Study of Attitude and Post-hospital Adjustment." *J. Nerv. and Ment. Dis.* 1969, **149**, 443–449.
[9]B. Kaplan (ed.), *The Inner World of Mental Illness.* Harper and Row, New York, 1964.

Anton Boisen, perhaps more than anyone, paid attention to the possibility of growth potential inherent in various forms of psychosis. His ideas are all the more relevant because of his personal involvement in the question. He states:

> This survey of the wilderness of the lost tends to support the hypothesis with which we started, that many of the more serious psychoses are essentially problem-solving experiences which are closely related to certain types of religious experience. . . . we have also discovered that such ideas are not to be found in all cases but only in those who are trying to face their difficulties . . . We may therefore draw the conclusion that such disturbances are not necessarily evils but, like fever or inflammation in the physical organism, they are attempts by regression to lower levels of mental life to assimilate certain hitherto unassimilated masses of life experience. They represent the deliquescence of the old sets and attitudes which make possible new formations. They are essentially purposive; in this group we even found individuals whose lives had been changed for the better.[10]

We have previously cited other instances in which patients somewhat covertly expressed their growth strivings in material written just prior to an acute psychotic episode. Thus a 23-year-old nurse, just prior to her psychotic outbreak, submitted a research proposal containing a rationale for the development of a manual for breast-feeding mothers. In the proposal, her own personal struggle with issues of feminine self-confidence are only thinly veiled.

> This researcher feels that the mother needs support in her decision to breast feed and a basic understanding of how to do it. If a mother is motivated to breast feed, it is her right as an individual to do it, and it is the responsibility of those who know how to help her, to give her the help . . . perhaps the reason they can't really help her is because they make her feel she shouldn't have the right to do what she wants because they feel they can't . . . the confidence is based on the fact that the mother is a woman who has the facilities to breast feed and then assumes she can. However, the mother will quickly lose this confidence when she finds that there can be obstacles to breast feeding if she doesn't know what to do with them. When a mother decides how to feed her baby, she needs confidence that she can do it, and her ability to do it demonstrates that she knows how and so has reason for her confidence.[11]

Similarly, material written by a 21-year-old student just prior to hospitalization for psychosis contained analogous evidence of the essential internal

---

[10]A. T. Boisen, *The Exploration of the Inner World.* Harper and Brothers, New York, 1962.
[11]M. B. Bowers, Jr., "Pathogenesis of Acute Schizophrenic Psychosis." *Arch. Gen. Psych.,* Vol. 19, 1968.

struggle he was having with a rather rigid moral code coming into conflict with recent sexual experiences.

> I spent the summer thinking about my nationalism paper. If my concept of nationalism is correct, it has implications for 19th century romanticism, much of which needs revising. According to some sources this is all that happened in the 19th century. But somehow the old concept didn't take care of all the facts. The old boundaries couldn't handle all the material. In addition to nationalism and romanticism, there was also liberalism and individualism. I was trying to feel my way through a whole body of material which had been largely unexplored.[11]

Not only are patients sometimes seemingly aware at various levels of the growth issues involved in acute psychosis, they also experience many of the cognitive and affective shifts which may accompany certain forms of major personality reorientation. Thus creative experience, religious conversion, and other "peak experiences" may involve much of the affective lability and "psychedelic" form of inner experience which can accompany the acute psychotic reaction.[7] Psychotic experiences, by creating upheaval at the very core of the individual, may offer, in some instances, opportunities for psychological growth potentially greater than those in neurotic states and character disorders where certain defensive patterns may be relatively fixed. It appears that

> Psychedelic and psychotomimetic phenomena are closely related. Our hypothesis is that these states demonstrate to varying degrees the subjective phenomena of intrapsychic alteration, that they are fluid states whose outcome is determined by both intrapsychic and environmental factors. There are clearly quantitative, interindividual differences in the ways such experiences can be tolerated, interpreted, terminated, and assimilated into the ongoing context of experiences.[7]

Further, if the "psychedelic" insight frequently seen at the onset of certain psychoses is illusory, such illusion cannot be disqualified from forming in whole or in part the basis of "healthy" illusion for the future. That is, such experience can be seen as prophetic, hopeful, a glimpse of potentiality. For instance, although the following quote from a 23-year-old man is "psychotic" in one sense, it also expresses a certain capacity for the anticipation of a healthier level of functioning.

> Before my marriage I was bothered by premature ejaculation. I tried to control this by developing my lower abdominal muscles. I became aware that my sexual ability was related to a burning sensation in my lower back. When this sensation was in front, in my loins, I felt like a totally different person, a real man. I worked for a man named Butch who was a very strong person. When Butch made certain movements with his feet

I could feel the burning sensation move into my loins. I really thought that should happen with my father, but it never did. When these things are in the right place I feel whole and vibrant inside, there is something there to push me. It is a pleasure to look at someone else's eyes, feel healthy yourself, and see a healthy gaze in their eyes. I know this burning feeling inside me did happen and was affected by people.[11]

Thus with regard to acute psychosis there may be "a relationship between pathological disillusion, and illusion and disillusion as normal processes playing an essential part in the establishment of external object relations and the development of a creative relation to the world."[12]

Finally, whereas patients may see the psychosis as involving the potential achievement of growth and including some of the cognitive and affective experiences of major personality alteration, they also seem to regard the psychosis itself as essentially a growth impasse, or deadlocked struggle. Time and again this idea is expressed in patient accounts. Ronald Laing has discussed the nature of the intrapsychic struggle in certain schizoid patients in his book *The Divided Self*.[13] One individual expressed the idea of growth impasse, stating "I cannot escape it—I cannot face it—how can I endure it?"[9] Another, somewhat poetically, seemed to be expressing a similar kind of inner dilemma.

> When Madness comes—a strange anesthesia follows. A sleep akin to death, but more mysterious. A rest from the dim regions of unconsciousness—a state which is neither death nor living; lethal, mysterious—evil perhaps to some, but only to those who do not know the blind, intolerable horror that comes from seeing something which cannot be borne—nor escaped.[9]

The emphasis here should be on the fact that attempting to face and endure is as much a part of the inner struggle as the desire to escape. Frequently neither growth nor regression is the entire matter, and it may make a difference whether therapists focus on growth strivings or avoidance tendencies. Better still, how can we learn properly to assess and foster the former while taking appropriate account of the latter?

Similarly, if acute psychosis can be seen as a growth struggle, chronic psychosis may be viewed as an unsuccessful struggle toward continuing development. This view has been supported by information obtained in amytal interviews with chronically hospitalized patients. These individuals, often mute, under amytal seemed preoccupied with events at the time of their initial psychotic episode often many years before.[14]

[12]C. Rycroft, *Imagination and Reality*. International Univ. Press, Inc., New York, 1965.

[13]R. D. Laing, *The Divided Self*. Penguin Books, Inc., Baltimore, 1965.

[14]F. Ehrentheil, "Thought Content of Mute Chronic Schizophrenic Patients: Interviews after injection of amobarbital sodium (sodium amytal) and methamphetamine hydrochloride (methedrine)." *J. Nerv Ment. Dis, Vol. 137*, pp. 187–97, 1963.

Therefore, I am suggesting that the essence of the acute psychosis is impasse and stalemate in human growth and this notion implies a collision of both progressive and retrogressive forces. In fact, the literature on prognostic factors shows that the intensity surrounding the acute episode is a favorable prognostic sign, suggesting that the impetus for growth is greater in such instances. All clinicians know the ominous portent of a psychosis where the onset is insidious. It is as if the relative force of the collision during growth presages the strength of the determination to push on later.

III. ACCOUNTS FROM THERAPISTS

Thus far we have argued that, from the subjective, experiential point of view, many psychoses have the form and content of growth struggles which have reached an impasse. However, not only patients but also some therapists have noted progressive aspects of certain acute psychotic episodes. I have previously reported a diary account by a patient which contained vivid examples of the progressive forces in a psychosis.[15] Jackson and Watzlawick have reported a case in which the psychosis was seen and interpreted as a crisis in growth by the therapists involved.[16] Carlson has described an "acute confusional state," sometimes seen in adolescents, as a stage in ego development which is potentially maturational.[17] Particularly noteworthy are two cases reported by French and Kasanin. These cases were followed with minimal treatment for a number of years and their outcome was characterized not only by loss of psychotic symptoms but by clear personality growth. Of interest is the observation that neither case would have been predicted to do well based on pre-morbid variables alone. In both cases the authors refer to a "constructive impulse to solve the problem of reconciling conflicting needs." Indeed with these two cases in mind, the authors come to the rather remarkable conclusion that:

> In attempting to estimate the probable outcome of a psychosis, it is helpful to try to reconstruct the problem in adaptation which the psychosis is attempting to solve and then to estimate the possibilities for a successful solution in view of the actual life situation of the patient. Such an estimate is probably more important than the form of the psychosis as an index of prognosis.[18]

[15]M. B. Bowers, Jr., "The Onset of Psychosis, a Diary Account." *Psychiatry*, Vol. 28, 1965.
[16]D. Jackson and P. Watzlawick, "The Acute Psychosis as Manifestation of a Growth Experience." *Psychiatric Research Report*, No. 16, 1963.
[17]H. Carlson, "The Relationship of the Acute Confusional State to Ego Development." *Int. J. Psychoanal.*, Vol. 42, 1961.
[18]T. French and J. Kasanin, "A Psychodynamic Study of the Recovery of Two Schizophrenic Cases." *Psychoanal. Quarterly*, Vol. 10, 1941.

IV. MINIMUM REQUIREMENTS FOR GROWTH

In a sense, the vicissitudes of human growth are highlighted as a result of the phenomenon of psychosis. As is so often the case in medicine, a malfunctioning system lays bare the intricacy of inner structure and gives rise to renewed respect for and understanding of the function of component parts. Psychotic reactions, seen as struggles for growth, point to some of the true rate-limiting processes in growth. Some capacities seem to be crucial simply for growth to continue.

One of these seems to be the presence during development of some constructive relationship between felt need and object gratification. This basic groundwork for future transactions between the human organism and his object environment must be seen as essential for growth. Prior to all other qualifying statements about object relations lies the pre-requisite that the growing human organism seek and achieve relationships with the external world. Rycroft puts this principle as follows:

> It is Winnicott's contention, I believe, that early infancy is such a critical phase and that the importance of the early mother-infant relationship lies not only in the amount of satisfaction received by the infant but also in the degree of correspondence between the infant's latent impulses, wishes, or needs and the mother's provision of the kind of stimuli necessary for their release. Insofar as the mother arouses the infant's expectations and maintains them by a modicum of satisfaction, its perception and conception of reality will accord with the pattern of its inherent instinctive tendencies, and impulses will not merely tend to be directed toward an external reality which is subjectively felt to be good but will actually be developmentally bound to the imagos of the reality that has released them.[12]

By contrast, in chronic psychotic states, it could be said of a patient

> That he cathected the process of thinking itself and derived pleasure from passively watching his intellectual processes idling in neutral . . . the thoughts which in psychical truth have become bereft of significance come to be regarded as precisely the only objects to have any significance.[12]

The classic papers of Jonathan Lang[19] (pseudonym, himself a paranoid schizophrenic) substantiate the impression that in psychosis affectivity becomes centred around *ideation* instead of external objects, thus short-circuiting the relationship between felt need and object gratification which is crucial for psychological growth. White seems to be dealing with this same principle when he discusses the importance of a "feeling of efficacy" in

---

[19]J. Lang, "The Other Side of the Affective Aspects of Schizophrenia." *Psychiatry, Vol. 2,* 1939.

development. He notes that "we learn about reality by exploring it and by experiencing the consequences" and adds

> I believe that this feeling of efficacy is one of our most fundamental and biologically important affects, the basis of our persisting attempts to achieve whatever mastery we can over the environment, the thing that lies behind our unceasing attempts to enlarge the sphere of our competence. It is the root of the sense of competence that is so central in self esteem.[20]

White feels that the lack of a sense of efficacy is a central factor in the schizophrenic life style.

> Poor direction of attention and action, poor mastery of cognitive experience, weak assertiveness in interpersonal relations, low feelings of efficacy and competence, a restricted sense of agency in leading one's life—all these crop out in almost every aspect of the schizophrenic disorder.[20]

Thus I would suggest that, speaking tentatively, the abruption in growth which a psychotic episode represents may ultimately promote continuing personality development if the individual does not abandon the struggle of engaging objects for the satisfaction of inner needs. When the psychosis leaves a serious paranoid experiential style—such that the object world is seen as pervasively non-gratifying and menacing—or when massive withdrawal from striving takes over (certain "hebephrenic" reactions), we might expect prognosis to be relatively poor.

V. CASE HISTORIES

Although a detailed differential analysis of the specific aspects of the experiential phenomenology in psychotic reactions related to growth potential is beyond the scope of this paper, we will examine four case histories in an effort to highlight certain qualitative variations in this factor.

Case 1. A 21-year-old, unmarried woman was admitted to the hospital for treatment of an acute psychotic reaction. Although graduated from high school and having worked as a clerk in a department store, she had had very little heterosexual experience and her acute symptoms, of only 2 to 3 weeks' duration, seemed related to rather strong sexual advances recently made by a married male acquaintance. She brought with her to the hospital a rather detailed written account of her experience covering approximately the week prior to admission. This account was characterized by yearning for love vaguely associated with various sequences of numbers which she felt had magical significance. She described various events as "clues" to understanding what was happening to her.

[20]R. White, "The Experience of Efficacy in Schizophrenia." *Psychiatry, Vol. 28,* 1965.

A comic talked about sex, everyone was in hysterics but me; a strange feeling of euphoria came and enveloped me. He said that to sum it up girls do not know what love is, that they receive it in the wrong way and that there is no one in the audience who is pure . . . I went for a Pap test to Dr. . . . who said he couldn't believe I was a virgin, they are so hard to find these days. . . . Tonight there are shooting stars in space, something's coming, maybe tonight. If and when I find the face of faces, even when that face smiles, then and only then will I know love.

Men she had known since childhood were listed, phone numbers and birth dates were added and subtracted in such a way that a certain significance was supposedly derived. The entire record had the characteristics almost entirely of wishful fantasy and magical thinking regarding her sexual concerns. Her clinical course in the hospital was characterized by rather uneventful recovery from her psychotic symptoms but little in the way of social gain. Eight months after discharge she still works, has essentially no social life, and lives at home under almost complete direction by her parents. There has been, in essence, no psychological progression.

Case 2. A 28-year-old married woman was admitted to the hospital approximately two months after the birth of her second child. The patient was a rather markedly insecure woman with extremely low self-esteem. She had married a man in whom she saw all the positive qualities which she did not possess. Marriage—rather than fostering an improvement in her own self-concept—had resulted simply in further confirmation of her own basic worthlessness. During the acute psychotic episode she was pre-occupied with a desire to die and thus to relieve her husband and children of her negative influence. Delusional material centered primarily around various schemes which she felt were being devised to "put her away," including the possibility that she would be thoughtlessly exploited sexually. Ecstatic mastery of the experience was minimal, her emotional experience was primarily one of worthlessness and depression. Subsequent therapy over a 2 year period has resulted in a return of her ability to function as a mother and wife somewhat satisfactorily. Improvement in her negative self-image has been slow but definite. I cite this case as an intermediate example with regard to growth potentiality. Conscious desire to "make sense" out of the experience was minimal and there was a tendency toward delusional mastery of the core conflict. Nevertheless, her depressive affect may be seen as at least signifying a more mature level of intrapsychic conflict than was present in the first example cited above.

Case 3. A 33-year-old woman was admitted to the hospital with symptoms of an acute psychosis of approximately 6 weeks' duration. Her difficulty ostensibly arose from her marriage in which she had maintained a very subservient status for 8 years. She wrote an account of the week preceding her hospitalization which contained in part the following notations.

> Thoughts spun around in my head and everything, objects, sounds, events took on special meanings for me. Childhood feelings began to come back, as symbols and bits from past conversations went through my head. I felt like I was putting the pieces of a puzzle together. I thought understanding myself better would help me with conflicts that *I felt compelled to* resolve (my italics). I wanted to grow up and feel the way a 33-year-old woman was supposed to . . . I thought that my parents had supplied information about the nursery school teacher . . . with the hope that I would be able to straighten myself out by remembering the earlier years . . . I felt as if I were love and hate with nothing in the middle, that everything was opposites, but that I was fighting myself so that the little girl of four and a half would grow up quickly so that I could be a woman and a good mother to my children.

This account was filled with expressions of felt conflict and a drive toward conflict resolution. There were ecstatic periods but these were interspersed with periods of terror and fear. This individual was discharged after two months of hospitalization and was doing well at a three year follow-up examination. She had weathered a difficult period of marital therapy which had led to divorce, although she had maintained custody of her children and was working successfully.

Case 4. A 20-year-old college student who was hospitalized very briefly for a stormy, self-limited psychotic episode wrote a personal interpretation of his struggle prior to hospitalization. He was an intelligent young man who had always taken pride in his academic and rational abilities. These faculties had been developed much more extensively than his social skills and affective life, and he regarded himself as unattractive and particularly unappealing to women. The increasingly competitive pressures of academic and social life in college led to a personal crisis which he described, in part, as follows.

> I cannot bear what I have uncovered. It is not an emotional collapse. It is due, not to depression, but to knowledge—pure, abstract knowledge in whose terrible light the will to live must wither and die. I can seek surcease only in forgetfulness. What is a life in which all values, all pleasures are dissected and laid bare by the light of reason. It is horror! This cannot be treated in the normal psychiatric manner. This horror has resided in my brain for days, months, years, but the merciful clutter of my mind prevented me from realizing this horror. My life, in all its facets, has been an insatiable quest for knowledge. I recognized the highest form of knowledge, self-knowledge, toward which I strove. Finally I have discovered myself and its purpose. My self is an automaton, my purpose is nonexistent. How I wish that I was anywhere than where I am now, for I would have found my identity which I have now lost.

Whatever one might say about this account, it is clearly filled with struggle and anguish. Personal deficiencies are recognized as crucially involved. Follow-up in this instance has been brief, although the psychotic panic was shortlived and the patient was able to leave the hospital rapidly to continue his personal struggle in individual outpatient therapy. If the notion of growth potentiality as described here has any validity, this young man would have to be considered a good prospect for using his psychotic episode for maturational gains.

These cases do little more than point the way to some of the possible differentiating features related to growth potential as manifest in the early experiential aspects of some psychoses. Nevertheless, they do demonstrate that early psychotic experience can be examined and evaluated along a dimension of felt experience of conflict and desire for psychological growth. A systematic predictive study relating such evaluations to pre-morbid factors, treatment, and outcome would seem a logical step for further research.

To evaluate psychotic experiences with regard to evidence of growth potential is not necessarily to be overly optimistic about the phenomenon of psychosis. It may allow us to be more precisely optimistic where the clinical data warrant, however, and urge us to re-examine our therapeutic strategies so that we foster growth whenever possible.

VI. IMPLICATION FOR TREATMENT

I have suggested that some psychoses, when examined from the standpoint of the existential situation and experience of the patient, can be seen as impasses in human growth. What are the implications of this view for a treatment aimed at supporting the continuation of growth? To begin with, it seems appropriate that therapists devote at least as much time trying to understand what the patient is trying to accomplish as they routinely do to describing his handicaps. There is clearly inherent in most of us a certain resistance to looking at the adaptive capabilities of patients. This is an interesting phenomenon in itself, but for the present discussion it is sufficient to point to it and to urge that clinical assessment of psychotic patients include an evaluation of growth potential. In some instances the patient's strivings will be relatively clear, in others they will be fragmented and inapparent. Both Sullivan and Boisen call attention to the fact that "catatonic" patients and others with intense religious ideation are often most clearly struggling (frequently at a conscious level) with growth issues. I have noted in the present report how such conflicts may be manifest in material patients have written. At other times, skilled clinical assessment of the status of the patient's relationships with important loved ones (parents, heterosexual objects, siblings) may lay bare the essential conflict. Further, the patient should be made aware of the fact that his therapists view him not simply as having had an illness or "breakdown" but as being essentially involved in important purposive activity that has gone awry. A therapist should share his tentative hypotheses about the specific nature of such activity with the patient. It is possible to say, for instance, "I think, from what you have told me, that you are trying to gain some independence from your mother but are feeling very guilty about doing so." Such a statement gives the patient some idea of the structure of the task at hand and frequently helps him begin to organize his view of the psychotic episode. It should be acknowledged as tentative and provisional. The patient should know that he and his therapist have the joining task of continuing revision and sharpening of such an hypothesis. I want to emphasize that it is *from the patient's point of view* that hypotheses must be validated and reformulated. Having made this point it is well to remember Sullivan's caveat:

> The degree of "insight" which the patient brings from his psychosis is quite generally accepted as having an important relation to the stability of recovery. Insight, however, is never perfect, and there are a large proportion of recovered or arrested schizophrenics who have achieved a reasonably unified personality fairly adapted to the social integration, without any ability for the conscious formulation and expression which we generally seek as evidence of insight.[5]

Finally, there are patients, primarily those called "hebephrenic," "process schizophrenics," or "poor pre-morbids" who may appear least understandable in terms of the growth model presented here. Far from being caught in a bind of progressive and retrogressive strivings, these individuals appear peculiarly ill-equipped and poorly motivated to master the minimal social concomitants of biological maturation. Under such circumstances, in promoting growth one may have to fall back upon elemental processes referred to above. A therapeutic program which fosters, even demands, interaction with real people and activities can prevent severe regression and foster new social learning.

VII. CONCLUSIONS

Prognosis in acute psychotic reactions is likely to be a result of multiple influences. Pre-morbid social factors and certain characteristics of the acute episode have been shown to be important. Most studies have implied that prognosis may be relatively pre-determined and not particularly affected by contingencies (including treatment) related to individual assimilation of the psychotic experience. Nevertheless, as we have attempted to show, a case can be made for viewing some psychotic episodes as essentially maturational struggles and for viewing prognosis as, in part, related to relative success or failure in dealing with such a struggle. Proper therapeutic assistance should take into account the maturational strivings inherent in many psychotic episodes.

SECTION III

Research

Inner experience, personal as it may be, can be studied by proper application of fundamental scientific methodology. The development of "state-specific" science (Tart, 1971), or techniques to investigate different states of consciousness, is opening the way for objective assessments of personal accounts.

While there have been decades of purely psychological research concerning madness, the present thrust is toward more basic examinations, especially at the neurological and behavioral levels. The psychoanalytic notions of cathexes and libido, of traumas and complexes, while useful in treatment, have not proved useful to this kind of fundamental research. Thus, clinical descriptions are giving way to laboratory analogues, simulations of mental states, and biological investigations of physical and chemical interactions.

Analysis of accumulated subjective reports indicates that persons undergoing "psychotic" experience look upon the world with a radically different viewpoint from normal people. Different styles of perception seem to correlate with the content and the outcome of such experience.

Researchers recognize that an unused key to understanding madness lies in comprehending the perceptual differences in abnormal experience. The primitive state of laboratory technology in this field has been a major obstacle to the attainment of extensive knowledge of the physiological and psychological processes involved in an alteration of consciousness. One researcher, for example, suggests that using the EEG to describe altered states is like trying to diagnose a problem in an automobile engine over the telephone, with the receiver held on the closed hood of the car. Yet the evidence is beginning to emerge. Julian Silverman's work on evoked brain responses and other measures of attention has shown physiological correlates of altered perception. John Lilly and Bernard Aaronson have produced "psychotic" alterations in consciousness in normal research subjects in laboratory settings.

149

The research reported here displays a variety of procedures and conclusions, including strict laboratory results and work in clinical settings. Silverman is concerned with the modulation of afferent stimuli in abnormal psychological states. Aaronson's work involves the effects of consciously altering the basic parameters of space and time. McNeil, Rosenbaum, and Luce all report evidence from different avenues of laboratory investigation. All these studies, looking for major factors that lead to mental malfunctioning, give intriguing, but as yet inconclusive, results. Reading them all forces one to realize that no matter what we know or do not know about madness, we can be sure that its genesis is complex; it can be affected by a host of mutually exclusive factors. Also, the movement from madness to normal reality can be facilitated in a variety of ways from change of diet to orthodox psychoanalysis.

The biochemical considerations that McNeil discusses offer possibilities in gross control of madness. Gay Luce's report on rhythmic variations in body chemistry offers insights into the natural ecology of the human personality. Silverman's work with perception in altered states of consciousness has been partially responsible for the redesign of certain treatment centers.

The value of the research presented here is twofold: (1) Each of the strands has immediate practical applications that might alleviate the situation presently faced by most mental patients while representing thrusts of scientific curiosity into the central darkness of the inner world. (2) We are beginning to understand madness; the cloud of ignorance and fear is beginning to lift, giving us new insights into consciousness.

REFERENCE

Tart, C. Scientific foundations for the study of altered states of consciousness. *Journal of Transpersonal Psychology*, 1971, **3**, 93–124.

Perceptual and Neurophysiological Analogues of "Experience" in Schizophrenia and LSD Reactions

Julian Silverman

Silverman presents evidence from laboratory experiments that physiological mechanisms may account for the changes in perception reported by individuals during altered states of consciousness. He points out that differences in perceptual style (the way the organism handles incoming sensory information) among psychotics are reflected in the form and content of the experience. These perceptual styles are also found in normal individuals; however, the abnormal person seems to develop a hypersensitivity to stimulation that appears to be a prerequisite to altered states of awareness.

In earlier papers (1967, 1968) Silverman suggests that the eventual outcome of abnormal experience is determined not by the severity of the symptoms, but by the degree of cultural acceptance. A nonsupportive atmosphere in early stages of the break-up of normal thought and perceptual patterns predisposes the person to lose control and to require extensive treatment and custodial care. The lack of value assigned by the culture to the initial experience leads to the need for treatment. A "bizarre" individual is considered sick, and resources are expended on effecting a recovery from the illness. Neither the patient nor his family usually questions the wisdom of the treatment. The patient may hate or fear the hospital, but rarely does he challenge the diagnosis itself. Individuals within a culture share a common belief system about abnormal experience, allowing the system to work. This basic agreement is often confused with understanding, while the fundamental premises of the system go unquestioned.

Silverman offers insight into the difficulty of communicating with a "disturbed" individual. Not until we realize that the psychotic person truly sees the world differently can we begin to understand him and recognize that his world makes as much "sense" as our own.

This long and complex article is divided into three subsections. Proceed carefully, reviewing the main points covered at the end of each section. The first part suggests that many kinds of laboratory studies are self-limiting; the data observed are not central to the phenomenon. Silverman emphasizes that this review of research focuses primarily on the "experience, control, and inhibition of sensory stimulation."

The second portion is a concise review of fundamental differences between the perceptual world of the schizophrenic and that of the normal person. Silverman's examples are drawn from extensive clinical interviews of persons in the early stages of a schizophrenic or psychotic episode.

The final section of the article describes investigations that have revealed physiological correlates of perceptual experience for schizophrenics and normal people. Modulation of sensory information is examined using measures of size judgment and average evoked responses to stimuli under laboratory conditions. This kind of experimental investigation allows the isolation of key variables that may play an important part in the mediation of abnormal experience.

Isolation of critical physiological processes opens the possibility of modulating abnormal experience by training individuals to control specific sensory phenomena using biofeedback equipment, yoga, autogenic training, and so on. These are alternative forms of treatment in addition to the currently accepted methods of medication and psychotherapy.

The basic premise of this paper is that experiential reports of schizophrenic and LSD-drugged individuals are extremely significant data. The failure to consider these reports seriously has served to limit our understanding of mental disorder. In the following pages, an evaluation of this area of inquiry is presented. The information derived from the approach is systematically related to important perceptual and neurophysiological researches.

"SCIENTIFIC" BIASES REGARDING EXPERIENCE IN SCHIZOPHRENIC AND LSD-DRUGGED SUBJECTS

Most research psychologists and psychiatrists do not realize the scientific value of studies of the subjective world of schizophrenic and LSD-drugged individuals. Among the factors which can be cited as reasons for this are the following:

> 1. Most laboratory studies of behavior are evaluated in terms of *reffectiveness of performance* criteria (adequacy, accuracy, efficiency). Typically the performances of schizophrenic and LSD-drugged subjects on psychological laboratory procedures are less adequate, accurate, and efficient than "normal" subjects. Individuals who evidence such generally ineffective behavior usually are presumed to be unreliable informants regarding their experiences during laboratory testing (e.g. Silverman, 1967, pg. 234).

From *Schizophrenia: Current Concepts and Research*, 1969. Edited by D. V. Siva Sankar. Reprinted by permission of PJD Publications, Ltd.

2. Clinical studies of schizophrenic and LSD-drugged subjects are evaluated traditionally in terms of *appropriateness of behavior* and of *degree
of reality testing* criteria. Often, these subjects do not behave according
to standards of personal and social appropriateness and evidence a
reduced degree of reality testing. If they make comments, which are
indicative of keen awareness, the comments are regarded by the
average clinician as *extra*-ordinary and accidental. All too often, individuals evidencing indications of mental and emotional disorder are
presumed to be unreliable informants regarding their experiences
during clinical interviews. A monumental example of how such an
attitude has affected our conceptualizations in this field NEGATIVE-
LY is found in Eugen Bleuler's (1950) famous (and in almost all respects excellent) monograph on the schizophrenias:

> "Sensory response to external stimulus is quite normal. *To be sure
> the patient will complain that everything appears to be different and frequent-
> ly we can observe the absence of the "feeling of familiarity" with known
> things.* However, this strangeness is usually attributable to a deficit
> in customary associations and particularly to an alteration in emo-
> tional emphasis, *not to* disturbances of sensation (pg. 56) [My
> Italics]."

Bleuler's subsequent remarks regarding this issue also were to the
effect that what the patient says is one thing and what really is happening within him is quite another. How wrong he was!

3. Most ordinary "normal" people (including scientists) experience contact with schizophrenic and LSD-drugged subjects as mildly-to-
moderately stressful. Manfried Bleuler (1963) has written on this issue
as follows: "Something in us reacts to this experience [of encountering
an insane person] as a serious threat to our own existence." Sullivan
(1927) wrote of the *aversion* of the "normal" for the "insane." In order
to protect himself from this stressful experience, the average clinician
acquires distance-taking techniques. (M. Bleuler, 1963; H. Wiener,
1967, III). These techniques necessarily interfere with personal communications between patient and clinician. Thus, rather than effecting
open and direct contact with a schizophrenic or LSD-drugged person,
the person is "treated." One consequence of this at-arms-length approach is that essential signs of disorganization are not uncovered
in soon-to-become psychotics (McGhie and Chapman, 1961; Wiener,
1967, II) and erroneous and often ineffable signs are relied upon
(Temerlin, in press; Wiener, 1967, III).

OVERVIEW

Attempts to obtain detailed information about experiences of schizophrenic and LSD-drugged subjects have yielded a number of interesting
and reliable findings (e.g. Bowers, 1968; Bowers and Freedman, 1966; Chapman, 1966; Hoffer and Osmond, 1966; McGhie and Chapman, 1961). Examined in relation to perceptual and neurophysiological researches in this

area, these findings indicate that sensory behavior and sensory experience are fundamental considerations in any explanation of altered psychological states (Silverman, 1968).

Incipient schizophrenic and LSD-drugged subjects experience stimulation of ordinary-range intensities more strongly than others. They also report unusual sensitivities to low intensity stimuli (e.g. Bowers and Freedman, 1966; McGhie and Chapman, 1961). Sights and sounds are experienced as brilliant, intense, more alive, vivid, rich, full of energy, compelling. Inputs to the other senses also are experienced as being more acute. Apparently because of this hypersensitivity, the sensory attributes of meaningful stimuli (e.g. intensity, magnitude, color) often are responded to more strongly than perceptual and ideational attributes of stimuli (e.g. configuration, quality, quantity). In effect, attention is "captured" by the compelling sensory attributes of stimulus configurations. Distractability is markedly increased. Even normally stable and automatic aspects of perception, such as body-boundaries are affected by this new way of experiencing sensory input. Pronounced increases in responsiveness to sensory events, inside and outside of the body, also are associated with decreases in attention to other aspects of the environment, *including the fundamental self-environment differentiation.* The dedifferentiation of body boundaries makes it difficult to distinguish between external sensory events and sensations which have their origins within the body. Thought-images and feelings may be experienced as external sensations (realities). For example, it literally becomes possible to *perceive* a person as a figure of ice if he or she is experienced as *cold* and not understanding (e.g. Sechehaye, 1951, pgs. 27–30). (This translation of emotion or feeling into sensory experience, is a highly common report.) The extraordinary vividness and strangeness-of-feeling-and-thoughts may have the quality of revelation and often is experienced as coming from outside. It is as if "boundaries" which enable one to differentiate inner and outer sensations no longer function properly. For example, an individual under the influence of LSD was asked his associations to an idea (Savage, 1955). "Instead of producing verbal associations, he had an hallucination of two men carrying in a heavy box, the plastic representation of the idea he was seeking. So real was the hallucination that he said aloud: "O.K., boys, you can set it down right here" (pg. 13).

Norma McDonald (1960) a one-time schizophrenic patient, explained such experiences in the following way:

> the mind must have a filter which functions without our conscious thought, sorting stimuli and allowing only those which are relevant to the situation in hand to disturb consciousness . . . What had happened to me . . . was a breakdown in the filter and a hodge-podge of unrelated stimuli were distracting me from the things which should have had my undivided attention (pg. 218). By the time I was admitted to the hospital

I had reached a stage of "wakefulness" when the brilliance of light on a window sill or the color of blue in the sky would be so important it could make me cry. I had very little ability to sort the relevant from the irrelevant. The filter had broken down. Completely unrelated events become intricately connected in my mind (pg. 219).

It is most interesting to compare McDonald's interpretation of her breakdown, derived primarily from her experiences, with neurophysiology theorist Donald Hebb's (1960) explanation of a comparably awesome experience:

The normally complete dichotomy of self from other depends entirely on the efficacy of the distinguishing sensory cues (pg. 743).

A number of abnormal perceptual phenomena:

can be accounted for by the failure of an inhibition which is normally present and necessary for the integration of higher processes. . . . The integration of the thought process, the attainment of veridical perception, and a unified control of response, evidently depends as much on the suppression of some central activities as on the excitation of others (pg. 743).

In this paper, the experience, control, and inhibition of sensory stimulation are considered as the primary variables. Other characteristics of incipient schizophrenic and LSD reactions are derived strictly from these considerations. Part I of this presentation is elaborated primarily from the point of view of the individual who is going "out of his mind." Part II is concerned with the integration of these experiential reports with important behavioral researches.

I. THE SUBJECTIVE WORLD

1. Heightened Sensory Experience—The Key Characteristic

The usual boundaries which structure thought and perception become fluid; awareness becomes vivid . . . (Bowers and Freedman, 1966).

Heightened sensitivity to stimulation is a primary characteristic of incipient schizophrenic and LSD reactions. More than fifty years before Bleuler's monograph on the "Group of Schizophrenias" appeared, Conolly (1849) wrote of "a sensible excitement of the mind, more or less partial" in psychotic patients; their "senses become disturbed." The famous schizophrenic Judge, Daniel Schreber, whose autobiography was so extensively studied by Freud, was evaluated by a well known medico-legal expert of the time, G. Weber, as follows:

I have in no way assumed *a priori* the pathological nature of these ideas, but rather tried to show from the history of the patient's illness how the appellant first suffered from severe hyperaesthesia, hypersensitivity to light and noise, how to this were added massive hallucinations and particularly disturbances of common sensation which falsified his conception of things, how on the basis of these hallucinations he at first developed fantastic ideas of influence which ruled him to such an extent that he was driven to suicidal attempts and how from these pathological events, at last the system of ideas was formed which the appellant has recounted in such detail and so vividly in his memoirs . . . (Macalpine and Hunter, 1955, pg. 319).*

More recently McGhie and Chapman (1961), Chapman (1966), and Bowers and Freedman (1966), employing specially designed interview techniques, reported that alterations in color and sensory quality precede other perceptual disturbances. Most schizophrenic individuals experiencing these changes report that for a time, everything around them looks "fascinating, objects standing out vividly in contrast to the background"; "noises all seem to be louder . . . It's as if someone had turned up the volume." These initial changes in sensory experiences often are regarded as pleasant and a number of patients at this stage go through a period of mild-to-marked elation.

One night I woke up and started feeling good again . . . I felt alive and vital, full of energy. My senses seemed alive, colors were very bright. They hit me harder. Things appeared clear-cut. I noticed things I had never noticed before (Bowers, 1968, pg. 350).

Patients report that they regarded everything during this period with a new significance. "There was a general tendency for interest to be directed to ruminating about the world and life in general, religion, philosophy, art, and literature (Chapman, pg. 240)."

Identical kinds of observations are documented in the literature on subjective reactions to psychedelic drugs (e.g. Cohen, 1964; Savage, 1955). The citation of a unique case study reported by Bowers and Freedman (1966) is appropriate here. Two years prior to hospitalization, their patient had taken LSD. During his admission interview he judged his LSD and schizophrenic reactions to be essentially the same.

I feel my tactile senses are enhanced as well as my visual ones, to a point of great power. Patterns and designs begin to distinguish themselves and take on significance. This is true for the LSD-25 experience also. It's the same now as it was with the drug, only then I knew I was coming back (pg. 242).

---

*This quote is the most incisive summary statement of the development of a schizophrenic reaction that the present writer has ever read.

In all cases the individual is acutely aware that he has stepped beyond the bounds of his usual state of awareness. Sensory impressions are awesome and attention is directed, in large measure, by them. This "openness" to stimulation often is associated with a fear of being swamped by sensations and images. Laing (1960) terms this the "implosion" of reality—the danger of losing all control, of being hurt, of being obliterated. The natural tendency is to engage in psychological and physical maneuvers which the overwhelmed individual thinks will restore sensory control.* From a clinical viewpoint, these defensive maneuvers are familiar symptoms of early schizophrenia and of LSD reactions—distractibility, blocking, withdrawal, loss of spontaneity in movement and speech. From the viewpoint presented here, their initial purpose is to reduce the overwhelming intensity of, ordinarily regarded, minimal-to-moderate intensity stimulation (Silverman, 1968).

2. Distractibility and Figure-Ground Disorders

> In psychotic states, where the fate of the whole universe may be at stake, awareness of material objects and of trivial events can be heightened to an extent that is outside the range of sane experience (Coate, 1965).

The sensory attributes of complex information exert a particularly strong influence on highly sensitive individuals. The term "stimulus-bound" describes this effect well (Silverman, 1967). The experience of this effect is one of being "caught," or being "compelled-to-attend" to irrelevant, and otherwise innocuous events in unpredictable ways. Furthermore, it may be especially difficult for the schizophrenic or LSD-drugged person to stop attending to incidental stimuli. The consequences of this failure in inhibition of attention range from annoyance and perplexity all the way to fragmentation of perceptual configurations.

> e.g.   Everything seems to grip my attention although I am not particularly interested in anything. I am speaking to you just now but I can hear noises going on next door and in the corridor. I find it difficult to shut these out and it makes it more difficult for me to concentrate on what I am saying to you. Often the silliest little things that are going on seem to interest me. That's not even true; they don't interest me but I find myself attending to them and wasting a lot of time this way (McGhie and Chapman, 1961, pg. 104).

> e.g.   If something else is going on somewhere, even just a noise, it interrupts my thoughts and they get lost (ibid, pg. 105).

*An experienced LSD-guide usually has no difficulty in guiding a subject through such disturbances by encouraging him to "engage in the experience and surrender to it" (Kast, 1967). It is conceivable that comparable techniques will be used widely with incipient schizophrenic reactions, in the not-too-distant future.

Small details like paint brush markings on a wall, dirt, or slight imperfec-
tions in furniture may be experienced forcefully and in effect, temporarily
exclude other stimuli from awareness (e.g. Cohen, 1964; McGhie and Chapman, 1961; Savage, 1955). "The way one walks, the rubbing of the nose,
the crossing of the knees, the arrangement of the chairs on the ward and
of the knives and forks on the table, the smoking of a cigarette, the color
of a necktie, are all supposed to have meaning . . . (Boisen, 1942, pg.
25)." Hyperattentiveness to details of stimulus configurations also results
in pronounced perceptual changes. Under the effects of LSD, in which
attention to sensory events shifts unpredictably from moment to moment,
these perceptual changes may occur with amazing frequency:

> e.g.   I feel like I don't have a head, just my mouth is moving . . . My
> mouth or my lips feel very dry. I feel very squished now, sort of narrow
> (Pollard and Uhr, 1965, pg. 50).

Arieti (1961) describes an effect, termed "awholism," in which extreme
perceptual disorganization is associated with hyperattentiveness to ordinarily disregarded aspects of a stimulus configuration.

> For instance, a patient looking at the nurse could not see or focus on
> her as a person but perceived only her left or right eye or her hand
> or her nose, etc. Another patient who, while she was in a state of dangerous
> excitement was put in a seclusion cell, remembered that she could not
> look at the whole door of the cell. She could see only the knob or the
> keyhole or some corner or the door (pg. 8).

Chapman (1966) and McGhie and Chapman (1961) cite excerpts from interviews which are in accord with Arieti's report.

> e.g.   I have to put things together in my head. If I look at my watch
> I see the watch, watchstrap, face, hands and so on then I have got to
> put them together to get it into one piece (Chapman, 1966, pg. 229).

Hyperresponsiveness to details and hyporesponsiveness to organiza-
tional aspects of the perceptual field (involving abstracting and relating)
are underlying determinants of so-called "thought disorder."

3. Thought Disorder

> In the abstract attitude we transgress the immediately given specific
> aspects or sense impression . . . We detach ourselves from the given
> impression and the individual thing represents to us an accidental sample
> or representative of a category . . . (Goldstein, 1954).

Marked increases in the strength and significance with which sensory
stimuli are experienced are associated with decreases in the immediate

significance of meaningful symbols. Attention becomes passively directed; that is, it is controlled to a greater extent by the compelling aspects of stimulus configurations than by concentration (Bleuler, 1924). Difficulties in differentiating salient from irrelevant stimuli in problem-solving situations occur. Anticipation and logical organized thinking are interfered with. Thinking is "Stimulus-bound." In the extreme, stimulus-boundedness may result in dissolution of the ordinary experience of continuity from moment to moment; goal-directed thinking may be impossible.

> e.g. It's like being a transmitter. The sounds are coming through to me but I feel my mind cannot cope with everything (McGhie and Chapman, 1961, pg. 104).

> e.g. I can hear what they are saying all right, it's remembering what they have said in the next second that's difficult—it just goes out of my mind. I'm concentrating so much on little things, I have difficulty in finding an answer at the time (Chapman, 1966, pg. 237).

> e.g. Everything is in bits. You put the picture up bit by bit into your head. It's like a photograph that's torn in bits and put together again (Patient 3, McGhie and Chapman, 1961, pg. 106).

> e.g. I get fogged up with all the different bits and lose the important things in the picture (Patient 6, ibid, pg. 108).

Under the effect of LSD, these experiences usually are not unpleasant and often there is little concern about the fragmented ways in which thinking goes on.

4. Blocking

> The most extraordinary formal element of schizophrenic thought processes is that termed "blocking." The associative activity often seems to come to an abrupt and complete stand-still (Bleuler, 1911).

In his excellent paper on "The early symptoms of schizophrenia," Chapman (1966), observed that hyperresponsiveness to sensory input is closely linked to the occurrence of blocking phenomena ("trances," "blank spells," "thought-deprivation," "dazes"). Blocking phenomena are regarded as transient disturbances in consciousness which are associated with a failure to exclude irrelevant stimulation. Many of the patients interviewed by Chapman stated that they had experienced some kind of blocking effect on countless occasions and that this effect was associated with being over-stimulated.

> e.g. I just get cut off from outside things and go into another world. This happens when the tension starts to mount until it bursts in my brain. It has to do with what is going on around me—taking in too much of

my surroundings—vital not to miss anything. I can't shut things out of my mind and everything closes in on me. It stops me thinking and then the mind goes a blank and everything gets switched off . . . I can't control whats coming in and it stops me thinking with the mind a blank.

e.g. I don't like dividing my attention at anytime because it leads to confusion and I don't know where I am or who I am. When this starts I just go into a trance and I just turn off all my senses and I don't see anything and I don't hear anything.

This extraordinary statement regarding a kind of all-or-none control of sensory input actually is quite consistent with recent neurophysiological researches by Petrie (1967); Buchsbaum and Silverman (1968), and others and will be considered in detail, at a later point.

e.g. You can very easily go into a trance—it goes on as soon as the mind stops and then you realize you are not actually seeing anything or hearing anything. It's a delight—you don't feel anxious until you come out of it.

e.g. My mind goes blank when I listen to somebody talking to me—telling me a story and my eyes just stare and I'm not aware of anything . . . I go into a daze because I can't concentrate long enough to keep up the conversation and something lifts up inside my head and puts me into a trance or something but I always wake up later.

Chapman (1966) also reported a blocking effect which he observed first hand. If the interviewer talked a lot, and particularly if the communication was conceptually difficult, the patient would become confused, distracted, and be unable to maintain his line of thought. When this occurred, the patient lost his initial composure and became manifestly anxious. A perceptible increase in the pressure of the patient's talk was noted at this time. Also, the patient nearly always continued or initiated talk at this point. With further increases in distractibility, there occurred a sudden cessation of talk and/or an apparent lack of attention to what the interviewer was saying. These episodes ranged from a few seconds to one or two minutes in patients "within the first two years of the illness," and for much longer periods of time in longer-term patients and in patients with "additional catatonic symptoms." During these episodes,

the patient does not move, speak, or respond to verbal stimulation. Eye-blinking is either infrequent or absent and the patient looks fixedly at some point in the room, usually the floor. The observer may deliberately introduce new stimuli at this stage, such as questions, noises, movements, etc.; but the patient fails to attend to them (Chapman, 1966, pgs. 232–233).

Blocking phenomena also are common during LSD intoxication. Often words and thoughts are totally inadequate for describing the intense kaleidoscope of feelings and visions.

When you ask a psychedelic subject what is happening, he can't tell you. He looks at you blankly or he gasps: "WOW"! (Leary, 1966, pg. 71).

5. Withdrawal

The most striking aberration of behavior of the schizophrenic patient is his tendency to retreat from reality: not a surprising reaction with nerves made raw by warped input . . . (Wiener, 1967).

The hypersensitive person's avoidance of other people is part of an overall effort to reduce his intake of sensory stimulation. Sensory input may be reduced by minimizing conversation, voluntarily maintaining fixed gaze, closing one's eyes, and in more severe cases, plugging one's ears, or hiding in a corner. Note that some of the illustrations of the blocking phenomenon, cited above, involve other people being a prominent source of overstimulation. The desire to avoid others certainly is a "sensible" one. It is no wonder that some schizophrenic and LSD-drugged individuals interpret their difficulties in controlling sensory input as being due to other people exercising the control.*

6. Loss of Spontaneity in Movement and Speech

Loss of spontaneity in moving and speaking . . . is associated with a heightened awareness of mental and bodily processes and flooding of consciousness with excess sensory data (Chapman, 1966).

Kinesthetic and proprioceptive responses are reduced in schizophrenic and LSD reactions. Apparently they have to be because they are experienced as over-stimulation. McGhie and Chapman (1961) cite some very good examples.

e.g. I can't move if I am distracted by too much noise. I can't help stopping to listen. That's what happens when I am lying in bed. If there's too much noise going on I can't move.

e.g. I get stuck, almost as if I am paralyzed at times. It may only last too quickly. If I move quickly I don't take things in. My brain is working the floor and someone suddenly switches on the wireless, the music seems to stop me in my tracks and sometimes I freeze like that for a minute or two.

e.g. If I could walk slowly I would get on all right. My brain is going too quickly. If I move quickly I don't take things in. My brain is working

*Sullivan (1953), Boisen (1942) and others have discussed withdrawal from a different perspective—the absorption of the individual with awesome, cosmic and profoundly serious events. Since the concern here is primarily the defensive character of withdrawal, consideration is not given to withdrawal in terms of the self-absorption of the individual with his inner world. The reader is referred to such sources as Sullivan (1953), Boisen (1936) and Cohen (1964).

all right but I am not responding to what is coming into it. My mind is always taking in little things at the side.

e.g.   When I move quickly it's a strain on me. Things go too quick for my mind. They get blurred and it's like being blind. It's as if you were seeing a picture one moment and another picture the next. I just stop and watch my feet. Everything is all right if I stop, but if I start moving again I lose control.

Examples of speech difficulties due to over-stimulation are the following:

e.g.   My brain is not working right—I can't speak properly—the words won't come.

e.g.   If people talk to me about anything—say the weather—my mind feels no response and I have difficulty in finding an answer at the time. There's nothing there and I can't get the ideas quick enough.

Retardation of movement and speech is characteristic of most individuals while under the effects of LSD (e.g. Klee, 1963). The association of heightened sensitivity to stimulation with reduction in motor responsiveness also is characteristic of day-dreaming and so-called sensory deprivation. Fischer (1969) emphasizes that in all of these conditions there is a high sensory to motor ratio; that is, there is a predominance of the sensory over the motor component of behavior. The prototypic example of this is in the catatonic hallucinatory state with its very high sensory involvement and no motor performance.

7. Changes in Space Perspective

Immediate-raw and uninterpreted, i.e., a-logical, sensations are the content of experience in non-Euclidian hyperbolic *sensory space-time*, whereas *survival space-time* is the realm of active waking experience, a modified sensory space constructed by and reflecting life experience (Fisher, 1969).

During schizophrenic and LSD, reactions, attention to visual stimuli is captured by dominant objects in the field. Relatively minimal attention is payed to less impressive stimuli. This has the effect of changing the way in which objects are perceived in space (Silverman, 1968). In nearby space, objects are experienced as even larger than they are ordinarily, whereas distant objects are experienced as smaller. Events are perceived "in a world-space . . . from which the actors suddenly emerge much larger nearby than in ordinary (learned) life (Fischer, 1968)." Considered in relation to changes which occur in the experienced intensity of stimulation, it is no wonder that schizophrenic and LSD-drugged individuals report that things appear "strange," "unfamiliar," "different." They are indeed strange, unfamiliar and different.

The strange and unstable quality of depth perspective also contributes to the loss of spontaneity in coordinating body movements in space.

> e.g. I am not sure of body movements anymore. It's very hard to describe this but at times I am not sure about even simple actions like sitting down (McGhie and Chapman, 1961, pg. 107).

> e.g. The things I look at seem to be flatter as if you were looking just at a surface. Maybe its because I notice so much more about things and find myself looking at them for a longer time (ibid, pg. 105).

Similar behaviors are reported by normal-state subjects who have been given the hypnotic suggestion that there is no depth to space (Aaronson, 1968). Under this condition, subjects may evidence such symptoms as disturbances of gait, movement, and posture, dysphoria, blunted affect and withdrawal. Movement in a world which may appear "as though painted on a glass window (Savage, 1955, pg. 11)" is beyond the empathic comprehension of normal-state individuals. When no reasonable explanations are available as to how this can be, hidden explanations may be sought by the schizophrenic or LSD-drugged subject.

8. Stimulus Intensity Reduction

> For the living organism, protection against stimuli is almost a more important task than reception of stimuli (Freud, 1920).

There is a paradoxical quality to sensory experience which is exemplified in some of the experiential reports of schizophrenic and LSD-drugged individuals. On the one hand, hypersensitivity is reported in response to ordinary range stimulation. On the other hand hyposensitivity is reported to extremely strong stimulation (Silverman, 1968). (The perceptual and neurophysiological bases for this paradoxical effect will be elaborated upon in Part II of this presentation.) Feelings of numbness and paresthesias of the entire body are common (e.g. Klee, 1953). Despite this kind of subjective experience, registration and differentiation of minimum intensity sensations is not lost. An example of this superficially contradictory state is provided by a patient examined by Bowers and Freedman (1966). The subject reported that during the week prior to his hospitalization "My senses were sharpened;" several sentences later he stated in regard to this same period of time: "There was a fog around me *in some sense** and I felt half asleep (pg. 241)."

Paradoxical complaints of blurred vision and a fuzziness in the quality of sensory input also are common (e.g. Savage, 1955). The metaphor of the "trance" is used by a number of patients interviewed by Chapman

---

*Italics mine.

(1966) and McGhie and Chapman (1961). In many individuals the experience of _non_feeling becomes pronounced.

> e.g. I am starting to feel pretty numb about everything because I am becoming an object and objects don't have feelings (McGhie and Chapman, 1961, pg. 109).

In it's extreme form, the feeling commonly reported is one of having died (Chapman, 1966; Cohen, 1964; Savage, 1955).*

It is most interesting to note that when schizophrenic and LSD-drugged individuals are placed in reduced sensory-input situations (e.g. sensory isolation) they evidence less pronounced indications of being in an altered state of consciousness (Chapman, 1966; Cohen, S. I., et al., 1963; Pollard, Uhr, and Stern, 1965; Wiener, 1967). This suggests that indications of markedly reduced responsiveness to stimulation are compensatory responses to the experience of being overstimulated. In physiological terms, they are the result of an "attempt" by the sensory control apparatus of the central nervous system to reduce the experienced intensity of sensory stimulation. Unfortunately, this type of sensory adjustment has disruptive effects on other sensory, perceptual and cognitive functions. When overstimulated individuals are placed in a sensory-isolation situation the degree of aberrant behavior and experience is lessened, apparently, because exaggerated sensory-input-reduction responses are evoked to a lesser extent (see Silverman, 1968).

II. PERCEPTUAL AND NEUROPHYSIOLOGICAL ANALOGUES OF EXPERIENCE

In Part I of this paper a relationship was elaborated between the experience of being hypersensitive to stimulation and various aspects of incipient schizophrenic and LSD reactions. Gross alterations in perception and thinking were ascribed to a sensory input modulating system which does not dampen (as it formerly did) the intensity of ordinary-range stimulation. Perceived much more intensely than normally, this stimulation serves to "bind" behavior and experience to the immediate here-and-now.† Inhibitory responsiveness in the sensory nervous system (sensory input reduction) has little affect in attenuating the overwhelming experience of ordinary-intensity stimulation. Feelings of "nonfeeling" co-occur with feelings

---

*Other aspects of the experience of having died probably relate to the perception of space-time as being different from moment to moment and of one's self as being "discontinued" or diffused.

†"Immediate experience, that is, the accommodation of thought to the surface of things, is simply empirical experience which considers, as objective datum, reality as it appears to direct perception (Piaget, 1954, pg. 381)."

of being overstimulated. The overall result is a radically different-than-normal way of experiencing one's self and one's environment.

Part II of this presentation is concerned with a discussion of the experimental literature relevant to these issues. Hypersensitivity in schizophrenic and LSD-drugged subjects *is* found in the laboratory. Paradoxically, reduction of the experienced intensity of strong stimulation also is found in the same types of subjects. For example, very unpleasant stimulation is tolerated less well by nonpsychiatric subjects than by schizophrenic and LSD-drugged subjects. Additional researches indicate a neurophysiological basis for the paradoxical association of feelings of being hypersensitive to minimal-intensity stimulation and feelings of anesthesia. Because a good deal of this evidence has already been integrated elsewhere (Silverman, 1967, 1968), this discussion is concerned primarily with updating the review of the experimental literature and with a consideration of some important issues relevant to research with nonreality-oriented subjects.

1. Sensitivity to Low-Intensity Stimulation

Until recently, results of experiments on the sensitivity of schizophrenic and LSD-drugged individuals were inconsistent with the subjective reports of these subjects. Hence, statements about extraordinary sensitivity were regarded by most scientists merely as exaggerations and distortions. After all, the experimental evidence indicated that, at most, sensory responsiveness was within normal limits and all too often was "impaired" just like cognitive and emotional responsiveness was impaired. However, within the past several years a number of researchers have reported laboratory performances indicative of hypersensitivity in these nonreality-oriented subjects (Fischer and Kaelbling, 1967; Fischer, Ristine, and Wisecup, 1968; Henkin, *et al.*, 1967; Hill, Fischer and Warshay, 1968; Keeler, 1965; Lapkin, 1962; Maupin, 1963; Rockey and Fischer, 1967). In contrast with earlier laboratory reports these studies are consistent with the subjective report literature; they indicate that during a schizophrenic reaction and under the influence of psychedelic drugs, 1) ordinary-intensity stimuli are experienced more intensely than normally and 2) less sensory information is necessary in order to report that a stimulus is present. Previous failures to demonstrate hypersensitivity in the laboratory quite likely occurred for several reasons. To begin with, it is very difficult for an experimenter to control the stimuli to which individuals in an altered psychological state are responding. Considering that these subjects disattend to requests or communications when demands are made on them (e.g. Chapman, 1966) and, that they are extra-ordinarily distractible (Silverman, 1968), it should not be at all surprising if their laboratory performances did not reflect their stimulus-detection capacities. Secondly, a strong presumption on the part of the experimenter that subjects would perform in an abnormally inefficient manner actually may have contributed to the outcomes of some of the earlier experiments (see Rosenthal, 1966). Katz, Waskow and Olsson (1968), commenting on such issues in regard to research with psychedelic-drugged subjects wrote:

> The available research literature does not indicate that the psychological states which are produced have been as carefully and unemotionally described or analyzed as they could be, or that the appropriate methods for their study have generally been applied . . . (pg. 2).

Finally, the problem of individual differences has undoubtedly contributed confusion to the sensitivity issue. This problem probably has been less in psychedelic drug studies. Thus, Fischer, et al., (1968) and McGlothlin, Cohen, and McGlothlin (1967) have found that many volunteers for psychedelic drug studies tend to be of a similar personality type in which hypersensitivity to stimulation is common. Nevertheless, considerable personality and perceptual style differences have been found in individuals who respond differently under the effects of psychedelic drugs (Fisher, et al., 1968; Silverman, in press). In laboratory studies of schizophrenic subjects, the problem is more pronounced. Performances of heterogeneous groups of schizophrenics tend to define the *extremes* of behavior on several basic sensory response dimensions, including hypersensitivity and hyposensitivity to stimulation (e.g. Fischer, et al., 1968; Silverman, 1967). Contrary to popular clinical impression, the paranoid type of schizophrenic is not hypersensitive to minimal intensity stimulation. Rather, the essential or nonparanoid schizophrenic (Sullivan, 1953), who maintains a perceptually undifferentiated orientation toward his environment, is the one who is hypersensitive to stimulation (Silverman, 1968). Indeed, in studies of normal subjects by Allison (1963), Kaswan, Haralson and Cline (1965), and others, the maintenance of a perceptually *un*differentiated orientation to input is associated with greatest sensitivity to low intensity stimulation. In accord with these findings Sullivan (1953) has noted that the development of a differentiated delusional system (characteristic of the paranoid type) has the effect of toning down the intensity of an acute schizophrenic reaction. Apparently a delusional system functions as a buffer, which somehow lessens the impact of sensory stimulation. It is interesting to note that Sullivan considers this to be an abortion of the schizophrenic process and a poor-prognosis sign.

> The patient, caught up in the spread of meaning, magic, transcendental forces, suddenly 'understands' it all as the work of some other concrete person or persons. This is an ominous development in that the schizophrenic state is taking on a paranoid coloring. If the suffering of the patient is markedly diminished thereby, we shall observe the evolution

of a *paranoid schizophrenic state*. These conditions are of relatively much less favorable outcome. They tend to be permanent distortions of the interpersonal relations, though the unpleasantness of the patient's experience gradually fades and a quite comfortable way of life may ultimately ensue . . . (pg. 153). A paranoid systematization is therefore, markedly beneficial to the peace of mind of the person chiefly concerned, and its achievement in the course of a schizophrenic disorder is so great an improvement in security . . . (Sullivan, 1953, pg. 157).

Laboratory sensitivity studies have not differentiated between schizophrenic subjects in terms of degree of systematized delusional activity. No doubt consideration of this aspect of behavior will shed further light on the nature of hypersensitivity in schizophrenic states.* At present it appears that in incipient schizophrenia (and under the effects of psychedelic drugs) hypersensitivity and, associated with it, undifferentiated perceptual and cognitive activity are fundamental response characteristics; they emerge earlier in time than "paranoid coloring," and "paranoid systematization." At least, in part, paranoid adjustments may be considered as attempts to free oneself from the hypersensitive, high excitation state, from the "implosion" of reality. In this context, a delusional construction is literally an attempt at making NONSENSE out of intense SENSE experience.

2. Hypersensitivity, Overstimulation and Paradoxical Reduction Responsiveness

Individuals who are hypersensitive to low intensity stimulation react strongly to ordinary sensory events in the here-and-now. Experimental studies indicate that these subjects have difficulty in inhibiting responsiveness to irrelevant, contextual stimuli when the stimuli are of low-to-moderate intensity (Palmer, 1966; Silverman, 1967). However, inhibition of response is observed in hypersensitive individuals when the intensity of stimulation presented is "very strong" (Silverman, 1967). Pavlov (1957) suggested an explanation for such findings. He observed that organisms who are hypersensitive to stimulation are most likely to become overstimulated. If overstimulation occurs, he hypothesized that a generalized state of "protective inhibition" is induced in order to protect the nervous system from further stimulation. If further strong stimulation is registered in this state, more protective inhibition is generated; the organism now is observed to evidence reduced responsiveness to strong stimuli. *Thus, hypersensitivity and overstimulation are among the basic precursors of reduced responsiveness to strong stimulation and reduced responsiveness to strong stimulation is characteristic of schizo-*

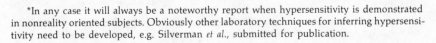

*In any case it will always be a noteworthy report when hypersensitivity is demonstrated in nonreality oriented subjects. Obviously other laboratory techniques for inferring hypersensitivity need to be developed, e.g. Silverman *et al.*, submitted for publication.

phrenic and LSD-drugged subjects. Excellent illustrations of this kind of response to strong stimulation are provided by Donoghue (1964) and Kast (e.g. 1966).*

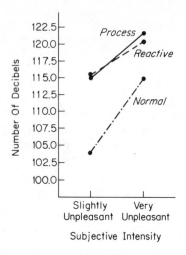

Fig. 1.   Degree of unpleasantness ratings of a 440 cps. tone presented at different intensities to normal subjects and to process and reactive schizophrenics (from Donoghue, 1964).

Donoghue (1964), using the psychophysical method of single stimuli, recorded the judgments of sounds of different intensities by sixty schizophrenic subjects and thirty nonpsychiatric control subjects. (I.Q. scores and years of education were not significantly different in the two groups; mute and uncooperative patients were excluded from the study). Sound intensity ratings were made by subjects on a six point scale ranging from pleasant to unpleasant. Median values (in decibels) of the sound intensities rated "slightly unpleasant" and "very unpleasant" were computed for each subject. Schizophrenic subjects were found to require a significantly more intense stimulus than nonschizophrenics in order for them to rate a stimulus as "slightly unpleasant." An intensity which was rated as "very unpleasant" among control group subjects was likely to be rated as only "slightly unpleasant" by schizophrenic subjects (Fig. 1). The results of a number of pain reactivity experiments also have indicated the occurrence of reduced responsiveness to strong stimulation in schizophrenic subjects (Silverman, 1967).

Recent electroneurophysiological studies by Buchsbaum and Silverman (1968) and others (Blacker, Jones, Stone and Pfefferbaum, 1968; Silverman,

*For a more extensive survey of the literature in this and related areas see Silverman, 1967, pgs. 229-235 and pgs. 239-243.

Buchsbaum and Henkin, submitted for publication) have indicated that reduced responsiveness to strong stimulation occurs on the electroencephalographic averaged evoked response (AER) procedure. By averaging electrical potentials, recorded from the scalp, for long series of stimuli, such as light flashes, an averaged evoked response waveform is produced. For a given individual, the amplitudes of certain peaks of the waveform change systematically with changes in stimulus intensity. In the moderate-to-high range of stimulus intensities, amplitudes of one particular peak of the waveform (Peak 4) are found to change in different ways for individuals with different perceptual judgment characteristics. In brief, subjects who *reduce* the sizes of tactile judgments of width, following a period of tactile stimulation, evidence quite different AER patterns than subjects who *augment* the sizes of tactile judgments following stimulation. Size judgment "reducers" evidence relatively decreased AER amplitudes at the higher stimulus intensities. Size judgment "augmenters" evidence increases in AER amplitudes with increases in stimulus intensity (Fig. 2). This effect is found in normal subjects and in various psychiatric patient and medical patient groups.

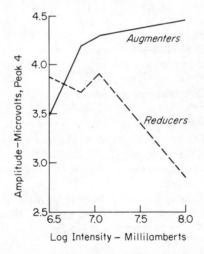

Fig. 2.   Amplitudes of averaged evoked responses to four intensities of photic stimulation for normal size-judgment-augmenter and normal size-judgment-reducer subjects' (from Buchsbaum and Silverman, 1968). Note: Peak 4 designation is based upon numbering system of Kooi and Bagchi (1964). Light values in lumen seconds range from 32 to 980 lumen seconds.

The AER reduction curve was found to be pronounced in a small group of college-age, reducer, essential schizophrenic males (Buchsbaum and Silverman, 1968).

Most recently, it has been observed that an AER reduction curve also occurs among normal, male subjects whose performances on traditional sensory threshold procedures are indicative of greater sensitivity to low intensity stimulation (Silverman, Buchsbaum and Henkin, submitted for publication). Individuals with augmenter AER curves tend not to be as sensitive to low intensity stimulation. Consistent with this finding are others which indicate that administration of phenothiazines to schizophrenic subjects changes baseline AER reduction to AER augmentation (Singer, et al., in press), and that phenothiazines also cause individuals to be *less* sensitive to low intensity stimulation (Fischer and Kaelbing, 1967). Thus, the hypersensitivity formulation elaborated here receives considerable support. Experimental studies turn out to be consistent with subjective reports.

Taken together these researches indicate that the study of the sensory nervous system is of fundamental importance for our understanding of schizophrenic and LSD reactions. Furthermore, the value of carefully listening to and examining the subjective reports of our nonreality oriented subjects is confirmed; they do have substantive things to teach us about altered psychological states.

REFERENCES

Aaronson, B. S. Hypnotic alterations of space and time. In *Proceedings of an International Conference on Hypnosis, Drugs, Dreams, and PSI, 1967*. Garrett Press Inc., New York, 1968.

Allison, J. Cognitive structure and receptivity to low intensity stimulation. *J. abnorm. soc. Psychol.* **67**, 132–138, 1963.

Arieti, S. The loss of reality. *Psychoanal. Rev.* **3**, 3–24, 1961.

Bleuler, E. *Textbook of Psychiatry.* Macmillan, New York, 1924.

Bleuler, E. (Orig. publ. 1911). *Dementia Praecox or the Group of Schizophrenias.* (Translated by Zinkin, J.) International University Press, New York, 1950.

Bleuler, M. Conceptions of schizophrenia within the last fifty years and today. *Proc. Roy. Soc. Med.* **56**, 945–952, 1963.

Boisen, A. T. *The Exploration of the Inner World.* Harper, New York, 1936.

Boisen, A. T. The form and content of schizophrenic thinking. *Psychiat.* **5**, 23–33, 1942.

Bowers, M. B. Pathogenesis of acute schizophrenic psychosis: an experimental approach. *Arch. Gen. Psychiat.* **19**, 348–355, 1968.

Bowers, M. B. and Freedman, D. X. "Psychedelic" experiences in acute psychoses. *Arch. Gen. Psychiat.* **15**, 240–248, 1966.

Buchsbaum, M. and Silverman, J. Stimulus intensity control and the cortical evoked response. *Psychosom. Med.* **30**, 12–22, 1968.

Chapman, J. The early symptoms of schizophrenia. *Brit. J. Psychiat.* **112**, 225–251, 1966.

Coate, M. *Beyond All Reason*, Lippincott, New York, 1965.

Cohen, S. *The Beyond Within: The LSD Story*. Athenium Press, New York, 1964.

Cohen, S. I., Silverman, A. J. and Shmavonian, B. M. Psychophysiological studies in altered sensory environments. *J. Psychosom. Res.* **6**, 259–281, 1963.

Conolly, J. *The Croonian Lectures, 1849*. Reprinted from the Lancet by C. B. Birnie, St. Bernard's Hospital, Southall, England, 1960.

Donoghue, J. R. Motivation and conceptualization in process and reactive schizophrenia. Unpublished doctoral dissertation, University of Nebraska, 1964.

Fischer, R. Space-time coordinates of excited and tranquilized states. In *Psychiatry and Art*, Jakob, I. (Editor) S. Karger, Basel, New York, 1968.

Fischer, R. On creative, psychotic and ecstatic states. In *Proceedings of the American Society of Psychopathology of Expression*, Jakob, I. (Editor) Karger, Basel, 1969.

Fischer, R. and Kaelbling, R. Increase in taste acuity with sympathetic stimulation: The relation of a just-noticeable taste difference to systemic psychotropic drug dose. *Recent Advances in Biological Psychiat.* **9**, 183–195, 1967.

Fischer, R., Marks, P. A., Hill, R. M., and Rockey, M. A. Personality structure as the main determinant of drug induced (model) psychoses. *Nature*, **218**, 296–298, 1968.

Fischer, R., Ristine, L. P. and Wisecup, P. Increase in gustatory acuity and hyperarousal in schizophrenia. *Soc. Biol. Psychiat.*, in press.

Freud, S. *Beyond the Pleasure Principle*. (Originally published in 1920). The Complete Works of Sigmund Freud. Standard Ed. **18**, London, 1955.

Goldstein, K. "Methodological approach to the study of schizophrenia. In *Language and Thought Schizophrenia*. Kasanin, J. S. (Editor), University of California Press, Berkeley, 1954.

Hebb, D. The American Revolution. *Amer. Psychol.* **15**, 735–745, 1960.

Henkin, R., Buchsbaum, M., Welpton, D., Zahn, T., Scott, W., Wynne, L., Silverman, J. Physiological and psychological effects of LSD in chronic users. Presented at the Eastern Meeting of the American Federation for Clinical Research, December, 1967.

Hill, R. M., Fischer, R. and Warshay, D. Effects of psychodysleptic drug psilocybin on visual perception: changes in brightness preference. Submitted for publication, *Experientia*, 1968.

Hoffer, A. and Osmond, H. Some psychological consequences of perceptual disorder and schizophrenia. *Int. J. Neuropsychiat.* **2**, 1–19, 1966.

Kast, E. C. LSD and the Dying Patient. Chicago Med. School Quarterly, **26**, 80–87, 1966.

Kast, E. C. Attenuation of anticipation: A therapeutic use of lysergic acid diethylamide. *Psychiat. Quart.*, **41**, 1–12, 1967.

Kaswan, J., Haralson, Sally and Cline, Ruth. Variables in perceptual and cognitive organization and differentiation. *J. Pers.*, **33**, 164–177, 1965.

Katz, M. M., Waskow, I. E. and Olsson, J. Characterizing the psychological state produced by LSD. *J. Abnorm. Psychol.*, **73**, 1–14, 1968.

Keeler, M. H. The effects of psilocybin on a test of after-image perception. *Psychopharm.*, **8**, 131–139, 1965.

Klee, G. D. Lysergic acid diethylamide (LSD-25) and ego function. *Arch. Gen. Psychiat.*, **8**, 461–474, 1963.

Kooi, K. A. and Bagchi, B. K. Visual evoked responses in man: Normative data. *Ann. N.Y. Acad. Sci.*, **112**, 254, 1964.

Laing, R. D. *The Divided Self.* Tavistock, London, 1960.

Lapkin, B. The relation of primary-process thinking to the recovery of subliminal material. *J. Nerv. Ment. Dis.*, **135**, 10–25, 1962.

Leary, T. The experiential typewriter. *Psychedelic Rev.*, No. 7, 70–85, 1966.

Macalpine, Ida and Hunter, R. A. Daniel-Paul Schreber—*Memoirs of my Nervous Illness.* W. M. Dawson and Sons, Ltd., London, 1955.

Maupin, Barbara, A. M. The Effect of Altered Ego States on the Utilization of Subliminal Registrations of Color, unpublished dissertation, University of Michigan, 1963.

McDonald, Norma. Living With Schizophrenia. *Canad. Med. Assoc. J.* **82**, 218–221, 1960.

McGhie, A. and Chapman, J. Disorders of attention and perception in early schizophrenia. *Brit. J. Med. Psychol.* **34**, 103–116, 1961.

McGlothlin, W., Cohen, S. and McGlothlin, M. S. Long lasting effects of LSD on normals. *Arch. Gen. Psychiat.* **17**, 521–532, 1967.

Palmer, R. D. Visual acuity and excitement. *Psychosom. Med.* **28**, 364–374, 1966.

Pavlov, I. P. General types of animal and human higher nervous activity. In I. P. Pavlov's *Experimental Psychology and Other Essays.* Philosophical Library, New York, 1957.

Perry, J. W. Reconstitutive process in the psychopathology of the self. *Annals New York Acad. Science* **96**, 853–876, 1962.

Petrie, Asenath. *Individuality in pain and suffering, Chicago.* University of Chicago Press, 1967.

Piaget, J. *The construction of reality in the child.* Basic Books, New York, 1954.

Pollard, J. and Uhr, L., and Stern, Elizabeth. *Drugs and Phantasy, The Effects of LSD, Psilocybin, and Sernyl on College Students.* Little, Brown and Company, Boston, 1965.

Rockey, M. and Fischer, R. An interpretation of the aesthetic experience of non-artists under psilocybin. *Proceedings of the Fifth International Congress on Psychopathology of Expression*, 1967, in press.

Rosenthal, R. *Experimenter effects in behavioral research.* Appleton-Century-Crofts, New York, 1966.

Savage, C. Variations in ego feeling induced by D-Lysergic Acid Diethylamide (LSD-25). *Psychoanal. Rev.* **42**, 1–16, 1955.

Sechehaye, M. *Autobiography of a schizophrenic girl.* Gruen and Stratton, New York, 1951.

Silverman, J. Variations in cognitive control and psychophysiological defense in the schizophrenias. *Psychosom. Med.* **29**, 225–251, 1967.

Silverman, J. The study of individual differences in the effects of LSD-25 on sensory-perceptual functioning. A report of a pilot study. In *Proceedings of the Conference on Adverse Reactions to LSD, 1967.* NIMH Publication, in press.

Silverman, J. A paradigm for the study of altered states of consciousness. *Brit. J. Psychiat.* **114**, 1201–1218, 1968.

Silverman, J., Buchsbaum, M. and Henkin, R. Stimulus sensitivity and stimulus intensity control. *Perceptual and Motor Skills,* **28**:71–78, 1969.

Singer, M., Borge, G., Almond, R., Buchsbaum, M., Silverman, J. and Wynne, L. C. Correlation between phenothiazine administration, clinical course and perceptual (neurophysiological) measures. *Clinical Res.,* **17**:133, 1969.

Sullivan, H. S. The common field of research and psychiatry. *Psychiatric Quart.* **1**, 276–291, 1927.

Sullivan, H. S. (Originally written in 1940). *Conceptions of Modern Psychiatry,* New York, 1953.

Temerlin, M. K. Suggestion effects in psychiatric diagnosis. *J. Nerv. Ment. Dis.,* in press.

Wiener, H. External Chemical Messengers. I. Emission and Reception in Man, *New York State J. Med.* **66**, 3153–3170, 1966.

Wiener, H. External Chemical Messengers. II. Natural History of Schizophrenia, *New York State J. Med.* **67**, 1144–1165, 1967.

Wiener, H. External Chemical Messengers. III. Mind and Body in Schizophrenia, *New York State J. of Med.* **67**, 1287–1310, 1967.

Biochemistry and Psychosis
Elton B. McNeil

A survey of the literature of the biochemistry of mental illness indicates that each biochemist apparently has his own theory. Each theory, while comprehensive in its ramifications, is based on inconclusive evidence. This is a field floating with "ifs," with large banks of data emerging and disappearing as new research results are accumulated. With the growing sophistication of research methodology and reporting, it is not unduly optimistic, however, to predict even better ways and means of controlling or mitigating "psychotic" symptoms. This does not mean that we will be able to understand psychotic experience by understanding the correlated chemical changes—only that we will improve our capacity to control or alter states of consciousness biochemically. Laing and other theorists, having reservations as to the "curative" value of such biochemical modulation, propose that biochemical and psychological changes occurring naturally during psychosis may have beneficial effects. The argument is far from settled.

Unfortunately for the student of psychology, it is difficult to appraise the evidence presented by biochemical researchers, an extensive technical and technological background being a prerequisite for sophisticated evaluations. But to understand madness it is important to acquire an overview of the range and focus of investigations currently underway. Elton McNeil presents a brief appraisal of current biochemical investigations, minimizes the uncertainties and conflicts among the researchers, and links major theoretical positions objectively into a general comprehensive viewpoint.

Biochemists have always dreamed of establishing control over man's behavior, but this dream has not yet been fulfilled (Himwich and Himwich, 1967).

Since the patient's blood and urine are easily accessible to observation, they have frequently been subjected to study. Theorists assume that if psychopathology is a generalized physiological reaction it is reasonable to suppose that its presence ought to be reflected in some fashion in the fluid medium that surrounds the tissues of the body, in the body chemistry, or in human waste products. Study of the state of the body fluids seeks to discover the presence of substances that affect the brain, producing disordered patterns of behavior.

In this quest, pharmacologically active substances (drugs) have been introduced into the body to provoke reactions that may serve as models for those chemical-behavioral causes and effects produced naturally in the patient. A large number of drugs such as LSD (lysergic acid diethylamide) has been employed in research, and a great many tranquilizers, stimulants, and depressants have been used to alter the characteristic mood of the patient. It is, in fact, the promising response of patients to these mood-changing drugs that has recently encouraged researchers in their pursuit of other biochemical keys to behavior (Woolley, 1962).

Biochemical studies have explored the energy metabolism of patients—abnormalities of basal metabolism and glucose, carbohydrate, and phosphate utilization by the body—but have not managed, convincingly, to connect biochemical anomalies to human behavioral disorder. Most studies marked by initially glowing accounts of statistical significance simply fail to provide adequate experimental control (comparison with nondisordered persons) for other possible "causes" of the condition (Benjamin, 1958; Kety, 1959).

The discovery of a high correlation between catatonic schizophrenia and some element of blood chemistry must, for example, demonstrate that the same chemical finding *cannot* be traced to the patient's diet or lack of physical exercise that occurs for all hospitalized patients. Bulle and Konchegul (1957), for example, found a substance very much like the compound serotonin in the cerebrospinal fluid of psychotics and a substance with the properties of adrenaline in manic-depressives. When dosages of these substances were administered to the patients, alterations in their symptoms appeared. A detailed theory of biochemical action in the psychoses was developed based on these findings, but the raw biochemical data were not enough to rule out the possibility of a great many other interacting events that could produce such chemical changes independent of the psychotic state of the patient. Biochemistry furnishes interesting *clues* to psychosis, but a careful appraisal of the data suggests that conclusions such as "Schizophrenia is regarded as starting with a failure to form enough serotonin in the brain" (Woolley, 1962, p. 183) are more than a little premature.

The list of possible biochemical "causes" investigated has included: amino acid and monoamine metabolism, endocrine gland excretions, and serum proteins. We know, for example, that the neuro hormones mediate the transmission of nerve impulses and that the primary neuro hormones (acetylocholine, histamine, noradrenalin, serotonin, and gamma amino butyric acid) make up a kind of internal "tide of life" that is thought to influence the direction of mental activity (Rubin, 1962). Experimental reactions produced in animals and the discovery of similar or related substances in the brain and nervous system of some of the victims of psychopathology encourage the biochemist's hope for the discovery of keys that will unlock some of the mystery of man's behavior (Bulle and Konchegul, 1957).

Biochemical study of the schizophrenias presents a wildly scattered set of findings—findings that do not always fit into a reasonable pattern. Reaction to reports in the professional literature depends, in great part, on the initial optimism or pessimism with which one approaches the field (Durell and Schildkraut, 1966). For a variety of reasons, significant and meaningful "breakthroughs" in biochemical research most often fail to be confirmed by the next researcher to try the experiment (Jackson, 1962). There is a close kinship of genetic and biochemical studies in this respect since a number of theorists have suggested that genetic or constitutional defects might take the form of biochemical disarray. Research to explore this possible connection is almost nonexistent.

Much of what we know of biochemistry and disorder comes from comparisons between normal and pathological groups. It is in the faulty comparisons of these that many errors are made. As Kety (1959) has noted, the concept of schizophrenia is so loose and incapable of definition that it is difficult to know if two geographically separated researchers are working on comparable populations. The easy availability of captive populations of schizophrenic patients in mental hospitals has always been seductive to researchers and has provoked a number of indiscretions in experimental design. As long as biochemical studies are carried out on patients who have been hospitalized for a great many years, it is impossible to determine whether findings relate to fundamental differences between normals and schizophrenics, or to hospital diets and chronic infections of the digestive tract, or to the consequences of prolonged courses of medication, drugs, or convulsive shock. Cause and effect relationship is the issue to be resolved, and this has most often been treated in a very cavalier and unscientific fashion.

In addition, diagnostic categories are woefully unreliable; control subjects are not easily available (volunteers cannot be used since they may have special psychological characteristics); normal chemical base lines may not be known (and these may wax and wane in unknown ways); and observed chemical changes may be a response to psychotic disorder rather than a cause of it. It is not a hopeless arena for scientific grappling with issues, but it is a demanding and challenging one. Refinements in theory and technique still hold promise, but researchers may one day be forced to make friends with the psychological enemy in order to achieve their aims.

Biochemists view psychosis as a disease, and it is reasonable, then, to suppose the "disease" is a function of body chemistry. It is interesting that the neuroses are seldom seen as disease in the same fashion as the psychoses. Perhaps the psychoses are so alien to our notions of normal human behavior that, for those who think "chemically," the psychotic population is a prime candidate for biochemical disorder.

The psychoses are obviously some mixture of mental and physical but they are not simply either/or. One form of causation does not automatically exclude the other. It is most reasonable to say that an interactive effect of the two is necessary to produce so serious a disorder in human kind. The question is, "How far do you reduce causes?" i.e., beginning with the demands of adult social life, how much distance must be travelled before we can achieve some understanding of the disorder? At what juncture do we declare that we have unearthed the true causes? Must we return, ultimately, to the level of the cell structure?

Horwitt (1956) in discussing schizophrenia and biology said, "The sum total of the differences reported [in the literature] would make the schizophrenic patient a sorry specimen indeed: his liver, brain, kidney, and circulatory functions are impaired; he is deficient in practically every vitamin; his hormones are out of balance, and his enzymes are askew" (p. 430). Claims of new chemical answers to schizophrenia come and go with time but it is unfortunate that so many generations of biologists must repeat the theoretical errors of those who went before them.

This is not to suggest that biochemistry has seen its heyday. It is still in its infancy and we would be presumptuous to expect that in biochemistry a single, simple answer to severe human disorder is soon to be found (Throne and Gowdey, 1967). If biochemical studies are to contribute to our understanding of the nature of the psychoses, they must mature to a point where they recognize the complicated nature of man and cease to treat him as though he were an uncomprehending vial of chemicals.

REFERENCES

Benjamin, J. D. Some considerations in biological research in schizophrenia. *Psychosom. Med.*, 1958, **20**, 427–45.

Bulle, P. H. and Konchegul, L. Action of serotonin and cerebrospinal fluid of schizophrenics on the dog-brain. *J. clin. exp. Psychopathol.*, 1957, **18**, 287–91.

Durell, J. and Schildkraut, J. J. Biochemical studies of the schizophrenic and affective disorders. In S. Arieti (ed.), *American Handbook of Psychiatry, Vol. III.* New York: Basic Books, Inc., Publishers, 1966. Pp. 423–57.

Himwich, W. A. and Himwich, H. E. Neurochemistry. In A. M. Freedman and H. I. Kaplan (eds.), *Psychiatry.* Baltimore: The Williams & Wilkins Co., 1967. Pp. 49–67.

Horwitt, M. K. Fact and artifact in the biology of schizophrenia. *Science,* 1956, **124,** 429–30.

Jackson, D. D. Schizophrenia. *Scientific Amer.,* 1962, **207,** 65–75.

Kety, S. S. Biochemical theories of schizophrenia, Part II. *Science,* 1959, **129,** 1590–96.

Rubin, L. S. Patterns of adrenergic-cholinergic imbalance in the functional psychoses. *Psych. Rev.,* 1962, **69,** 501–19.

Throne, M. L., and Gowdey, C. W. A critical review of endogenous psychotoxins as a cause of schizophrenia. *Can. Psychiatr. Assoc. J.,* 1967, **12,** 159–74.

Woolley, D. W. *The Biochemical Bases of Psychoses.* New York: John Wiley & Sons, Inc., 1962.

The Effects of Biological
Rhythms in Mental Illness
Gay Gaer Luce

Gay Luce presents evidence that the emotional states of normal and abnormal individuals are affected by biological rhythms that are similar to other normal changes in body chemistry and emotional disposition, such as hunger, sleep, or seasonal allergies.

Rhythmic changes can be detected in more dramatic emotional states such as psychosis, catatonia, and manic-depression. Careful observation of individuals classified under other categories of mental illness also reveals rhythmic swings in mood, food intake, susceptibility to drugs, and other characteristics. A mapping of these rhythms may show underlying patterns that could lead to the development of more effective coping strategies. Scheduling of daily activities, psychotherapy, or medication, in harmony with a person's individual biorhythms, could lead to more rapid and lasting improvement than do traditional methods, which tend to be arbitrarily set for all patients in accordance with normal working hours.

As we become aware of our own personal cycles, we gain in understanding of the unusual feelings we have "for no apparent reason." This insight may eventually lead to wide-scale changes in our attitudes toward certain kinds of mental disturbance. Just as scurvy and diabetes were once termed mental illnesses, it is possible that manic-depression and other forms of psychosis may someday be seen and treated as irregularities in biological rhythms.

MENTAL ILLNESSES: CYCLIC PSYCHOSIS

Most dramatic of all the periodic illnesses are the recurrent emotional or mental illnesses. Some plunge an individual through rapid alternations of normalcy and symptoms of illness every forty-eight hours, while others span weeks or months. By way of example, Mary Lamb, the sister of the great English essayist Charles Lamb, suffered a cyclic psychosis for fifty years, beginning at age thirty. During one of her psychotic attacks, she killed her ailing mother of whom she was very fond. A lawyer friend was fortunately able to save her from prosecution and placed her in her brother's custody where she lived a long and fruitful life to the age of eighty-three. Between her thirty-eight attacks, she was normal. The attacks were regular and at the first sign of a slight irritability in her manner, her brother would rush her to a hospital or put her in a straitjacket. Immediately after recovering, she went on her usual round of entertaining literary friends and writing books or stories until the next attack.

This famous case is of interest because Mary Lamb showed no signs of physical or mental deterioration, except that of old age later in her life. It is possible that some signs of deterioration in mental patients derive from interference with normal development and stimulation. The routine of hospital life deprives a person of his usual modes of expression and fulfillment; it is often humiliating, and the impairment observed among mental patients may be a result not only of illness but of the way we treat the mentally ill. Diary information might be used to restrict hospitalization for mental patients in the way we restrict it to the acute phases of physical illness. Chronic patients might lead more normal lives in the interstices between bouts of illness if the calendar of attacks permitted. Sometimes, however, the intermission is too brief, and then a hospital setting becomes crucial.

PERIODIC CATATONIA

A number of patients who alternated between a few weeks of normalcy and a few weeks of psychosis have been studied throughout their adult lives in what may be the single most thorough long-term study of an illness. In Oslo, Norway, at the community hospital, Dr. Leiv Gjessing and his father, Dr. Rolv Gjessing, before him, have been trying to discover what biochemical mechanisms cause periodic catatonia, an illness in which people swing from a normal state into one of hyperexcitability and violence or into a frozen state resembling paralysis.

The Dikemark Sikhus where the Gjessings studied these patients is the Oslo community hospital and was founded in 1905. The old stuccoed pastel buildings have high arched windows and towers, and the setting, on steep, wooded hills with lawns high above a small lake, is unusual for a mental institution, at least by American standards. Among farmland and lakes, the hospital grounds have an atmosphere of nineteenth-century New England. Patients are not isolated from the surrounding life of the community. Many of them work on the hospital farm or in its small industrial shops, treating the place as a home where they live, paint, practice the piano, construct furniture, and assist in the laboratories.

In the 1920s, Dr. Rolv Gjessing observed that some of his patients had fortnightly stupors interspersed with normal periods of behavior, and that when behavior changed radically, so did the physical appearance of the patient. During stupor, one man had sputum so thick it could be drawn out like chewing gum. His skin became very oily. Using the instruments available at the time, Dr. Gjessing measured nitrogen retention and other physiological functions, maintaining his patients on a controlled diet, and training nurses to get exceedingly accurate measurements. With his own funds, he furnished a biochemistry laboratory in one of the men's wards, for he suspected that metabolic flaws involving the thyroid gland underlay the illness. His work has been continued by his son, Leiv Gjessing, who has had the advantage of studying and caring for old men who once knew him as a little boy. Exacting around-the-clock studies have won extraordinary cooperation from these patients, who treated him as a young nephew.

Since catatonic patients have normal periods, they develop pretty much in pace with their peers. The periodic psychosis often begins in the early twenties, sometimes abruptly following a stress. Dr. Gjessing has speculated that stress, brain damage, or perhaps a metabolic shock due to some autoimmune reaction might damage a metabolic regulator and thus produce the clocklike symptoms of catatonia. When catatonic, a patient may seem to be out of contact, mute, and immobile for several days at a time, but according to the diaries and reports of such patients they are internally experiencing an implosive intensity. One man, who has been hospitalized since 1935, always begins to talk to himself during his transition; for a day or two he would babble aloud in a manic fashion, reclining with his head and feet raised. He would stay for several days in a position that is practiced a few seconds at a time by gymnasts. Eyes open and frozen, his hands clammy, skin oily, he lost his appetite, and had a high pulse rate and blood pressure. He looked like a wax doll until he began to recover.

This paralyzed state masks an intense hallucinogenic state resembling experiences under mescaline, as can be seen in these recollections of one patient:

> In the stupor many strange events enter the soul. The soul is bewitched. [Ordinary experiences, such as being washed, displeased him, and the sensation was strange.] Everything was polar. . . . In order that the sun should shine, the soul had to have psychic trouble, the trouble corresponding in strength in proportion to the strength of the sun. . . . Like the Tree of Knowledge, everyone who eats the fruit must die.
>
> If you ask a simple question, I hear it, but it's as if from outside the room. People help but the people become transformed into words, and from words people are transformed into a kinemagraphic picture . . . thought stops but for a few fixed points that act as a lighthouse. . . .

Asked why he did not move in bed, he answered:

> The soul and thinking prevent moving, prevent muscles from doing what
> I want them to. Impulses are not carried out, and this seems natural.
> Not to want anything and to have no interest in anything is important.
> Former interests do not penetrate.

This state suggested a kind of intoxication to Dr. Gjessing, the kind which might come from mishandled nitrogen. Over years of daily biochemical studies, it has become clear that nitrogen metabolism is faulty in these catatonic patients. Nitrogen is a key element of all protein and all body tissue. It is absorbed from plant and animal protein and metabolized in the liver. In general, the body maintains a balance, excreting about as much as it takes in. During intervals between stupor attacks, the urine shows a retention of nitrogen, but the balance is shifted noticeably during attacks of illness. In patients with catatonic excitement, nitrogen was over-excreted during the normal interval and retained during the phase of excitement. Thus, urinary ammonia was higher at the beginning of an attack than at the end. The electrolytes, phosphate and sodium chloride, are excreted more during attacks.

Graphs of daily temperature or of urine pigmentation in individual patients taken over ten years show such regular changes that one could predict, to within a day, when an attack would fall in the coming year. The oscillation between normal behavior and illness has been found to correspond to major oscillation in many metabolic functions. The periodic catatonic swings between phases resembling certain aspects of patients with underactive or overactive thyroid glands. Thyroxin, a thyroid extract, has prevented nitrogen retention and has successfully ameliorated the symptoms in a number of patients. These people have lived normal lives for years. When they stop thyroid treatment, however, they relapse.

MANIC-DEPRESSION

During the late nineteenth and early twentieth centuries in Munich and Vienna, a number of doctors kept careful diaries of mood change in patients. These showed weight and behavior fluctuations over many years, sometimes revealing a manic-depressive trend unfolding over fifteen months or two years. The person who has manic-depressive symptoms today is fortunate if his mood changes swiftly, for he is likely to be diagnosed and studied. Dr. Curt Richter has written about the famous case of a man with forty-eight-hour manic-depression. A foremost salesman in the Washington, D.C., area, he would be so morose and apathetic during his depressed twenty-four hours that he would drive to a customer's office and find himself unable to move from the car, sitting miserably there for hours. Yet, on good days, he was the epitome of the aggressive, garrulous salesman. He finally adapted to his illness by accepting appointments only on alternate days.

Manic-depressives with long cycles are likely to go undetected and may do themselves harm, for in their manic phases they are prone to serious misjudgments and grandiose illusions. Such people seem to go through a transformation of character, from normal diffidence and activity to super-confidence and unbounded energy, often coupled with pretentious business plans and outrageous gambles. The ceaseless activity of a person in an elated phase involves an astonishing output of energy.

At present a number of forty-eight-hour manic-depressive patients are being studied at various hospitals around the world. Dr. F. A. Jenner in Sheffield, England, has been watching a former boxer from Yorkshire who became manic-depressive after a bad accident in the 1950s. For twenty-four hours he is overactive, talkative, sometimes testy, with grandiose ideas about science and the world; typically, at some time in his sleep he changes. He awakens feeling lethargic and bleak, rises reluctantly, later than usual, and falls asleep earlier that night. On his sluggish days he urinates and excretes more but eats and drinks less than on manic days.

For eleven years this man has lived in a clinic, eating a controlled diet and being measured and tested every day for physiological changes that might match behavior. He has taken performance tests; his urine and blood are repeatedly tested for a variety of hormones, sugars, and amino acids. When he stayed in bed on a liquid diet, he showed a forty-eight-hour alternation of weight, urine volume, and volume of red blood cells. It appears that the amount of fluid within and around cells was shifting with his moods. Fluid retention within and around nerve and other cells has been thought to be controlled by a balance of charged elements. The sodium and potassium content of this man's saliva and urine did coincide with his alternating moods. On depressed days, the saliva sodium was very low and saliva potassium was very high; on manic days it was exactly the opposite. The influence of electrolytes on behavior did not, however, seem very strong in the light of a subsequent experiment.

In 1963 Dr. Jenner took his patient into a hospital isolation room where a team of observers supplied meals and collected urine samples from both of them. The lighting was regulated so that the day was twenty-two hours long, but neither Jenner nor his patient knew the exact day length. The experiment lasted eleven real days in which they lived twelve cycles. Throughout this period, Dr. Jenner, living in the compartment, took notes on his patient while unseen observers outside made behavior and physiological notes on him and his patient. His patient, meanwhile, alternated between morose silence and an uncontrollable railing, scheming, and incessant shouting; when manic he yelled and thrashed about in an agitated manner that was almost too much for Dr. Jenner to endure. Curiously enough, the patient's moods adapted to a twenty-two-hour day; he alternated from lethargy to mania in a forty-four-hour cycle. Yet, excretion of water and electrolytes largely remained on a twenty-four-hour cycle, and did not explain the adaptation of his moods to a twenty-two-hour day.

Since the balance of electrolytes in the nervous system seems critical to the function of nerve cells, the effects of lithium, an alkali metal, have attracted great interest among psychiatrists. In 1967 Dr. Jenner gave his patient lithium salts, and for the long period when he was taking them, the man remained essentially normal. When he stopped taking the drug for a couple of weeks, the hints of his old alternation began to show through. One day he was articulate, even over-talkative, and responsive. The next day he was slow at finding words, less ebullient, and less volatile. His manic-depressive cycle had been obliterated by lithium, yet when he was given doses of sodium, the alternating mania and depression returned. Similar results have been seen with lithium use throughout the world. It is the one medication that seems to be effective in "normalizing" people with manic-depression and it also works with other cyclic psychoses. The mechanisms by which lithium effectively damps these mood cycles is not fully understood.

REFERENCES

Gjessing, L. R. Studies of periodic catatonia, II: The urinary excretion of phenolic amines and acids with and without loads of different drugs. *Journal of Psychiatric Research*, **2**(3): 149–162, 1964.

Gjessing, L. R. A review of the biochemistry of periodic catatonia. Excerpta Medica International Congress Series, No. 150, 1967.

Gjessing, R., and Gjessing, L. R. Some main trends in the clinical aspects of periodic catatonia. *Acta Psychiatrica Scandinavica*, **37**(1): 1–13, 1961.

Gjessing, L. R.; Jenner, F. A.; Harding, G. F. A.; and Johannessen, N. B. The EEG in three cases of periodic catatonia. *British Journal of Psychiatry*, **113**(504):1271–1282, 1967.

Jenner, F. A. Studies of recurrent and predictable behavior. *Proceedings: Leeds Symposium of Behavioral Disorders*, 1965.

Jenner, F. A. Periodic psychoses in the light of biological rhythm research. *International Review of Neurobiology*, 11:129–169, 1968.

Jenner, F. A.; Gjessing, L. R.; Cox, J. R.; Davies-Jones, A.; Hullin, R. P.; and Hanna, S. M. A manic-depressive psychotic with a persistent 48-hour cycle. *British Journal of Psychiatry*, **113**(501): 895–910, 1967.

Jenner, F. A.; Goodwin, J. C.; Sheridan, M.; Tauber, I. J.; and Lobban, M. C. The effect of an altered time regime on biological rhythms in a 48-hour periodic psychosis. *British Journal of Psychiatry,* **114**:213, 1968.

Richter, C. P. Biological approach to manic-depressive insanity. *Proceedings of the Association for Research in Nervous and Mental Disease,* **11**:611, 1930.

Richter, C. P. Abnormal but regular cycles in behavior and metabolism in rats and catatonic-schizophrenics. In: Reiss, M. (ed.), *Psychoendocrinology.* New York: Grune and Stratton, 1958, pp. 168–181.

Richter, C. P. Psychopathology of periodic behavior in animals and man. In: Zubin, J., and Hunt, H. F. (eds.) *Comparative Psychopathology.* New York: Grune and Stratton, 1967.

Genetic Studies of Schizophrenia
C. Peter Rosenbaum

In recent years, the popular belief that "insanity runs in the family" has received widespread critical examination from a variety of branches of psychology and psychiatry. Most investigators have come to recognize the importance of environmental variables in the etiology of abnormal behavior. Many theories, such as Bateson, Jackson, Haley and Weakland's (1956) analysis of communication patterns, have served to stimulate interest in the investigation of social-psychological variables in the development of abnormal behavior.

However, research into the genetic factors that might cause or contribute to madness remains important. Rosenbaum summarizes the methods and results of many different investigations into the inheritability of schizophrenia. Similar research is being pursued in the genetic studies of other kinds of mental illness as well as various personality characteristics such as IQ.

One of the major difficulties of such studies is separating environmental from genetically inherited variables. Currently one of the most fruitful investigations involves studying the incidence of abnormal behavior among adopted individuals. Rosenbaum presents this research and states the difficulties in formulating a genetic model that will explain the patterns of incidence revealed by researchers.

GENETIC STUDIES

Introduction

The question of the importance of genetic factors in the schizophrenias has, at its worst, given rise to acrimonious and naïve nature-nurture controversies. Some have attributed the schizophrenias solely to genetic factors, others solely to environmental factors. Both concepts are global and nonpredictive; they have given way to more sophisticated and thoughtful attempts to integrate evidence from several sources.

The major sources of data in deciding on genetic influences have been

From *The Meaning of Madness: Symptomatology, Sociology, Biology and Therapy of the Schizophrenias*, Science House, New York, 1970. Reprinted by permission.

studies of families of schizophrenic patients, with special interest focused on twins. Other sources have been sociological and psychologically oriented studies of families of schizophrenics. Each of these major areas is important in considering the birthright with which the patient starts life. Genetic makeup, intrauterine influences, and constitution at birth are one kind of birthright, a class of factors that have both genetic and environmental components. The socioeconomic condition of the family is another kind of birthright, and the modes of parental thinking, feeling, and relating are a third. Even at birth these congenital "givens" can interact with each other. For instance, suppose a newborn is a constitutionally active, wakeful, alert, wriggling creature, and his mother conceives of the model and well-mothered child as being passive, quiet, and sleeping long hours. Already there would exist the basis for a good deal of mother-child anxiety, tension, and conflict. Had the child been fortunate enough to have been born passive and quiet, in accord with its mother's preconceptions, or if the mother had been so organized psychologically that she could accept and respond positively to a wide range of neonatal behaviors, the early relationship would obviously have started off on a better footing. Such an example points to only one of the myriad possibilities of the interactions of the genetic, constitutional, social, and psychological forces operant at birth and shifting throughout life.

General Studies

The investigators whose family and twin data are most often cited are Rosanoff[14] and Rosenthal,[15-21] of the United States; Kallmann[8,9] of Germany and the United States; Shields and Slater[5,22] in England; and Luxenberger,[12] Böök,[2] and Essen-Möller,[4] of Scandinavia. Their data are summarized in Table 1.

The two major measures used are morbidity-risk rate and concordance rate, both expressed as percentages. An identified schizophrenic patient is called the "proband" or "index case." Relatives of the proband are rated for psychiatric condition, age, and (often left unreported) sex. Morbid risk expresses the probability that a given family member, not a twin, of the proband has or will become schizophrenic by the time he has passed through the age of risk, thought to be from the ages of 15 to 45 years, for the illness. Such computations include parameters of first admissions in the general population by age and sex, prevalence in the population, etc.

Concordance rates are used in the twin studies. The proband's co-twin is examined for the presence of schizophrenia; if it is found, the twins are said to be concordant; if it is not, they are said to be discordant; again, these figures are expressed as a percentage.

Table 1.   A summary of family and twin morbid risk and concordance rates in the schizophrenias.

Non-Twin Studies				
		Morbidity Risk Range, Average (in percentages)		
Proband (Index Case)	Relative	High	Low	Average
I. General Population				1
II. Both Parents	Child	68[b]	35[f]	
III. Mother	Child	17[e]	16[b]	
IV. Half-sibling	Child			7[d]
V. Full sib, same sex	Sibling	16[b]	4[c]	12
Twin Studies				
I. Dizygotic Twins	Co-twin	27[c]	10[c]	17
II. Monozygotic[a, b, c, d]	Co-twin	94[a]	0[g]	35[g]

[a]Gottesman, I. I., and Shields, J.[5]
[b]Kallmann, F. J.[9]
[c]Rosenthal, D.[18]
[d]Shields, J., and Slater, E.[22]
[e]Heston, L. L.[6]
[f]Rosenthal, D.[15]
[g]Kringlen, E.[11]

In Table 1, for instance, the morbidity risk rate for the child of two schizophrenic parents ranges from 35 to 68 percent, depending on the investigator. The concordance rates between pairs of male dizygotic (DZ) twins varies from 10 to 27 percent; those for male monozygotic (MZ) twins range from 0 to 78 percent.

The table shows that the more nearly the control case resembles the index case in genetic makeup, the higher the probability that he will become schizophrenic. The morbid-risk rate for a half-sibling is 7 percent; where the index case is a schizophrenic parent, a full sibling, or a dizygotic (DZ) twin, the probabilities range from 10 to 27 percent; for a pair of schizo-phrenic parents the probabilities range from 35 to 68 percent; for an MZ twin, concordances range from 0 to 94 percent. Meehl[13] has pointed out that the only way to win an even money bet predicting that a given, un-known person is schizophrenic is by finding that he has an identical twin who is schizophrenic. (To this he might have added, find that the unknown person's parents are both schizophrenic, depending on which study is being used.)

There are slight but consistently higher percentages whenever sibling or twin pairs are same-sexed instead of opposite-sexed, and whenever the index case is a female rather than a male.

The accuracy of these figures has been challenged by several authors on a number of grounds; a summary of the major criticisms follows: first are criticisms of case finding and diagnosis. Kallmann's sample is drawn largely from a chronically and severely ill state hospital population. In fact, when the concordance rate for MZ twins where the index case is judged to be only slightly or moderately ill (i.e., eliminating the "severely ill" group) is computed, it drops from 86 to 54 percent. Furthermore, because Kallmann's interest in finding twin pairs for studying was well known to his colleagues, the possibility that cases brought to his attention were unconsciously biased toward higher concordance rates must be considered.

Even in matters of diagnosis, a good deal of confusion exists. European and American uses of the concept of schizophrenia are different. Kallman, quoted in Rosenthal, puts forth these characteristics of his diagnostic criteria: "Constellative evaluation of basic personality changes, . . . bending curve of personality development, . . . xenophobic pananxiety, . . . loss of capacity for free associations, . . . compulsive tendency to omnipotential thought generalizations." Even though Kallman always employed independent judges to review his diagnoses, interjudge reliability was not studied, and it would seem that consistent application of such criteria to a patient population would be quite difficult. Even if such criteria were consistently applied, whether the group so diagnosed would reliably resemble what others consider to be schizophrenia is open to question.

Morbidity and concordance rates vary also, depending on the investigator and the sophistication of the statistical measures he uses.[19] Hence the figures derived from family and twin studies are at best rough approximations and cannot yet be used as firm data from which to construct and test hypotheses.

Even assuming the figures to be reasonably accurate, genetic, constitutional factors, and environmental heritages have not been adequately separated. Nearly all twins studied were raised together until early adolescence; the major substrates of personality development have already been determined by then, according to psychodynamic theory.

One of the lesser defects has been that the reliability of tests of monozygosity in differentiating MZ from DZ twin pairs has sometimes been found wanting.

Summary of Genetic Studies

The question, "Are the schizophrenias hereditary or environmental?" is a naïve and unanswerable question. Questions such as "How much do genetic, constitutional, social, and psychological factors contribute to the different kinds of schizophrenia?" are much more to the point, and these questions are only beginning to be answered.

There is considerable evidence to suggest that the closer in consanguinity to a schizophrenic patient a person is, the greater the likelihood he will develop schizophrenia. The likelihood is slightly increased if one is of the same sex as the index patient, or if the index patient is a female.

The reported probabilities vary widely and reflect artifacts in case finding, diagnostic criteria and reliability, choice of statistical tests, insufficient separation of genetic and social heritages, unreliability of tests of zygosity in twin studies, and other factors. Hence the reported figures must be taken as suggestive rather than established.

Children of schizophrenic mothers, raised away from the mother, show a morbid-risk rate of 16 percent, compared with a rate of about 1 percent for children of nonschizophrenic mothers, also raised apart. If children of schizophrenic mothers did not become schizophrenic, they showed a higher incidence of psychopathology and more interesting, varied, and creative lives than did the control-group subjects.

In two studies of MZ twins discordant for schizophrenia, investigators found that the premorbid adjustment of the afflicted twin, as compared with his co-twin, was poorer and marked by greater parental concern, slower development, greater docility, dependency, sensitivity, introversion, and inhibition. The incidence of schizophrenia in families of discordant MZ twins is lower than in the families of concordant MZ twins, a fact suggesting a greater genetic contribution in the latter.

Monogenic and polygenic hypotheses have been proposed to fit the observed data. Within these hypotheses, varying degrees of dominance, recessivity, penetrance, and manifestation have been invoked. Of the monogenic theories, models of simple dominance or recessivity with complete penetrance do not fit the data and can be discarded. More complex models also do not yield a good fit, and in their present form are not sufficient. Furthermore, monogenic theories demand a rate of genetic mutation that far exceeds the rate generally observed.

Polygenic theories, some of which posit benign modifying genes that protect against the appearance of schizophrenia in carriers, have also been advanced. Supporting data for these theories is still equivocal at best.

In summary, Shields and Slater say:

> On this basis [genetic studies], some 70 percent of all persons carrying an adequate genetical predisposition to schizophrenia would not fall ill, leaving therefore a considerable margin for the operation of environmental factors.[22]

Rosenthal says:

> If we keep in mind that what is called schizophrenia is probably not a unitary disease, biologically speaking, that sampling procedures must

be exceptionally rigorous, that criteria of diagnosis must be specified in reliable detail, that rating and testing procedures should be liberally employed, that future research should be hypothesis-oriented and that both hereditary and environmental factors are probably contributing in varying degree to different types of the disorder, we may only now be on the threshold of discovery with respect to the basic issues surrounding the origin and transmission of schizophrenic behavior.[19]

REFERENCES

1. Baldessarini, R. J., and Snyder, S. H. A critique of recent genetic-biochemical formulations. *Nature,* 1965, **206,** 1111-1112.

2. Böök, J. A. A genetic and neuropsychiatric investigation of a North Swedish population, with special regard to schizophrenia and mental deficiency. *Acta Genetica et Statistica Medica,* 1953, **4,** 1–100.

3. Erlenmeyer-Kimling, L., and Paradowski, W. Selection and schizophrenia. *American Naturalist,* 1966, **100,** 651–665.

4. Essen-Möller, E. Psychiatrische Untersuchungen an einer Serie von Zwillingen, *Acta Psychiatrica et Neurologica* (Suppl.) 1941, **23,** 1–30.

5. Gottesman, I. I., and Shields, J. Schizophrenia in twins: 16 years' consecutive admissions to a psychiatric clinic. *British Journal of Psychiatry,* 1966, **112,** 809–818.

6. Heston, L. L. Psychiatric disorders in foster home reared children of schizophrenic mothers. *British Journal of Psychiatry,* 1966, **112,** 819–825.

7. Huxley, J.; Mayr, E.; Osmond, H.; and Hoffer, A. Schizophrenia as a genetic morphism. *Nature,* 1964, **204,** 220–221.

8. Kallmann, F. J. *Heredity in health and mental disorders.* New York: W. W. Norton & Company, Inc., 1953.

9. ———. The genetic theory of schizophrenia: an analysis of 691 schizophrenic twin index families. *American Journal of Psychiatry,* 1964, **103,** 309–322.

10. Karlsson, J. L. *The biologic basis of schizophrenia.* Springfield, Ill.: Charles C Thomas, Publisher, 1966.

11. Kringlen, Einar. *Schizophrenia in male monozygotic twins.* Oslo, Norway: Universitetsforlaget, 1964.

12. Luxenberger, H. Some factors associated with concordance and discordance with respect to schizophrenia in monozygotic twins. Cited by David Rosenthal, Problems of sampling and diagnosis in the major twin studies of schizophrenia. *Journal of Psychiatric Research,* 1961, **1,** 116–134.

13. Meehl, P. Schizotaxia, schizotypy, schizophrenia. *American Psychologist,* 1962, **17,** 827–838.

14. Rosanoff, A. J.; Handy, L. M.; Plesset, I. R.; and Brush, S. The etiology of so-called schizophrenic psychoses. *American Journal of Psychiatry*, 1934, **91**, 247–286.

15. Rosenthal, David. Some factors associated with concordance and discordance with respect to schizophrenia in monozygotic twins. *Journal of Nervous and Mental Disease*, 1959, **129**, 1–10.

16. _____. Confusion of identity and frequency of schizophrenia in twins. *Archives of General Psychiatry*, 1960, **3**, 297–304.

17. _____. Sex distribution and the severity of illness among samples of schizophrenic twins. *Journal of Psychiatric Research*, 1961, **1**, 26–36.

18. _____. Familial concordance by sex with respect to schizophrenia. *Psychological Bulletin*, 1962, **59**, 401–421.

19. _____. Problems of sampling and diagnosis in the major twin studies of schizophrenia. *Journal of Psychiatric Research*, 1962, **1**, 116–134.

20. _____. *The Genain quadruplets.* New York: Basic Books, Inc., 1963, p. 609.

21. _____. The offspring of schizophrenic couples. *Journal of Psychiatric Research*, 1966, **4**, 169–188.

22. Shields, J., and Slater, E. Heredity and psychological abnormality. In H. J. Eysenck (ed.), *Handbook of abnormal psychology.* New York: Basic Books, Inc., 1961, pp. 298–343.

Mental Effects of Reduction
of Ordinary Levels of
Physical Stimuli on
Intact, Healthy Persons
John Lilly

A distinct advantage in using laboratory procedures over clinical or field studies is that, by controlling a number of variables simultaneously, the experimenter can focus on those factors which he feels are affecting the variable studied. The advantages in field work are that conditions that cannot be duplicated in the laboratory can be found, and procedures too difficult or dangerous for controlled work can be observed.

Using a combination of both procedures, John Lilly has effectively studied experiences analogous to psychosis evoked by extreme sensory deprivation. His research allows systematic observation of possible mechanisms that affect perceptual and psychological experience. Information derived from personal accounts can be simulated and studied in a controlled setting using laboratory techniques.

Lilly's work demonstrates that normal individuals do manifest acute psychotic symptoms in certain controlled environments.

INTRODUCTION

We have been seeking answers to the question of what happens to a brain and its contained mind in the relative absence of physical stimulation. In neurophysiology, this is one form of the question: Freed of normal efferent and afferent activities, does the activity of the brain soon become that of coma or sleep, or is there some inherent mechanism which keeps it going, a pacemaker of the "awake" type of activity? In psychoanalysis, there is a similar, but not identical problem. If the healthy ego is freed of reality stimuli, does it maintain the secondary process, or does primary process take over? *i.e.*, Is the healthy ego independent of reality or dependent in some fashion, in some degree, on exchanges with the surroundings to maintain its structure?

From *Psychiatric Research Reports*, Number 5, 1956, 1–9. Copyright 1956 by the American Psychiatric Association. Reprinted by permission.

In seeking answers, we have found pertinent autobiographical literature and reports of experiments by others, and have done experiments ourselves. The experiments are psychological ones on human subjects. Many psychological experiments in isolation have been done on animals, but are not recounted in detail here; parenthetically, the effect on very young animals can be an almost completely irreversible lack of development of whole systems, such as those necessary for the use of vision in accomplishing tasks put to the animal. No truly neurophysiological isolation experiments on either animals or man have yet been done.

AUTOBIOGRAPHICAL ACCOUNTS

The published autobiographical material has several drawbacks: In no case is there a sizeable reduction of all possibilities of stimulation and action; in most cases, other factors add complications to the phenomena observed. We have collected 18 autobiographical cases from the polar and sea-faring literature (see References) which are more frank and revealing than most. We have interviewed two persons who have not published any of their material. In this account, we proceed from rather complicated situations to the more simple ones, *i.e.*, from a maximum number of factors to the most simple experimental situation.

From this literature we have found that isolation *per se* acts on most persons as a powerful stress. The effects observed are similar to those of any extreme stress, and other stressful factors add their effects to those of isolation to cause mental symptoms to appear more rapidly and more intensely. As is well known, stresses other than isolation can cause the same symptoms to appear in individuals in an isolated group.

Taking our last point first, we have the account by Walter Gibson given in his book, "The Boat." This is the case in which four persons out of an initial 135 survived in a lifeboat in the Indian Ocean in World War II. Gibson gives a vivid account of his experiences, and the symptoms resulting from loss of hope, dehydration, thirst, intense sunburn, and physical combat. Most of the group hallucinated rescue planes and drank salt water thinking it fresh; many despaired and committed suicide; others were murdered; and some were eaten by others. The whole structure of egos was shaken and recast in desperate efforts at survival. (It is interesting to note that many of those who committed suicide tried to sink the boat by removing the drain plugs before jumping overboard, *i.e.*, sink the boat [and other persons] as well as the self; this dual destruction may be used by some of the non-surviving solitary sailors; see below.)

I cite this case because it gives a clue as to what to expect in those who do survive isolation in other conditions: Gibson survived—how? He says: (1) by previous out-of-doors training in the tropical sun for some years; (2) by having previously learned to be able to become completely passive (physically and mentally); (3) by having and maintaining the conviction that he would come through the experience; and, we add, (4) by having a woman, Doris Lim, beside him, who shared his passivity and convictions. In all cases of survivors of isolation, at sea or in the polar night, it was the first exposure which caused the greatest fears and hence the greatest danger of giving way to symptoms; previous experience is a powerful aid in going ahead, despite the symptoms. Physical passivity is necessary during starvation, but, in some people, may be contra-indicated in social isolation in the absence of starvation. In all survivors, we run across the inner conviction that he or she will survive, or else there are definite reassurances from others that each will be rescued. In those cases of a man and a woman together, or even the probability of such a union within a few days, there is apparently not only a real assurance of survival, but a love of the situation can appear. (Such love can develop in a solitaire; see below.) Of course, such couples are the complete psychological antithesis of our major thesis of complete isolation; many symptoms can be avoided by healthy persons with such an arrangement.

Solitary sailors are in a more complex situation than the group of polar isolates. The sailing of a small boat across oceans requires a good deal of physical exertion, and the situation may be contaminated by a lack of sleep which can also cause symptoms. The solitary sailors, of which Joshua Slocum and Alain Bombard are outstanding examples, relate that the first days out of port are the dangerous ones; awe, humility, and fear in the face of the sea are most acute at this time. Bombard states that if the terror of the first week can be overcome, one can survive. Apparently, many do not survive this first period. Many single-handed boats have not arrived at their transoceanic destination. We have clues as to the causes from what sometimes happens with two persons on such crossings. There are several pairs of ocean-crossing sailors in which one of the couple became so terror-stricken, paranoid, and bent on murder and/or suicide, that he had to be tied to his bunk.

Once this first period is past, other symptoms develop, either from isolation itself or from isolation plus other stresses. In the South Atlantic, Joshua Slocum had a severe gastro-intestinal upset just before a gale hit his boat; he had reefed his sails, but should have taken them down. Under the circumstances, he was unable to move from the cabin. At this point he saw a man take over the tiller. At first he thought it was a pirate, but the man reassured him and said that he was the pilot of the Pinta and that he would take his boat safely through the storm. Slocum asked him to take down sail, but the man said, no, they must catch the Pinta ahead. The next morning Slocum recovered, and found his boat had covered 93 miles on true course, sailing itself. (His boat was quite capable of such a performance; he arranged it that way for long trips without his hand at the helm.) In a dream that night the pilot appeared and said he would come whenever Slocum needed him. During the next three years the helmsman appeared to Slocum several times, during gales.

This type of hallucination-delusion seems to be characteristic of the strong egos who survive: a "savior" type of hallucination rather than a "destroyer" type. Their inner conviction of survival is projected thoroughly.

Other symptoms that appear are: superstitiousness (Slocum thought a dangerous reef named M Reef was lucky because M is the 13th letter of the alphabet and 13 was his lucky number. He passed the reef without hitting it. Bombard thought the number of matches necessary to light a damp cigarette represented the number of days until the end of the voyage. He was wrong several times.); intense love of any living things (Slocum was revolted at the thought of killing food-animals, especially a goat given to him at one port. Ellam and Mudie became quite upset after catching and eating a fish that had followed the boat all day, and swore off further fish-eating.); conversations with inanimate objects (Bombard had bilateral conversations with a doll mascot.); and a feeling that when one lands, one had best be careful to listen before speaking to avoid being considered insane (Bernicot refused an invitation to dinner on another yacht after crossing the Atlantic alone, until he could recapture the proper things to talk about.). The inner life becomes so vivid and intense that it takes time to readjust to the life among other persons and to reestablish one's inner criteria of sanity (When placed with fellow prisoners, after 18 months in solitary confinement, Christopher Burney was afraid to speak for fear that he would show himself to be insane. After several days of listening he recaptured the usual criteria of sanity, and then could allow himself to speak.).

Life alone in the polar night, snowed-in, with the confining surroundings of a small hut is a more simple situation. However, there are other complicating factors: extreme cold, possibilities of carbon monoxide poisoning, collapse of the roof, etc. Richard Byrd, in his book "Alone," recounts in great detail his changes in mental functioning, and talks of a long period of CO poisoning resulting in a state close to catatonia. I refer you to his book for details. He experienced, as did Slocum and many others, an oceanic feeling, the being "of the universe," at one with it.

Christiane Ritter ("A Woman in the Polar Night") was exposed to isolation for periods up to 16 days at a time. She saw a monster, hallucinated her past as if in bright sunshine, became "at one" with the moon, and developed a monomania to go out over the snow. She was saved by an experienced Norwegian who put her to bed and fed her lavishly. She developed a love for the situation and found great difficulty in leaving Spitzbergen. For a thorough and sensitive account of symptoms, I recommend her book to you.

From these examples and several more (see References), we conclude the following:

(1) Published autobiographies are of necessity incomplete. Social taboos, discretion to one's self, suppression and repression of painful or uncomfortable material, secondary elaboration, and rationalization severely limit the scope of the material available. (Interviews with two men, each of whom lived alone in the polar night, confirm this impression.)

(2) Despite these limitations, we find that persons in isolation experience many, if not all, of the symptoms of the mentally ill.

(3) In those who survive, the symptoms can be reversible. How easily reversible, we do not know. Most survivors report, after several weeks' exposure to isolation, a new inner security and a new integration of themselves on a deep and basic level.

(4) The underlying mechanisms are obscure. It is obvious that inner factors in the mind tend to be projected outward, that some of the mind's activity which is usually reality-bound now becomes free to turn to fantasy and ultimately to hallucination and delusion. It is as if the laws of thought are projected into the realm of the laws of inanimate matter and of the universe. The primary process tends to absorb more and more of the time and energy usually taken by the secondary process. Such experiences either lead to improved mental functioning or to destruction. Why one person takes the healthy path and another person the sick one is not yet clear.

Experiments to clarify the necessary conditions for some of these effects have been done. One of the advantages of the experimental material is that simpler conditions can be set up and tested, and some of the additional stresses of natural life situations can be eliminated.

EXPERIMENTAL ISOLATION

The longest exposure to isolation on the largest number of subjects has been carried out in Dr. Donald Hebb's Department of Psychology at McGill University by a group of graduate students. We started a similar project independently with different techniques at the National Institute of Mental Health. In the Canadian experiments, the aim is to reduce the patterning of stimuli to the lowest level; in ours, the objective is to reduce the absolute intensity of all physical stimuli to the lowest possible level.

In the McGill experiments, a subject is placed on a bed in an air-conditioned box with arms and hands restrained with cardboard sleeves, and eyes covered completely with translucent ski goggles. The subjects are college students motivated by payment of $20 per day for as long as they will stay in the box. An observer is present, watching through a window, and tests the subject in various ways verbally through a communication set.

In our experiments, the subject is suspended with the body and all but the top of the head immersed in a tank containing slowly flowing water at 34.5°C (94.5°F), wears a blacked-out mask (enclosing the whole head) for breathing, and wears nothing else. The water temperature is such that the subject feels neither hot nor cold. The experience is such that one tactually feels the supports and the mask, but not much else; a large fraction of the usual pressures on the body caused by gravity are lacking. The sound level is low; one hears only one's own breathing and some faint water sounds from the piping; the water-air interface does not transmit air-borne sounds very efficiently. It is one of the most even and monotonous environments I have experienced. After the initial training period, no observer is present. Immediately after exposure, the subject writes personal notes on his experience.

At McGill, the subjects varied considerably in the details of their experiences. However, a few general phenomena appeared. After several hours, each subject found that it was difficult to carry on organized, directed thinking for any sustained period. Suggestibility was very much increased. An extreme desire for stimuli and action developed. There were periods of thrashing around in the box in attempts to satisfy this need. The borderline between sleep and awakedness became diffuse and confused. At some time between 24 and 72 hours most subjects couldn't stand it any longer and left. Hallucinations and delusions of various sorts developed, mostly in those who could stay longer than two days.

The development of hallucinations in the visual sphere followed the stages seen with mescaline intoxication. When full-blown, the visual phenomena were complete projections maintaining the three dimensions of space in relation to the rest of the body and could be scanned by eye and head movements. The contents were surprising to the ego, and consisted of material like that of dreams, connected stories sharing past memories and recent real events. The subjects' reactions to these phenomena were generally amusement and a sense of relief from the pressing boredom. They could describe them vocally without abolishing the sequences. A small number of subjects experienced doubling of their body images. A few developed transient paranoid delusions, and one had a seizure-like episode after five days in the box with no positive EEG findings for epilepsy.

Our experiments have been more limited both in numbers of subjects and duration of exposures. There have been two subjects, and the longest exposure has been three hours. We have much preliminary data, and have gained enough experience to begin to guess at some of the mechanisms involved in the symptoms produced.

In these experiments, the subject always has a full night's rest before entering the tank. Instructions are to inhibit all movements as far as possible. An initial set of training exposures overcomes the fears of the situation itself.

In the tank, the following stages have been experienced:

(1) For about the first three-quarters of an hour, the day's residues are predominant. One is aware of the surroundings, recent problems, etc.

(2) Gradually, one begins to relax and more or less enjoy the experience. The feeling of being isolated in space and having nothing to do is restful and relaxing at this stage.

(3) But slowly, during the next hour, a tension develops which can be called a "stimulus-action" hunger; hidden methods of self-stimulation develop: twitching muscles, slow swimming movements (which cause sensations as the water flows by the skin), stroking one finger with another, etc. If one can inhibit such maneuvers long enough, intense satisfaction is derived from later self-stimulations.

(4) If inhibition can win out, the tension may ultimately develop to the point of forcing the subject to leave the tank.

(5) Meanwhile, the attention is drawn powerfully to any residual stimulus: the mask, the suspension, each come in for their share of concentration. Such residual stimuli become the whole content of consciousness to an almost unbearable degree.

(6) If this stage is passed without leaving the tank, one notices that one's thoughts have shifted from a directed type of thinking about problems to reveries and fantasies of a highly personal and emotionally charged nature. These are too personal to relate publicly, and probably vary greatly from subject to subject. The individual reactions to such fantasy material also probably vary considerably, from complete suppression to relaxing and enjoying them.

(7) If the tension and the fantasies are withstood, one may experience the furthest stage which we have yet explored: projection of visual imagery. I have seen this once, after a two and one-half hour period. The black curtain in front of the eyes (such as one "sees" in a dark room with eyes closed) gradually opens out into a three-dimensional, dark, empty space in front of the body. This phenomenon captures one's interest immediately, and one waits to find out what comes next. Gradually forms of the type sometimes seen in hypnogogic states appear. In this case, they were small, strangely shaped objects with self-luminous borders. A tunnel whose inside "space" seemed to be emitting a blue light then appeared straight ahead. About this time, this experiment was terminated by a leakage of water into the mask through a faulty connector on the inspiratory tube.

It turns out that exposures to such conditions train one to be more tolerant of many internal activities. Fear lessens with experience, and personal integration can be speeded up. But, of course, there are pitfalls here to be avoided. The opposite effects may also be accelerated in certain cases. Fantasies about the experience (such as the illusion of "return to the womb," which is quite common) are dispelled; one realizes that at birth we start breathing air and hence cannot "return to the womb." One's breathing in the tank is extremely important: as a comforting, constant safeguard and a source of rhythmic stimulation.

In both the McGill experiments and in ours, certain aftereffects are noted: The McGill subjects had difficulty in orienting their perceptual mechanisms; various illusions persisted for several hours. In our experiments, we notice that after emersion the day apparently is started over. *i.e.,* The subject feels as if he has just arisen from bed afresh; this effect persists, and the subject finds he is out of step with the clock for the rest of that day. He also has to re-adjust to social intercourse in subtle ways. The night of the day of the exposure he finds that his bed exerts great pressure against his body. No bed is as comfortable as floating in water.

Experiments such as these demonstrate results similar to that given above for solitary polar living and sailing alone. If one is alone, long enough, and at levels of physical and human stimulation low enough, the mind turns inward and projects outward its own contents and processes; the brain not only stays active despite the lowered levels of input and output, but accumulates surplus energy to extreme degrees. In terms of libido theory, the total *amount* of libido increases with time of deprivation; body-libido reaches new high levels. If body-libido is not discharged somatically, discharge starts through fantasy; but apparently this is neither an adequate mode nor can it achieve an adequate rate of discharge in the presence of the rapidly rising level. At some point a new threshold appears for more definite phenomena of regression: hallucinations, delusions, oceanic bliss, etc. At this stage, given any opportunities for action or stimulation by external reality, the healthy ego seizes them and re-establishes more secondary process. Lacking such opportunities for a long enough interval of time, re-organization takes place, how reversibly and how permanently we do not yet know.

Apparently even healthy minds act this way in isolation. What this means to psychiatric research is obvious: We have yet to obtain a full, documented picture of the range available to the healthy human adult mind; some of the etiological factors in mental illness may be clarified and sharpened by such research. Of course, this is a limited region of investigation. We have not gone into details about loss of sleep, starvation, and other factors which have great power in changing healthy minds to sick ones.

I think that you can see the parallels between these results and phenomena found in normal children and in psychotics. And, if we could give you a more detailed account, possible explanations of the role of isolation factors in involuntary indoctrination and its opposite, psychotherapy, would be more evident.

REFERENCES

1. Small, Maurice H. April, 1900. On some psychical relations of society and solitude. Pedagogical Seminary, **VII**, No. 2.

Solitary Sailors

2. Slocum, Captain Joshua. 1948. Sailing Alone Around the World. Rupert Hart-Davis, London.
3. Ellam, Patrick and Colin Mudie. 1953. Sopranino. W. W. Norton and Co., Inc., N.Y.
4. Bombard, Dr. Alain. 1953. The Voyage of the Hérétique. Simon and Schuster, N.Y.
5. Merrien, Jean. 1954. Lonely Voyagers. G. P. Putnam's Sons, N.Y.
6. Merrien, Jean. 1954. Les Navigateurs Solitaires. Editiones Denoël.
7. Bernicot, Louis. 1953. The Voyage of Anahita—Single-Handed Round the World. Rupert Hart-Davis, Soho Square, London.

Drastic Degrees of Stress

8. Gibson, Walter. 1953. The Boat. Houghton Mifflin Company (The Riverside Press), Boston, Mass.

Living in the Polar Night

9. Scott, J. M. 1953. Portrait of an Ice Cap with Human Figures. Chatto and Windus, London.
10. Courtauld, A. July, 1932. Living alone under polar conditions. The Polar Record, No. 4. University Press, Cambridge.
11. Byrd, Richard E. 1938. Alone. G. P. Putnam's Sons, N.Y.
12. Ritter, Christiane. 1954. A Woman in the Polar Night. E. P. Dutton and Co., Inc., N.Y.

Forced Isolation and Confinement

13. Burney, Christopher. 1952. Solitary Confinement. Coward-McCann, Inc., N.Y.
14. Stypulkowski, Z. 1951. Invitation to Moscow. Thames and Hudson, London.

The Deaf and the Blind

15. Collingswood, Herbert W. 1923. Adventures in Silence. The Rural New Yorker, N.Y.
16. Ormond, Arthur W., C.B.E., F.R.C.S. 1925. Visual hallucinations in sane people. British Med. J., **Vol. 2.**
17. Bartlet, J. E. A. 1951. A case of organized visual hallucinations in an old man with cataract, and their relation to the phenomena of the phantom limb. Brain, **Vol. 74,** Part III, pp. 363–373.

Experimental Isolation

18. Heron, W., W. H. Bexton, and D. O. Hebb. August, 1953. Cognitive effects of a decreased variation to the sensory environment. The Amer. Psychol., **Vol. 8,** No. 8, p. 366.

Hypnotic Alterations of Space and Time: Their Relationship to Psychopathology
Bernard S. Aaronson

Bernard Aaronson explores the effects of altering fundamental perceptual constancies. The methods described here open another intriguing way of studying unusual mental states. By changing the way an individual organizes his world, Aaronson is able to evoke bizarre behaviors and schizophrenic-like feelings in normal persons. His work suggests that changes in perception (altering the way that time or form or space is viewed) can cause psychotic-like, euphoric, or other changes in consciousness.

The arresting aspect of this research is that massive changes in apparent personality organization can be brought about by a few words spoken by a hypnotist. It appears that behaviors that resemble various kinds of mental illness can be induced by a suggestion such as: "When you open your eyes the dimension of depth will be gone. There will be no depth." These findings lend support to the theory that much of what we call natural response is, in fact, a combination of suggestion and conditioning. Behaviorists like B. F. Skinner and esoteric psychologists like Idries Shaw and George Gurdijeff have come to similar conclusions. When their theoretical positions are applied to this research, they lead to the conclusion that perception itself may not be innate, but learned and therefore modifiable.

Aaronson reminds us that "abnormal" is a relative term meaning different or unusual; his research may allow us to decide which forms of abnormal functioning are debilitating and which are advantageous.

Carney Landis[20] quotes a psychiatric patient writing of his madness as saying, "The ideas of space and time, which are the fundamental conditions of all thought in rational minds, become confused, or wholly lost." There

This article has been specially edited for this volume. It is a partial summary of two articles: "Hypnosis, Time Rate Perception, and Psychopathology," presented to the Eastern Psychological Association, 1966, and "Hypnotic Alterations of Space and Time," from the *International Journal of Parapsychology*, 1968, **X**, pp. 5–36. Excerpts reprinted by permission.

may be other avenues into psychosis than just the disordering of the concepts of space and time, but certainly disordering of such major existential variables should be at least accompanied by psychopathology.

Previous studies carried out in my laboratory have suggested that hypnotic removal of depth perception is accompanied by schizophreniform behavior, while expansion of depth seems to produce a psychedelic experience.[1,4] Hypnotic alteration of the perception of future, present, and past also seems to produce marked changes in behavior, including a response indistinguishable from catatonia when suggestions are given that the present is gone or that the past and future are both gone simultaneously.[3]

Fogel and Hoffer,[14] studying the effect on personality of varying time rates hypnotically, observed that when time was speeded up with a metronome, their subject became manic and even maniacal. When time was slowed, their subject seemed to become depressed. When time was stopped, their subject froze in mid-gesture, in a manner suggesting catatonia.

A previous partially successful attempt to replicate the observations of Fogel and Hoffer in my laboratory has been reported.[2] In these studies with a single subject, when the metronome was speeded up, the subject showed manic behavior. When the metronome was slowed down, the subject showed bored withdrawal. When the metronome was stopped, the subject continued to hallucinate the beating of the metronome, but showed no other change in behavior.

Speeding time by verbal suggestion without a metronome again produced manic behavior. Slowing time produced a sense of fatigue and mild depression. Stopping time yielded a severe schizoaffective kind of response with marked depression, feelings of unreality, withdrawal, some paranoid mentation and some spatial distortion. The results of verbal suggestions were not identical with those from manipulating the metronome, although they were in the same direction.

SUBJECTS AND DESIGN

Subjects

Our sample comprised six subjects. All the subjects were male college students ages 20–27.

Hypnosis

Of the six subjects, only five were hypnotized. S-2 was a simulator, chosen for this role after extensive attempts to hypnotize him had failed to produce anything deeper than a light trance. The hypnotic subjects were trained to attain a state of deep somnambulism and to carry out posthypnotic instructions involving complex positive and negative hallucinations in all the major sensory modalities. The hypnotic training period ranged from 1½ to 11 months. Subsequently, each subject was exposed to as many experimental conditions as possible.

Tests, Interviews, and Records

Each subject first completed a Q-sort based on Plutchik's theory of emotions.[23] Next the subject took a battery of perceptual tests appropriate to the particular experimental condition of space or time. Then he was hypnotized and given a posthypnotic instruction pertaining to the experimental condition. The resultant behavior was allowed to develop over a period of two hours, during which the subject was questioned by the experimenter. One of the subjects, who had some experience as a painter, was asked to paint a picture of the view of the experimental room about 1½ hours after the instruction had been imposed. After completion of this initial interview, each subject was taken for a car ride over a standard course. Finally, he wrote an account of what his day had been like.

Once this set of tasks had been completed, the subject was questioned by an outside observer. The latter was a trained clinician who knew that the subject had been hypnotized, but did not know what, if any, posthypnotic instruction the subject had been given. After this second interview, the subject took the Minnesota Multiphasic Personality Inventory (MMPI), retook the Q-sort and the perceptual battery, and was again questioned by the experimenter. After completion of this third interview, the experimenter removed the posthypnotic instruction and asked the subject to describe what his day had been like.

The simulator, S-2, was required to keep a secret diary in which he recorded how he had gone about handling each instruction and how it had affected him.

Controls

Control conditions, in which the subject was hypnotized but not given any posthypnotic instructions concerning perceptual or conceptual changes, were run in conjunction with both series (space and time category). These control conditions also made it possible to assess a subject's behavior successively under similar conditions, so that the effects these experiments had on a subject could be evaluated.

PROCEDURE

Space Studies

Experimental Conditions.   The perceptual changes investigated in the space studies concerned the categories of depth and distance. The subjects were exposed to the following experimental conditions:

1. Depth
   (a) increased } controls
   (b) absent

2. Distance
   (a) increased } controls
   (b) decreased

Posthypnotic Instructions.   The posthypnotic instructions concerning altered perception of space were as follows:

No depth: "When I wake you up, the dimension of depth will be gone. There will be no depth."

Increased depth: "The dimension of depth will be expanded. Have you ever looked through a stereoscope? (The subjects had been given experience with the stereoscope earlier, without being told that this experience was to be applied to the subsequent studies.) Do you know how depth looks there? That's how the world will look to you."

Increased distance: "Everything you look at will be twice as far away as usual."

Decreased distance: "Everything you look at will be half as far away as usual."

Time-Category Studies

Experimental Conditions.   In the studies of time categories, the investigations involved the major categories of past, present, and future. First the categories were removed or expanded by posthypnotic instruction one at a time. Then they were removed or expanded in combination:

1. Past
   (a) removed   } control
   (b) expanded

2. Present
   (a) removed   } control
   (b) expanded

3. Future
   (a) removed   } control
   (b) expanded

Posthypnotic Instructions.   Concerning past, present, and future, the subjects' posthypnotic instructions were as follows:

Removed time: "Do you know how we divide time into the three categories of past, present and future? When I wake you, the _____ (name, or names of category) will be gone. There will be no _____ (name, or names of category).

Expanded time: "Do you know how we divide time into three categories of past, present, and future? When I wake you, the _____ (name, or names of category) will be expanded. The _____ (name, or names of category) will be expanded."

RESULTS

The results of these studies are not presented in the order in which the individual experimental conditions in each series were imposed on the subjects. A separate and different order of posthypnotic instruction was followed for each subject. The order of presentation was adopted for purely didactic reasons.

Spatial Studies

Five subjects were exposed to the conditions of depth and control (S-6, S-1, S-2, S-5, S-4). Only two subjects were exposed to the conditions of distance (S-5 and S-4).

No Depth.   When depth was removed, S-6 displayed a catatonic-like reaction. He engaged in many of the behaviors described by Clifford Beers in *A Mind That Found Itself.*[9] He showed disturbances of gait, posture, and movement, and during the ride, each hill seemed to him a cliff into which we would crash. He was also afraid to be left alone, and his affect was flattened.

S-1 also reacted with dysphoria and schizoid withdrawal. He felt that the people around him were inhuman robots and talking and plotting against him. He felt as if trapped inside a film, and everything around him was gray and dreary. He showed sensory disturbance and mild gait disturbance, which he was able to control.

The simulator (S-2) became captured by the instruction as he acted it out. He became withdrawn, irritable, and schizoid, and displayed some paranoid hostility when others infringed on him.

S-5 reacted with marked primitivization of behavior. He displayed shallow, inappropriate humor and could not conceive what lay over the brow of a hill or around a corner. He crossed himself repeatedly, although nothing in his background suggested this type of religious symbolism. His affect seemed shallow and blunted, his sense impressions seemed dulled, and his behavior was not unlike that of a chronic schizophrenic.

S-4 reacted with marked withdrawal and sleepiness. He felt that things had slowed down and that objects were closing in on him. Periodically, he developed strong paranoid feelings, especially about the experimenter. As the day progressed, the initial effects seemed to fade, though he remained sleepy and rather uncommunicative. After the experience, he reported that the relationship with the experimenter and with his wife (an assistant in the laboratory) had sustained him and helped him to overcome what, in the hypnotized state, he had perceived as a mysterious perceptual malady

Comment.   Exposed to absence of depth, all five subjects showed dysphoria and moved in a schizoid direction, but one subject was able to overcome the effects by using personal ties with members of the experimental staff. Gait disturbances were elicited in all subjects but the simulator. Dulling of sensation was reported by only three subjects, but all the hypnotized subjects reported perceptual disturbances. Delusional thinking of a paranoid sort was noted in four subjects. A feeling of being hemmed in was expressed by all five, but only two reported that the walls and the ceiling seemed to be closing in. These data support the contention that some correlation exists between loss of depth perception and schizophrenia, but they also suggest that interpersonal relationships may be used to provide enough emotional security to overcome the perceptual changes.

Increased Depth.   When depth was increased, S-6 was transported into an experience of great beauty: Sounds, colors, and contours all were enhanced; space seemed almost solid; each object and its placement seemed part of a Divine order. S-6 felt he could do no less than spend his life serving God.

S-1 felt that space transcended all boundaries and limitations. Like S-6, he reported sensory enhancement. He described the world as "at once a gigantic formal garden and an irrepressible wilderness of joyous space." He, too, felt lifted up in the world, although in him the religious overtones were not as vivid as in S-6.

The simulator concluded that our usual perception of depth is an illusion and, becoming engrossed with the tridimensionality of space, he became more spontaneous in the process.

S-5 also reported great expansion of visual and auditory perception, as well as a sense that anything that involved a repeated figure might go on forever. He felt greatly involved with the world, and became totally immersed in exploring his inner world as a result of listening to a record, "Music for Zen Meditation and Other Joys" (Scott, Yuize, and Yamamoto: Verve). His reaction to the condition is best summed up by the way in which he titled his postsession account: "And then there was Depth!"

S-4, because he was not given experience with a stereoscope during his training, could not conceive of expanded depth and hence was unable to respond to the instruction at first try. But when he was given the stereoscopic experience prior to the second attempt, he reacted with pleasurably enhanced perception of colors and shapes in the world. The only one of the subjects to have had experience with a psychedelic substance (marijuana), he described the experience as being similar to "pot high."

   Comment.   Exposed to increased depth, all five of the subjects responded with an expanded awareness of the world, similar to the experiences described by Huxley in *The Doors of Perception*.[16] They felt exuberantly happy, and all but the simulator went into a sort of psychedelic experience with mystical overtones. The initial failure of the instruction in S-4, because he could not conceive of increased depth, suggests how important it is to use imagination in devising experimental conditions of altered perception. Stolidity may be a protection against perceptual change which keeps the individual from the dangers of schizophrenia and the high adventure of mystic experience.

   Decreased Distance.   The response of S-5 was indistinguishable from a florid paranoid schizophrenia. Initially afraid that he would be set upon and injured, he hid all sharp and pointed objects from the experimenter. He accused the people around of stealing his air and engaged in other bizarre behaviors. Reassured that no one meant him any harm, he became grandiose and set the experimenter to cleaning the experimental room. Then he himself was about to start tidying up the laboratory, from which he meant to go on to the whole world.

   S-4 felt himself suddenly confronted by the world in which the walls were closing in on him and in which nothing seemed real. He retired to his bed and, when not asleep, spent the rest of the time intellectualizing about the world. No major personality changes occurred in him. He could be goaded into activity only with difficulty.

   Comment.   Of the two subjects exposed to decreased distance, one responded with a paranoid schizophreniform reaction. The other retreated from the experience and held on to a marginal existence by intellectualization. Withdrawal is an innate reaction to threat which sometimes works, provided it is simultaneously possible to focus one's attention on sufficiently small and abstract matters and to build these up to occupy the whole of consciousness.

   Increased Distance.   S-5 first reacted positively to this instruction. As the day wore on, however, he began to feel more and more isolated until at the end he felt trapped in a shallow world and was moving increasingly into a schizoid state.

   S-4 started out by feeling aloof. Subsequently he developed a stomach ache, and the feeling of aloofness disappeared. His time sense seemed slightly distorted and a mild colorblindness, which he has normally, seemed to become worse.

Comment. There seems to be an optimal conceptual distance people need between themselves and the world around them. Too little distance is encroaching, too much is isolating. The problem is to find the optimal arrangement of distance and how to maintain it.

Time-Category Studies

Three subjects were employed in this series (S-1, S-2, S-4). Because of the traumatic nature of the response of the first subject to the no present condition, the experiments involving ablation of the present in combination with the past and the future were not run with him.

No Past. When the past was ablated by posthypnotic instruction, S-1 became confused and disoriented. He maintained memory of important persons, such as his wife, but could recall little of the specific events of his past. He seemed to lose inhibitions and meanings.

The simulator felt that he could respond to this instruction by blocking past memories or by liberating himself from his past. He chose the latter course and responded with a feeling of rebirth. He responded to things as they were, not as previous experience had made them. He became oriented toward action and involvement with others.

S-4 lost memory. He became confused, unable to handle even simple questions, and spent as much time as possible asleep. He became rather repetitious in his handling of things and excessively primitive in his reactions.

Comment. The past, in its aspect of transference, keeps us from reacting to things as they are, but it is also the source of discriminations and of the controls we normally exercise in our daily lives. A person functioning without a past functions in a world in which meaning is impaired.

Expanded Past. When the past was expanded by posthypnotic instruction, S-1 became rather happy, but was much more difficult to relate to. As long as one wished to deal with what he happened to be interested in, everything went all right. If one attempted to deflect the conversation into any other direction, he would not relate.

The simulator devoted his time to considering how he now was against the preoccupations imposed by his past conditionings with neurotic authority figures. He, too, related well if one fell into what he was interested in, but poorly if one wished to relate in terms of any other topics than those in which he was interested.

S-4 also responded happily and spent the day reminiscing about his past. It was possible to turn the conversation to other things, but he quickly turned it back to his main area of preoccupation. As is true of most of us, his past was not entirely positive, and he tried to avoid the sad memories by increasing his activity when these occurred.

Comment. The past is a source of constantly recurring discriminations. As these increase, the span of attention diminishes so that more and more of what is going on becomes irrelevant to the person's interests. This results in the phenomenon of disengagement[11] and the general stereotype of personality change with aging experienced by persons in our culture.[7]

No Present. When the present was removed by posthypnotic instruction, S-1 became immobile and responded neither to his name nor to any other stimulation. To begin with, he displayed a mild, waxy flexibility, which turned into a catatoniclike rigidity. When awakened, he described his experience as a state of "unbeing," like death. He had been aware of what had gone on around him, but had simply recorded it as a tape recorder might. He had not even been frightened by the experience until he was brought out of it.

The simulator reacted with good-natured aggressiveness. He felt that in the clash of hostility, the masks and falseness that obscure being would be torn away. He felt that one must take violent action to affirm life in a world that denied it.

S-4 felt lonely and still, but was not in a terribly bad mood when he could get himself to wake up. He spent most of the day asleep. He reported without emotion a constant vision of graveyards. In the postsession interview, he stated that he had allowed his sense of the present to diminish, rather than letting it go, because of a presentiment that something bad would happen if the present disappeared.

Comment. The present is where we live. Any destruction of the sense of the reality of where we are is suggestive of death. Where the present is totally gone, a schizoid state may result. This suggests that schizophrenia may be a psychic analogue to dying.

Expanded Present. When the present was expanded by posthypnotic instruction, S-1 became interested in lines and textures. He seemed to be experiencing a mood of great luminosity, although he did not transcend his problems.

The simulator immersed himself totally in the experiences of the moment. Eventually the stimulation became more than he could bear, but he found himself unable to withdraw from it. At the end of the day he was still happy and active, but very tired.

S-4 became happy and relaxed. He felt much concerned with the clarity of objects and sounds around him. On the car ride, he had the experimenter stop and spent a long time being totally absorbed in watching cows chewing.

Comment. Expanding the present produces involvement. Stimulus input is increased and welcomed. As in the case of the simulator, the experience can eventually become fatiguing, and it is not possible to say what prolonged involvement beyond the time that elapsed during these experiments would produce.

No Future. When the future was removed by posthypnotic instruction, S-1 found himself in a boundless, immanent present. He was deeply attracted by colors and textures. He himself described his experience as "mystical."

The simulator at first became depressed, then calm and stoically resigned. He seemed content just to sit. He felt no anxiety, but also no sense of anticipation of pleasures to come.

S-4 became alert and interested in all that was going on. He found himself less anxious, as well as less motivated. He took things at they came and enjoyed himself.

Comment. The future is the repository of goals and deadlines. Removal of the future removes motivation, but also removes anxiety. Anxiety is a feeling about something that is going to happen and so is always located in the future.

Expanded Future. When the future was expanded by posthypnotic instruction, S-1 responded with joy to a state in which there seemed ample time for once to meet all the demands of the environment upon him. Deadlines became unimportant, and, in particular, death became merely the end of life rather than an event to be feared.

The simulator also reacted with a sense of ample time. He became happy and introspective. He felt that what his life had been to date was not the measure of what it might become. He looked forward to his future with confidence.

S-4 looked forward to his future with happiness and anticipation. He felt he could concentrate better and that he was more full and rich as a person.

Comment. Expanding the future seems to have the same effect on anxiety as ablating it. One source of anxiety is the fact that things rush on us too fast. With this suggestion, for once there seemed to be enough time.

DISCUSSION

These data suggest that profound changes in behavior occur as a result of altering the stance of an individual in space and time. The effects produced run from depression through mania, from schizophrenia through mystic experience. Each perceptual change seems associated with its own characteristic range of effects on behavior. When these changes are brought about by posthypnotic instructions, there seems to be an interaction between the experiences and the controlling verbal metaphors that function for us as instructions do in a computer program.

One of the central distinctions which may be drawn from these data is that between the psychotic and the mystical experience. A comparison of the descriptions of psychotic experience given by Landis[20] and those of mystical experience given by O'Brien,[21] Stace,[25] and Underhill[26] shows many parallels. Both, for instance, seem to involve transformations of the categories of space and time. Both seem to involve perceptual changes that are ineffable because they fall outside the range of socially communicated experience. The present data suggest that, although these two kinds of experience do indeed deal with similar phenomena, they are opposite: Mystical experience arises from the augmentation of perception, psychotic experience from its diminution. Huxley[17] has made a similar point when he contrasted a psychotic girl's perception of the landscape as bathed in a hideous electric light with the mystic's perception of the clear light.

Consideration of the data deriving from the spatial studies suggests that mystical experience tends to arise from conditions of high information input, as in the expanded depth condition, in which the sense of self expands. The naturally occurring sites for mystical experiences are in mountainous or desert places, where depth is accentuated. William James[18] notes the marked tendency for mystical experiences to take place out of doors. One aspect of this is the large amount of information the organism receives because of the clarity with which the contour lines are defined in such places.

Conversely, the loss of depth is associated with psychosis. Under conditions of no depth, the self contracts and the amount of sensory input diminishes. Two of the subjects in this series moved in a schizoid direction just from the imposition of a hypnotic suggestion of blurred vision. Dr. Harry Wierner (in a personal communication) has found evidence in the literature which sets forth an association between visual defects and sudden onsets of schizophrenialike syndromes.

In an earlier paper[8] I suggested that paranoid symptoms emerge when responsibility for a noxious state of affairs occurring within an interpersonal context is placed outside the self. The present study suggests that another source for paranoid feelings derives from a loss of distance perception. The breaking down of the usual Euclidean structure of space and the intrusion of objects and people into personal space[15] create a situation of panic if these intrusions cannot be accepted.

Time as such is seen as flowing through the self, in contrast to space which is seen as being around oneself. The classical view of eternity in which one steps outside the stream of time does not seem to be upheld here. Timelessness, death, and schizophrenia form a triad. The sense of here and now comes from being in perfect accord with the succession of instants, not moving apart from them. Whatever the structure of time, we are already in it.

Time as a flow derives in its conception from the experience of motion,[18] but the relation between time and movement perception is complex. Our moods appear to be a function of the rate at which time seems to move. The crux in the relationship between the self and the world in the time dimension is one of control. The conventional view of eternity is thus called into question here. When we move, other objects seem to remain stationary with regard to us. As we do not seem able in fact to go back to them, this is elaborated into the analogy of a river moving by its stationary banks. The past is not a set of events on the banks, but a description of the behavior of the water itself. When the river becomes a snapshot, we, too, become a snapshot and cease to be. We retain a record of the past in our memories, and this record is to all intents and purposes the past. What we are doing is the present, and from this vantage point the past is also in a state of flux as the present itself shifts. What we conceive may happen is the future, and the future itself is composed of events of varying probabilities, based on memory and current activity.

The present represents the dimension of involvement with the world. Thus, expansion of the present is associated with heightened involvement and, conversely, absence of the present is associated with "unbeing" and death. The present by itself, however, is not enough. It derives its meaning and conditionings from the past, which contains the successive discriminations which the organism has formed in the course of its life. The purposes and goals of the present extend into the conceptual area of the future. While both past and future shift as a result of one's stance in the present, at least one or the other of these is required for the present to exist at all.

The past represents the dimension of conditioning and discrimination. As discriminations are involved with one another and become finer, the experience of the present is elaborated in keeping with the pattern of conceived goals and likely events to come. When these events are projected over a shorter range relative to the past, a narrowing of span of interest occurs as a result of the finer conditionings. If this analysis is true, disengagement should not only be a function of aging, but should be found whenever anyone has reason to doubt his longevity.

Anxiety and motivation both belong to the future. We know what is happening, we may become afraid of what might happen. We act to produce not what is happening, but what we would like to have happen. When the future is long relative to the past, the span of interest is accordingly wide. It is conventional to think of the present as determined by the past, and this is true to a degree. On the other hand, any rat learning a maze for a food pellet at the far end gives the lie to this assertion.

Time and space comprise the matrix within which we exist and which we ourselves have created by virtue of our structure. We cannot know that what we experience is the way the world is, because we ourselves are events in that system. These studies suggest that we can and do influence how we experience the world. The veridicality of our usual perceptions derives from what is at base a system of statistical probabilities. There always may be something more.

ACKNOWLEDGMENTS

I wish to thank Drs. A. Moneim El Meligi, Frank Haronian, Harriet Mann, Humphry Osmond, Stanley R. Platman, Hubert Stolberg, and A. Arthur Sugerman for their assistance in this study.

REFERENCES

1. Aaronson, Bernard S., Hypnosis, depth perception, and schizophrenia. Presented at the Eastern Psychological Association meetings, Philadelphia, Pa., 1964.

2. _____, Hypnosis, time rate perception, and personality. Presented at the Eastern Psychological Association meetings, Atlantic City, N.J., 1965a.

3. _____, Hypnosis, being, and the conceptual categories of time. Presented at the New Jersey Psychological Association meetings, Princeton, N.J., 1965b.

4. _____, Hypnosis, depth perception, and psychedelic experience. Presented at the Society for the Scientific Study of Religion meetings, 1965c.

5. _____, "Behavior and the Place Names of Time," Amer. J. Clin. Hypnosis, 9 (1966), 1–17.

6. _____, "Hypnosis, Time Rate Perception, and Psychopathology." Read before the meetings of the Eastern Psychological Association, New York, N.Y., 1966.

7. _____, "Personality Stereotypes of Aging," J. Gerontol, 21 (1966), 458–462.

8. _____, "Hypnosis, Responsibility and the Boundaries of Self," Amer. J. Clin. Hypnosis, 9, 1968, 229–246.

9. Beers, C. W., A Mind That Found Itself. 7th ed. Garden City, N.Y.: Doubleday, 1950.

10. Cooper, L. F. and Erickson, M. H., Time Distortion in Hypnosis. 2nd ed. Baltimore: Williams and Wilkins, 1959.

11. Cumming, E. and Henry, W. E., Growing Old. New York: Basic Books, 1961.

12. Dunne, J. W., This Serial Universe. London: Macmillan, 1938.

13. _____, An Experiment with Time. 3rd ed. London: Faber & Faber, 1939.

14. Fogel, S. and Hoffer, A., "Perceptual Changes Induced by Hypnotic Suggestion for the Post-hypnotic State: I. General Account of the Effect on Personality," *J. Clin & Exper. Psychopathol,*" 23 (1962), 24–35.

15. Hall, E. T., *The Silent Language.* Garden City, N.Y.: Doubleday, 1959.

16. Huxley, A., *The Doors of Perception.* New York: Harper & Row, 1954.

17. _____, *Heaven and Hell.* New York: Harper & Row, 1956.

18. James, W., *Varieties of Religious Experience.* New York: Modern Library, 1929.

19. Kepes, G., Introduction. In G. Kepes (ed.), *The Nature and Art of Motion.* New York: George Braziller, 1965.

20. Landis, C., *Varieties of Psychopathological Experience.* New York: Holt, Rinehart, & Winston, 1964.

21. O'Brien, E., *Varieties of Mystic Experience.* New York: New American Library, 1964.

22. Palmer, R. D., "Visual Acuity and Excitement," *Psychosomat. Med.,* 28 (1966), 364–374.

23. Plutchik, R., *The Emotions: Facts, Theories, and a New Model.* New York: Random House, 1962.

24. Priestley, J. B., *Man and Time.* Garden City, N.Y.: Doubleday, 1964.

25. Stace, W. T., *The Teachings of the Mystics.* New York: New American Library, 1960.

26. Underhill, E., *Mysticism.* New York: Dutton, 1961.

Recommended
Reading

Castaneda, C. *A separate reality.* New York: Simon and Schuster, 1971.
A detailed account of the anthropologist-author's experience as the student of an Indian sorcerer. Castaneda encounters a system of knowledge based on a radically different way of viewing reality. It is an important work for the student of madness because it demonstrates the individual and cultural relativity of perception, as well as how altered states of consciousness are valued by a cultural system. The book offers an excellent description of a variety of altered states of consciousness, many of which closely resemble experiences reported by madmen.

Green, H. *I never promised you a rose garden.* New York: Holt, Rinehart, and Winston, 1964.
A profound story of a sixteen-year-old's voyage into the world of madness. The author presents an extremely lucid and detailed picture of a psychotic individual's experience with the inner-world, the impact of an institutional setting, and an exceedingly sensitive therapist.

Kaplan, B. (Ed.) *The inner world of mental illness.* New York: Harper and Row, 1964.
A comprehensive collection of personal accounts about madness.

Laing, R. D. *The politics of experience.* New York: Ballantine Books, 1967.
A collection of essays by a revolutionary psychiatrist. Exciting reading that bluntly challenges conventional ideas about insanity and proposes an alternative system, which treats madness as a natural and desirable psychological voyage.

Supplementary
References

PERSONAL ACCOUNTS

Boison, A. T. *The exploration of the inner world.* New York: Harper and Row, 1936.

Castaneda, C. *The teachings of Don Juan: A Yaqui way of knowledge.* New York: Ballantine Books, 1968.

Currey, A. E. Poetry of a schizophrenic: The language of an individual, *Review of Existential Psychology and Psychiatry,* 1963, **3**, 27–34.

Jefferson, L. (pseudonym). *These are my sisters.* Tulsa: Vickers, 1948.

Kesey, K. *One flew over the cuckoo's nest.* New York: Viking Press, 1962.

Lindner, R. The jet-propelled couch. In *The fifty-minute hour.* New York: Bantam Books, 1954.

Masters, R. E. L., & Houston, J. *The varieties of psychedelic experience.* New York: Holt, Rinehart and Winston, 1966.

Neihardt, J. G. (Flaming Rainbow). *Black Elk speaks.* Lincoln: University of Nebraska Press, 1961.

Nijinsky, R., (Ed.) *The diary of Vaslav Nijinsky.* New York: Simon and Schuster, 1936.

Sechehaye, M. *Autobiography of a schizophrenic girl.* New York: Grune and Stratton, 1951.

Sommer, R., & Osmond, H. Autobiographies of former mental patients. *Journal of Mental Science,* 1960, **106**, 648–662; 1961, **107**, 1030–1032.

Stone, A. A., & Stone, S. S., (Eds.) *The abnormal personality through literature.* Englewood Cliffs, New Jersey: Prentice-Hall, 1966.

THEORY

Adams, J. K. Psychosis: Experimental and real. *Psychedelic Review,* 1963, **1**(2), 121–144.

Adams, J. K. *Secrets of the trade.* New York: Viking Press, 1971.

Alexander, F. Buddhistic training as catatonia. *Psychoanalytic Review,* 1931, **19**, 129.

Assagioli, R. *Psychosynthesis.* New York: Viking Press, 1971. (Especially relevant is Chapter II titled Self-realization and psychological disturbances.)

Bateson, G., Jackson, D. D., Haley, J., & Weakland, J. Toward a theory of schizophrenia. *Behavioral Science*, 1956, **1**, 251–264.

Bowers, M. The onset of psychosis: A diary account. *Psychiatry*, 1965, **28**, 346–358.

Boyers, R., & Orrill, R., (Eds.) *R. D. Laing and anti-psychiatry*. New York: Harper and Row, 1971.

Brajinsky, B. M., Brajinsky, D. D., & Ring, K. *Methods and madness: The mental hospital as a last resort*. New York: Holt, Rinehart and Winston, 1969.

Cooper, D. *Psychiatry and anti-psychiatry*. New York: Ballantine Books, 1967.

Dabrowski, K. *Positive disintegration*. (Trans. and Ed., Jason Aronson) Boston: Little, Brown, 1967.

Diagnostic and statistical manual of mental disorders (DSM-II). Washington, D.C.: American Psychiatric Association, 1968.

Evans-Wentz, W. Y. (Ed.) *The Tibetan book of the dead*. New York: Oxford University Press, 1960.

Fisher, R. The perception hallucination continuum. *Diseases of the Nervous System*, 1969, **30**, 161–171.

Foucalt, M. *Madness and civilization*. (Trans. R. Howard) New York: Pantheon, 1965.

Grof, S. Beyond psychoanalysis: III. Birth trauma and its relation to mental illness, suicide and ecstasy. Presented as a preprint at the Second Interdiciplinary Conference on Voluntary Control of Internal States, Council Grove, Ka., April 13-17, 1970.

Grof, S. *Theory and practice of LSD psychotherapy*. Philadelphia: University of Pennsylvania Press, 1973.

Huxley, A. *Heaven and hell*. New York: Harper and Row, 1954.

Jackson, D. D., & Watzlawick, P. The acute psychosis as manifestation of a growth experience. In Acute psychotic reaction. *Psychiatric Research Report*, 1963, **16**, 89–94.

Kaplan, B. On "reason in madness" in King Lear. In J. Bugental (Ed.), *Challenges of humanistic psychology*. New York: McGraw-Hill, 1967.

Laing, R. D., *The divided self*. London: Tavistock, 1960.

Ornitz, E. M. Disorders of perception common to early infantile autism and schizophrenia. *Comprehensive Psychiatry*, 1969, **10**(4), 259–274.

Perls, F. S. *Gestalt therapy verbatim*. Lafayette, Calif.: Real People Press, 1969.

Rosen, G. *Madness in society*. New York: Harper and Row, 1968.

Silverman, J. Shamans and schizophrenia. *American Anthropologist*, 1967, **69**, 21–32.

Silverman, J. When schizophrenia helps. *Psychology Today*, 1970, **4**(4), 63–65.

Smythies, J. R. A logical and cultural analysis of hallucinatory sense-experience. *Journal of Mental Science*, 1956, **102**, 336.

Southwell, E. A., & Feldman, H. (Eds.) *Abnormal psychology: Readings in theory and research*. Monterey, Calif.: Brooks/Cole, 1969.

Szasz, T. The uses of naming and the origin of mental illness. *American Psychologist*, 1961, **16**, 59–65.

Szasz, T. *Ideology and insanity*. Garden City: Doubleday, 1970.

Ullmann, L., & Krasner, L., *A psychological approach to abnormal behavior*. Englewood Cliffs, N.J.: Prentice-Hall, 1969.

Van Duzen, W. The phenomenology of a schizophrenic existence. *Journal of Individual Psychology*, 1961, **17**, 80–92.

Wegroki, H. J. A critique of cultural and statistical concepts of abnormality. *Journal of Abnormal and Social Psychology*, 1939, **34**, 166–178.

Wilhelm, R. (Trans. and Ed.) & Jung, C. G. (Ed.) *The secret of the golden flower: A Chinese book of life.* New York: Harcourt, Brace and World, 1962.

RESEARCH

Aaronson, B. S. Hypnotic induction of colored environments. *Perceptual and Motor Skills*, 1964, **18**, 30.

Aaronson, B. S. Behavior and the place names of time. *The American Journal of Hypnosis*, 1966, **9**, 1–17.

Aaronson, B. S. Lilliput and Brobdignag—self and world. *The American Journal of Clinical Hypnosis*, 1968, **10**, 160–166.

Aaronson, B. S. Hypnotic alterations of space and time. *International Journal of Parapsychology*, 1968, **10**, 5–36.

Adams, F. Stereotypy, social responsiveness, and arousal in a case of catatonia. *British Journal of Psychiatry*, 1967, **113**, 1123–1128.

Angyal, A., Freeman, H., & Hoskins, R. G. Physiologic aspects of schizophrenic withdrawal. *Archives of Neurology and Psychiatry*, 1940, **44**(3), 621–626.

Benivieni, A. *The hidden causes of disease.* (Translated by C. Singer.) Springfield, Ill.: Charles C Thomas, 1954.

Boison, A. T. The form and content of schizophrenic thinking. *Psychiatry*, 1942, **5**, 23–33.

Boison, A. T. Onset in acute schizophrenia. *Psychiatry*, 1947, **10**, 159–166.

Buchsbaum, M. Average evoked response: Techniques and applications. *Schizophrenia Bulletin.* Chevy Chase, Md.: National Clearing House for Mental Health Information, 1970, **3**, 10–23.

Cameron, N. Deterioration and regression in schizophrenic thinking. *Journal of Abnormal and Social Psychology*, 1939, **34**(2).

Chapman, J. The early symptoms of schizophrenia. *British Journal of Psychiatry*, 1966, **112**, 225–251.

Curtis, G. C., & Zuckerman, M. A psychopathological reaction precipitated by sensory deprivation. *American Journal of Psychiatry*, 1968, **125**, 255–260.

De Ropp, R. S. *Drugs and the mind.* New York: Grove Press, 1957.

Eliade, M. *Shamenism: Archaic techniques of ecstasy.* New York: Pantheon, 1964.

Erickson, M. H. Experimental demonstrations of the psychopathology of everyday life. *The Psychoanalytic Quarterly*, 1939, **8**, 338–353.

Erickson, M. H. A special inquiry with Aldous Huxley into the nature and character of various states of consciousness. *The American Journal of Clinical Hypnosis* 1965, **8**, 14–33.

Fadiman, J. Behavior change following psychedelic therapy. Unpublished dissertation, Stanford University, 1965.

Fisher, S. Body image boundaries and hallucinations. In L. J. West (Ed.), *Hallucinations.* New York: Grune and Stratton, 1962.

French, T. M., & Kasanin, J. A psychodynamic study of the recovery of two schizophrenic cases. *Psychoanalytic Quarterly*, 1941, **10**(1).

Glendlin, E. T. Research in psychotherapy with schizophrenic patients and the nature of that "illness." *American Journal of Psychotherapy,* 1966, **20**, 4–16.

Goldstein, M. J. Premorbid adjustment, paranoid status, and patterns of response in phenothiazine in acute schizophrenia. *Schizophrenic Bulletin,* 1970, **3**, 24–37.

Hanfman, E. Analysis of the thinking disorder in a case of schizophrenia. *Archives of Neurology and Psychiatry,* 1939, **41**.

Harman, W., & Fadiman, J. Selective enhancement of specific capacities through psychedelic training. In B. Aaronson & H. Osmond (Eds.), *Psychedelics: The uses and implications of hallucinogenic drugs.* Garden City: Doubleday, 1970.

Higgins, J. Process-reactive schizophrenia: Recent developments. *Journal of nervous and mental disease,* 1969, **149**(6), 450–472.

Hoffer, A., & Osmond, H. *How to live with schizophrenia.* New Hyde Park, New York: University Books, 1966.(a)

Hoffer, A., & Osmond, H. Some psychological consequences of perceptual disorder and schizophrenia. *International Journal of Neuropsychiatry,* 1966, **2**, 1–19.(b)

Izumi, K. LSD and architectural design. In B. Aaronson & H. Osmond (Eds.), *Psychedelics: The uses and implications of hallucinogenic drugs.* Garden City: Doubleday, 1970.

Jackson, D. D. (Ed.) *The etiology of schizophrenia.* New York: Basic Books, 1960.

James, W. *The varieties of religious experience.* London: Collier-Macmillan, 1961.

Kantor, R. E. Theoretical and practical considerations of extreme regression in reactive schizophrenia. *Journal of Humanistic Psychology,* 1964, **4**(2), 154.

Kety, S. S. Biochemical theories of schizophrenia: Part I. *Science,* June 5, 1959, **129**, 1528–1532.

Kety, S. S. Biochemical theories of schizophrenia: Part II. *Science,* June 12, 1959, **129**, 1590–1606.

Kiev, A. The study of folk psychiatry. In A. Kiev (Ed.), *Magic, faith and healing.* New York: Glencoe Free Press, 1964.

Kitano, H. Mental illness in four cultures. *Journal of Social Psychology,* 1970, **80**(2), 121–134.

Kline, N. S. Non-chemical factors and chemical theories of mental disease. In M. Rinkel (Ed.), *Chemical concepts of psychosis.* New York: McDowell/Oblensky, 1959.

Lewis, I. M. *Ecstatic religion: An anthropological study of spirit possession and shamanism.* Baltimore, Md.: Penguin Books, 1971.

Ludwig, A. M. Altered states of consciousness. *Archives of General Psychiatry,* 1966, **15**, 225–234.

Meehl, P. E. Schizotaxia, schizotypy, schizophrenia. *American Psychologist,* 1962, **17**, 827–838.

Mogar, R. E. Psychedelic states and schizophrenia. *Journal of Existential Psychiatry,* 1968, **6**, 401–420.

Monroe, R. *Journeys out of the body.* New York: Doubleday, 1971.

Murphy, J. M., & Leighton, A. H. (Eds.). *Approaches to cross-cultural psychiatry.* Ithaca, N.Y.: Cornell University Press, 1965.

Naranjo, C., & Ornstein, R. *On the psychology of meditation.* New York: Viking Press, 1971.

Rinkel, M., De Shon, H. J., Hyde, R. W., & Solomon, H. C. Experimental schizo-phrenic-like symptoms. *American Journal of Psychiatry*, 1952, **108**, 572–578.

Rosenthal, D. *Genetic theory and abnormal behavior.* New York: McGraw-Hill, 1970.

Silverman, J. Shamans and schizophrenia. *American Anthropologist*, 1967, **69**, 21–32.

Silverman, J. A paradigm for the study of altered states of consciousness. *British Journal of Psychiatry*, 1968, **114**, 1201–1218.

Silverman, J., Berg, S. D., & Kantor, R. Some perceptual correlates of institution-alizations. *Journal of Nervous and Mental Diseases*, 1966, **141**(6), 651–657.

Skakow, D. Psychological deficit in schizophrenia. *Behavioral Science*, 1963, **8**(4), 275–305.

Soskis, D. A., & Bowers, M. B. The schizophrenic experience: A follow-up study of attitudes and post-hospital adjustment. *Journal of Nervous and Mental Disease*, 1969, **149**, 443–449.

Tart, C. (Ed.). *Altered states of consciousness.* New York: John Wiley and Sons, 1969.

Wallace, A. F. C. Cultural determinants of response to hallucinatory experience. *Archives of General Psychiatry*, 1959, **1**, 58–69.

West, L. J. (Ed.). *Hallucinations.* New York: Grune and Stratton, 1962.

Witkin, H. A. Psychological differentiation and forms of pathology. *Journal of Abnormal Psychology*, 1965, **70**, 317–336.

Wittkower, E. D., & Dubreuil, G. Cultural factors in mental illness. In E. Nor-beck, D. Price-Williams, & W. McCord (Eds.), *The study of personality.* New York: Holt, Rinehart and Winston, 1968.

TAPE RECORDINGS

Grof, S., Watts, A., & Silverman, J. Science in madness. (2 hours)

Perry, J., & Silverman, J. Mores, mysticism, and madness. (1½ hours)

Watts, A. Divine madness. (1½ hours)

(For catalog and orders, write Big Sur Recordings, 117 Mitchell Boulevard, San Rafael, California 94903.)

Index

223